MUHAMMAD IN THE SEMINARY

Muhammad in the Seminary

*Protestant Teaching about Islam
in the Nineteenth Century*

David D. Grafton

NEW YORK UNIVERSITY PRESS
New York

NEW YORK UNIVERSITY PRESS
New York
www.nyupress.org

Library of Congress Cataloging-in-Publication Data
Names: Grafton, David D., author.
Title: Muhammad in the seminary : Protestant teaching about Islam
in the nineteenth century / David D. Grafton.
Description: New York : New York University Press, 2024. |
Includes bibliographical references and index.
Identifiers: LCCN 2023049397 (print) | LCCN 2023049398 (ebook) |
ISBN 9781479831463 (hardback) | ISBN 9781479831470 (ebook) |
ISBN 9781479831487 (ebook other)
Subjects: LCSH: Islam—Relations—Christianity—19th century. |
Christianity and other religions—Islam—19th century. | Qur'an—
Christian interpretations. | Muḥammad, Prophet, –632—Christian interpretations.
Classification: LCC BP172 .G724 2024 (print) | LCC BP172 (ebook) |
DDC 261.2/7097309034—dc23/eng/20231026
LC record available at https://lccn.loc.gov/2023049397
LC ebook record available at https://lccn.loc.gov/2023049398

This book is printed on acid-free paper, and its binding materials are chosen for strength and durability. We strive to use environmentally responsible suppliers and materials to the greatest extent possible in publishing our books.

Manufactured in the United States of America

10 9 8 7 6 5 4 3 2 1

Also available as an ebook

For Andrew & Fatemeh, Rebekah, and Dan

CONTENTS

In 2012, the Association of Theological Schools (ATS) added a new standard to their expectation of theological education for master of divinity students, those students who were enrolled in graduate professional education to become clergy: "MDiv education shall engage students with the global character of the church as well as ministry in the multifaith and multicultural context of contemporary society." Since that time, American seminaries have undertaken a variety of methods to help sensitize their students to the "multifaith and multicultural context of contemporary" American society, and, dare I say, the pluralistic world as we experience it. While this standard has been reluctantly adopted by some seminaries and their faculty, others have wholeheartedly embraced the challenge. Protestant theological education has at its heart the education of Christian leaders for public ministry, however that may be construed. Historically, seminaries have focused on training seminarians within particular denominational or confessional traditions. It has been important to learn the theology, polity, and sociology of one's own "tribe." Dialogue was first introduced only between Protestant denominations, then with Catholics, and finally with the Jewish tradition. Prior to 2012, rarely did seminary education require students to engage other religious traditions as part of their professional education. However, 9/11 demonstrated how radically unprepared American clergy were to recognize the needs of a "multifaith and multicultural" society. Many clergy had no idea how to engage in dialogue with the Muslim community in their ministry.

Partly in response to the new ATS standards, in 2013, the Virginia Theological Seminary (VTS) undertook a research project on interfaith dialogue in Episcopal parishes. It surveyed over four thousand Episcopal priests (with a 20 percent response rate) regarding how they "engage in and foster interfaith relationships and dialogue."[1] One of the findings of this survey was that 90 percent of those priests who "offered educational forums in their congregations about another religion . . . had previous education in that religion."[2] Those who were active in interfaith education or relationships had received some education about other religions in seminary or college. The study also found that there was a correlation between perceived competence and action. In other words, if priests felt competent in their knowledge of another faith tradition, they would be more likely to initiate some type of activity with that community. Otherwise, many of the priests did not feel qualified to engage in or lead interfaith activities, and so often did nothing.

Of course, there have been other studies undertaken about how Christian congregations engage in interfaith education, or what Christians in America think and feel about people of other religious traditions. But the result of this study made me curious about exactly "what" or "how" seminary students were learning about other religions, particularly about Islam, in their seminary education. This also prompted me to wonder what has been taught about Islam in American seminaries.

I am not a sociologist or an anthropologist. I am a historian and a pastor—a member of the clergy. I am also trained in Islamic studies, with a specialization in Christian-Muslim relations. And so, I became interested in finding out what was being taught about Islam in the formative years of American seminary education in the nineteenth century. This was also the period when many graduates of these seminaries were initially sent out as missionaries to Muslim communities in India and the Ottoman Empire. I wondered if perhaps a historical study might lead to some fruitful thinking about how we approach contemporary theological education today, as we train seminarians to be equipped to do ministry with sensitivity and humility in a "multifaith and multicultural" America and world. Of course, I hope this research is not just of value to seminaries or even Christians. This book offers an important look into the American past and its self-identity in relation to the world. There is much that can be gleaned in it, I hope, for those interested in American history and American cultural identities. And, I hope that it provides insight for American Muslims into the experience of a dominant Protestant culture of the United States that is starkly visible and still very present.

The cover of this book highlights this important view of Islam as a religion shared by many Americans during the late nineteenth century and reflects much of what was taught in seminaries at this time. Edwin Bashfield's mural "The Evolution of Civilizations," located inside the dome of the south pavilion of the Library of Congress, depicts Islam in American Orientalist fashion as a turbaned man, and as one contribution among many to the development of a Western Protestant civilization. Between the experience of the Barbary pirates and the Turkish atrocities against the Armenians and Assyrians, that is the majority of the nineteenth century, Islam was taught in the seminaries as an important Semitic religion but morally and religiously deficient to America's culture and its particular Protestant Christianity.

The new multifaith and multicultural ATS standard was officially added to expectations in 2012, coincidentally the same year I began working on the Christian-Muslim Relations: 1500–1900 (CMR 1900) project with Dr. David Thomas at the University of Birmingham, England. The CMR 1900 was the second part of a research project, the first being the CMR 600, which had already published four volumes of material on the writings of Muslims and Christians on or about one another from the seventh to the fifteenth century. The second part of the project was to run from the sixteenth century up to 1915. That project is currently publishing its twenty-first volume!

The CMR has been an incredible undertaking that has involved thousands of scholars across the globe—Muslim, Christian, Jewish, and scholars of no religious tradition. The project has provided many of us access to documents, resources, and histories that have been previously otherwise unknown or unavailable. Readers will notice how influential that project was in this research. I am indebted to countless researchers and intellectuals who have contributed to the CMR.

Another group of individuals to whom I am greatly indebted are the librarians of the various institutions included in this study. I began researching before the 2020 COVID-19 pandemic began but was literally right in the middle of archival research when the world shut down. In fact, the librarians at New Brunswick Theological Seminary were kind enough to let me stay through the end of the day on March 15, when they locked the doors behind me as I left. Talk about research challenges! I was only halfway through my seminary library visits when things were put on hold. Thankfully, all the library staff were willing to answer my many questions via phone calls and emails and were more than accommodating in checking on the provenance of many books for me until I was able to conclude some site visits in the spring of 2022. Needless to say, I would not have been able to complete this project without the assistance of the librarians at Gettysburg, General, Hartford, New Brunswick, Princeton, and Union seminaries, as well as Yale Divinity School and Princeton University. To them and to their profession, I say, "Thank you!" I am also deeply grateful to the blind peer reviewers who read this manuscript and to my editors at New York University Press, Jennifer Hammer, Alexia Traganas, and Emily Wright, who have skillfully and patiently guided me along in this process. Their suggestions and comments have been an important part of strengthening the book. Naturally, of course, any misperceptions or errors in this work are mine alone.

Finally, this research could only have been generated from within the rich context of Hartford International University for Religion and Peace (formerly Hartford Seminary). I am deeply grateful to my colleagues there who have been ongoing conversation partners in all matters of faith and life and have contributed to this project in many official and incidental ways. Their insights, suggestions, questions, and support have shaped this work into something I could never have accomplished on my own.

Introduction

Sitting in his chair in Alexander Hall at Princeton seminary, Charles Hodge scribbled notes during a lecture on "Mohammedanism" being given by Professor Archibald Alexander, the first president of Princeton seminary. Alexander's course on Polemical Theology covered a wide range of subjects, including the major heresies of the Christian faith and the "errors" of the non-Christian world. On this day, Alexander was lecturing on Islam. Sitting in what must have been a cold room in Princeton, New Jersey, in January 1819, Hodge recorded the basics of the life of Muhammad, the formation of the Qur'an, the beliefs of Muslims and their ritual practices, and the major communities of Muslims in the nineteenth century. Alexander—who would become a mentor and encourage Hodge on his own path toward becoming a professor and the next theological giant at Princeton seminary—would provide his students with a lasting image of Islam and Muhammad: "Mohammed was a cruel, sensual man & a robber."[1] Alexander's views, transferred to Hodge and many other young and impressionable seminarians, would have an important impact on how Islam was viewed by many Protestant seminary students who would become America's clergy.

Throughout the nineteenth century, White Americans became acutely aware of Islam and garnered an increasing amount of information about Muslims. This occurred first through the traumatic experience of Americans being taken captive by North African pirates and the subsequent Tripolitan, or Barbary, Wars in 1801–1805 and 1815.[2] Americans who had been captive and later ransomed wrote about their experiences, which generated national attention. However, following the successful suppression of this threat of piracy, American merchants in Boston and Philadelphia developed an extensive trade with the Ottoman Empire. This culminated in a "most favored treaty" status in 1830, which provided more opportunities for interactions with Islamic cultures. As Ottoman wares began showing up in East Coast warehouses, American society began to develop a taste for all things "Oriental": clothing, coffee, and carpets. The curiosity about what was then called the "Orient" grew in North America after the publication of Comte de Volney's *Voyage en Syrie et en Egypte* in 1787, also published in English in London that same year. Constantin-François de Chasseboeuf (1757–1820), or Volney for short, had arrived in the United States in 1795 and hobnobbed with the likes of Washington and Jefferson. His images and descriptions of ancient Egypt, published fourteen years before the first volume of Napoleon's massive project *Description D'Egypte*, created an industry of interest in the "Orient" in the young republic of the United States.

The large swath of territory from what is now Turkey all the way to India was branded as the "Orient," as distinct from East Asia, which was known as the "Far East." The phenomenon of Western fascination and stereotypical representation of the peoples of the Middle East, North Africa, and South Asia through images, paintings, and literature is known as "Orientalism." For Americans, who held no colonies in this part of the world, the "Orient" was a mysterious land to be marveled at and feared at the same time.[3] The earliest firsthand American reports of the Orient were letters and journals written by the captives of the Barbary pirates. This captivity literature provided American readers with one particular way to learn about the manners, customs, and religion of the captors. The genre also generated both interest in and anger toward the despotic sultan of the Ottoman Empire, whose subjects carried out acts of piracy. The enslavement of White American sailors led to the United States' first international war with the city states of Algiers, Tunis, and Tripoli. Because the young republic did not have a navy to protect its merchants, the US Congress engaged in a bitter debate over whether the federal government had the right to create such a navy in the first place. In the end, Congress approved its creation and funded its operations, ultimately leading to two wars to free American captives.[4]

After the conclusion of the Barbary Wars, the Orient was opened to Americans, first to American merchants, then to missionaries, and then to other White Americans who became interested in and intrigued with the Orient. By the 1830s the Mediterranean had become safer for American shipping, due to American and European naval power. With a protected passage east and a growing number of American travelers, Muslims were no longer perceived as a threat but became an item of curiosity—that is, until the end of the century when violence against Armenians and Assyrians once again raised alarms about the despotism of the Muslim Turks.

However, for the likes of Archibald Alexander (1772–1851), the Barbary Wars were very much of recent memory and shaped his American experience of Islam. Alexander himself had never attended college but was tutored by and apprenticed under the Reverend William Graham at Liberty Hall Academy in Virginia. Graham himself had studied at the College of New Jersey under the leadership of John Witherspoon. Eventually, Alexander would become the first president of one of the newly organized Protestant seminaries in the United States at Princeton. For Alexander, Islam was not an intrigue or a passing cultural fad. On the basis of all that he had read about the pirates and their religious traditions from the English Orientalists Edward Gibbon, Bishop Humphrey Prideaux, and William Paley, he viewed Islam as a false religion. Alexander passed on to his students what he read and experienced about Islam as an American.

But Hodge was not the only seminary student who heard of Muhammad or "Mohammedanism" in his classes. Further up in New England, at Andover Theological Seminary outside of Boston, two recent graduates had determined that they were called to preach the Gospel in the very heart of the Turkish Empire. As early as 1819, these two graduates, Levi Parsons and Pliny Fisk, headed to the Ottoman Empire as missionaries. Their interest was first and foremost to reclaim Jerusalem for Christianity through their preaching and Bible distribution among the Jewish community. In a sermon he preached on the eve of his departure, Pliny Fisk highlighted that "the religions of the country are all strongly characterized by violent prejudice, and bigotry of the darkest hue. The principles of political liberty, and the rights of conscience are not understood."[5] Of these religions, "the empire of Mohammadenism" was the "more destructive enemy."[6]

While they did not succeed in their intended mission of conversion, they were the first of many American missionaries to set foot in the Near East. The missionaries, many of them graduates from Andover and Princeton seminaries, began sending information about the Near East and its people, including their own views about Islam, back to their former classmates and supporting churches in the United States. On occasion, they would return on furloughs to speak to various church communities or teach in the seminaries.[7] American missionary literature on the Orient and Islam, while not the only avenue of information on Islam for Americans, became the most significant source of knowledge production among American Protestants.[8] And by the beginning of the twentieth century, American missionaries and seminary professors were reading the Qur'an and Islamic sources in their original languages and translating them for American audiences, including seminary students. Islam appeared regularly throughout the Protestant seminary curriculum in different places.

In 1841, Yale College established the first professor of Arabic in North America, Edward E. Salisbury. In his inaugural address to the college, Salisbury presented an overview of Arabic studies and his views on Islam.[9] His appointment to this new field of study was a crucial moment for American colleges as they began catching up to European universities in the study of Islam and all things Oriental. As a founding member of the American Oriental Society in 1842, Salisbury was on the front line of a new movement that provided opportunities for the brightest and best to begin learning about Islam and Muslim societies, primarily through the reading of texts and philology. Salisbury would complain that there were too few students at Yale interested in his topics and lectures.[10] However, even before Salisbury's appointment, Protestant seminary students were processing information about Islam in various places throughout their curricula. In fact, seminaries were the first places in the United States to consistently engage in formal teaching and learning about Muhammad, the Qur'an, and Islam. The numbers of students involved in this educational system far outweighed any previous initiatives within the early American college system.

The Establishment of American Protestant Seminaries

American seminaries, like Andover and Princeton, had their origin and success by creating a novel system of education for large numbers of Protestant ministerial candidates at the beginning of the nineteenth century. As training schools for clergy, seminaries generated a professional industry of theological education to meet the spiritual needs of growing and diverse Protestant communities in America. Protestant religious revivals sweeping the country beginning in the 1790s (often called the Second Great Awakening) created an increased need for more charismatic pastors and preachers. Young men who had been so moved by the Spirit desired to follow their newly envisioned call to ministry. Various Protestant clergy wanted to have a direct hand in the training of this new generation and did not trust the college atmosphere to do so.[11] The primary focus of a new seminary education was to teach doctrine and methods of biblical interpretation for the denomination to which these exclusively male seminarians were going to serve. They were to be "learned interpreter[s] of the Christian faith."[12]

As the population of the young United States grew, so too did the number of Protestant denominations. Congregationalists and Presbyterians splintered into church bodies that differed in their understandings of Jesus, salvation, and the Bible. Different explanations of original sin, the imputation of grace, and a belief in the inspiration of scripture drove Protestant clergy to create their own centers of instruction. So, seminaries became the bastion to guard pure doctrine as understood by a particular tradition, as well as the center of suspicion around the teaching of heresy. The disagreement over what constituted orthodox teaching contributed to the proliferation of denominations and their schools. In addition to theological debates, other Protestant communities wanted to support their own cultural-linguistic-ecclesiastical traditions. After the War of Independence, the Dutch Reformed, German Lutherans, and, of course, the Anglicans realized that American churches could no longer look back to Europe for their pastors to be trained and needed to develop their own American theological institutions.

Biblical studies and Christian theology were the cornerstones of seminary education. However, other topics, specifically Islam, continually worked their way into educational curricula in surprising places. First, seminary students had access to a small but important library. English, Latin, and then German books from Europe about Islam found their way into these institutional libraries. The books were used by professors for recitations, or in their own preparations for teaching, and were recommended to students for further learning. Secondly, young seminarians began to hear about Islam through lectures and readings in church history. The story of Islam was also the story of Christianity. Through professors retelling the story of Eastern Christianity, students were exposed to the role Islam played in the destruction of Byzantium and Saladin's capture of Jerusalem from the Crusaders, for example. Third, one of the most intriguing ways in which seminarians began to learn about Islam was through the study of Hebrew. As a Semitic language, Arabic was considered an important tool for understanding and interpreting the Hebrew scriptures. Seminary curricula not only required the study of Hebrew and Greek but offered courses in "cognate biblical languages" such as Aramaic, Syriac, Arabic, and on some occasions Akkadian, Ethiopic, and Persian. By the 1870s, it was not unusual for students in their final year to be reading passages of the Qur'an to help them develop skills in interpreting the Psalms. By 1895, Professor Duncan Black Macdonald (1863–1943) began reading Islamic sources in Arabic with students at Hartford seminary as part of this language training.

Fourth, in the 1870s comparative religions became an exciting new field of study in seminaries. Seminary education responded to the growing interest in anthropological and ethnographic study of other cultures and religious traditions. These courses on comparative religions included various perspectives and interpretations of Islam. Fifth and finally, as previously noted, those seminarians who went out as missionaries to Muslim-majority lands wrote letters or returned to their alma maters to lecture about Islam. Becoming a foreign missionary was a popular field of service and a very realistic career opportunity for young seminarians to consider. Even if a graduate decided to stay in the United States and pursue more traditional parish ministry, or headed west for domestic missionary opportunities, the network of relationships of former professors and alumni ensured an active channel of communication among former classmates. Alums who served in Muslim-majority contexts abroad acted not only as recruiters for future potential missionaries but also as conduits of information to their colleagues who served in a variety of ministries in the United States. Thus, after graduating from seminary, Protestant clergy had some knowledge and could provide a significant voice in interpreting Islam in the young American republic—for better or worse.[13]

Throughout the nineteenth century, thousands of ministerial students learned about Muhammad and the Qur'an in a variety of surprising ways throughout their seminary education. Usually, their exposure to Islam was negative and pejorative. Islam was a foil for American values. It was portrayed as alien and backward. However, by the end of the nineteenth century, views of Islam became more complicated and nuanced. It was not uncommon for seminary students to learn that while Islam may still have been considered an inferior religion, it was a Semitic religion that held the key to understanding the roots of the Hebrew Bible and was a step in the moral development of humanity even though it fell short and gave way to a morally, spiritually, and intellectually superior American Protestantism.

This book examines not only how seminarians were educated in the new seminary system of the nineteenth century, but more specifically what they were taught about Islam during this seminal period of graduate theological education. How was Islam understood and conveyed to theology students? What books were being read? What was being discussed in classrooms and meetings? What was the general view among students about Muslims and Islam? Examining such questions adds to a growing body of literature about American views of Islam in the nineteenth century. Moreover, this work aims to offer insights into lessons that may be gleaned from the theological education about Islam that then may be applied to the training of Christian seminarians and clergy in the twenty-first century.

Previous Studies in American Views of Islam

American Christian reflection on Islam and engagement with Muslim-majority lands have been important themes in the study of Christian missions. Two of the earliest studies focused on American missionary activity in Muslim-majority lands are A. L. Tibawi's *American Interests in Syria, 1801–1901* and Lyle Van Der Werf's *Christian Mission to Muslims.*[14] However, more recently American Christian mission to Muslim-majority lands has come to be seen as an important contribution to American religious and historical studies more broadly. Habib Badr, Adam Becker, Samir Khalaf, Hans Lukas-Keiser, Ussama Makdisi, Heather Sharkey, Emrah Şahin, Uta Zeuge-Buberl, and I, for example, have examined the encounter of American Christian religious culture with late Ottoman society.[15] In addition, there has been a much-needed focus on the contributions and ideas of American women in their encounter with Ottoman cultures through the work of Beth Baron, Ellen L. Fleischmann, Christine B. Lindner, Deanna Ferree Womack, and Fruma Zachs.[16]

American missionaries and their projects were, however, only one aspect of American interest in Muslim cultures. In the 1830s, safer passages across the Atlantic due to the creation of a US navy and a favorable commercial treaty with the Ottoman Empire, combined with the development of the steamship, made it easier for more Americans than ever to travel to Europe and the eastern Mediterranean. And, as European colonial expansion over Muslim populations in the Near East increased, Americans took full advantage of traveling throughout the network of European empires. Americans would not only go westward to fulfill their manifest destiny, but they could now also go eastward to the Orient. Merchants, travelers, and diplomats wrote about their experiences and views of the peoples and religions of the Ottoman Empire. Historians have come to appreciate the American engagement with the Near East, what we now call the Middle East, as an important aspect of American cultural encounter with Muslims abroad. The pioneering works of James A. Field and David H. Finnie in the 1960s, and John A. DeNovo and Joseph L. Grabill in the 1970s, for example, focused on the American cultural and political encounter with the Middle East prior to World War II completely detached from any American spiritual motivations.[17] More recently there has been an increased interest in this topic within the field of American studies. Jacob Berman, Jeffrey Einboden, Thomas Kidd, Timothy Marr, Hilton Obenzinger, Denise Spellberg, and Karine Walther have all provided important contributions to our understanding of the deep and sustained cultural interactions of Americans with Islam and Muslims in Muslim-majority lands, on which much of this book relies.[18]

Another important critical area of research on the American interaction with the Muslim world has been in the record and contributions of enslaved African Muslims. As Kambiz GhaneaBassiri has stated, Muslims were "deeply embedded" in the history of the exploration and colonization of the Americas.[19] These voices have now found an important place in American historical studies through the work of Allan D. Austin, Edward E. Curtis IV, and Sylviane A. Diouf, among others. The United States has, since its founding, been part of the Muslim world as Muslims have either involuntarily or voluntarily made North America their home and have successfully contributed to its culture.

All these various areas of investigation demonstrate that what had once been considered a niche field restricted to those interested in Protestant American missions or missiology is now an important part of the general American story and encounter with the world. This book examines another addition to the American cultural encounter with Islam. It focuses on how American seminaries presented Islam to those students who were being trained as "Christian gentlemen" and later as ministerial professionals who were expected to contribute to the public moral discourse of American society. Because of the important role that Protestant clergy had in the shaping of American society during the early years of the republic, their views carried authority within American public discourse. In tracing this history, this book crosses several disciplines, including Christian theological studies, American cultural history, and the study of American education.

Methodology of the Research

In his extensive study of early North American seminaries, Glenn T. Miller notes the establishment of thirty-four Protestant seminaries between 1808 and 1839.[20] As Protestant denominations created seminaries to fill the pulpits for an expanding American population, Miller argues, every denomination and tradition sought to create its own seminary to serve its own community. This ideal could not be properly sustained as the United States became a land of numerous religious "sects." Seminaries were usually poorly funded, the faculty were overtaxed and underpaid, and resources were scarce. Nevertheless, the system has persisted and has been the foundation for the formation of Christian ministers into the twenty-first century.

Timothy Dwight, the president of Yale College, provided the inaugural sermon at the 1808 opening of Andover seminary, widely recognized as the nation's first formal seminary. In his sermon "The Evangelical Scribe," he provided the basic principles around which seminaries were founded: (1) a theological curriculum, (2) professional teachers who taught specific disciplines, (3) a student body, (4) sound trustee management that would oversee funding, and (5) a library.[21] These distinctive marks continue to be the basis of theological education today, even though its curricula, teachers, students, and libraries have changed dramatically since Dwight's time.

In his study, Miller categorizes the theological institutions established during the first half of the nineteenth century according to their founding dates, number of faculty, number of students, and the volumes of books in their library. This book uses Miller's classification of first-tier seminaries created before 1839 and focuses on seven of the original thirty-four: Andover, New Brunswick, General, Princeton, Gettysburg, Hartford, and Union. These seven institutions have been chosen for several reasons. First, they all follow the distinctive principles of seminaries as institutions of higher learning as set out by Timothy Dwight, and each fits Miller's criteria as a first-tier seminary.[22] Second, over time they were successful in drawing a significant number of students to study at their institution and created important alumni networks. Third, they developed distinctive theological libraries that served their own particular denominations. And last, they represent a cross-section of Protestant traditions that engaged in the new seminary system during the formative years of theological education. The seven seminaries are listed here in the order of their recognized establishment and denominational affiliation:

Andover Theological Seminary (1808)—Congregational
New Brunswick Theological Seminary (1810)—Reformed[23]
General Theological Seminary (1810)—Anglican
Princeton Theological Seminary (1812)—Presbyterian
Gettysburg Theological Seminary (1826)—Lutheran
Hartford Theological Seminary (1833)—Congregational
Union Theological Seminary, New York (1836)—Presbyterian

Two Congregational and two Presbyterian institutions are included in this list for two reasons. First, these two traditions made up the earliest and largest Protestant communities within American society in the East during the early nineteenth century, that is, until the Methodists and Baptists overtook them. Second, the missions of each of these seminaries were distinctly different. Princeton was founded to be "the seminary" of the Presbyterian Church for Presbyterian candidates under the auspices of the General Assembly. Union, however, was established as a freestanding seminary by Presbyterians in the city of New York to raise up pastors, regardless of their denominational background, for ministry in the city. For the Congregational seminaries, Andover was the first American graduate theological school, and Hartford seminary was chosen because its beginning is the classic Protestant seminary origin story, but it also transformed itself from a conservative Calvinist institution to a successful ecumenical school where Islamic studies as an area of study took root in the United States. In many ways, Andover and Hartford serve as book ends of the seminary experience during the period under investigation. In addition, Gettysburg, New Brunswick, and General provide important contributions to the story of American Protestant religion. Gettysburg was founded to serve the German Lutheran immigrants streaming into the United States. However, its leadership was caught in the debate over whether their identity would remain German Lutheran or become part of the mainstream Anglo Protestant culture. New Brunswick provides a similar story, being rooted in the Dutch Reformed tradition. It served a particular role among the Dutch immigrants in the Hudson Valley, western New York, and midwestern communities. Some of these churches later joined with the Congregationalists; others stood firmly rooted in their Dutch heritage. Finally, General seminary presents the important story of the sole Anglican institution that had to remake itself as a truly American Episcopal church from the remnants of the British Anglican Church in the American colonies.

Other seminaries could have been chosen as part of this study. The decision to use Miller's categorization and dates excludes two important Protestant traditions: the Baptists and the Methodists, the two largest Protestant denominations in America at the end of the nineteenth century. While these traditions did eventually establish theological schools, their leadership was by and large initially opposed to the creation of seminaries as a way to educate, train, and credential clergy.[24] In general for the Baptists and Methodists, pastoral authority was understood to derive from one's individual calling by the Holy Spirit and not through any educational process. They were suspicious of formal theological education. These suspicions did change, especially after the Civil War, when these denominations began founding successful seminaries throughout the United States. I recognize that some might object to this exclusion, and hope that further similar studies might include or focus on these denominational traditions. Nevertheless, the seven seminaries included provide a manageable number of institutions to study for the period selected, and they provide a significant cross-section of the American Protestant landscape, with the additional exception of the

African American Protestant communities. The first freestanding African American seminary of the African Methodist Episcopal Seminary at Wilberforce University, Payne Theological Seminary, opened its doors in 1892 and falls outside of the scope of Miller's time frame.

One final comment about the choice to exclude divinity schools or theology departments of universities is in order here. The earliest institutions of higher learning in the North American colonies, Harvard (1636), William & Mary (1693), and Yale (1701), were all founded for the purpose of delivering a classical education to White, male colonial North Americans. It had been assumed from their inception that some of the students in these colleges would continue their education to "read theology" to prepare for the Christian ministry. However, preparation was done on an ad hoc basis. Normally, students stayed on to read theology with the designated "professor of divinity," usually the president of the college. This system produced only a handful of students each year, and is one of the reasons why Congregationalists, Reformed, and Presbyterians wanted to establish schools specifically for the education of a cohort of ministerial students. While Harvard and Yale founded their own divinity schools in 1815 and 1822, respectively, the American seminaries, by contrast, were institutions created solely for the purpose of training clergy for ministry.[25] Their libraries, buildings, campuses, and boards were created for the expressed purpose of theological education, as opposed to more general studies. This is the reason why Princeton Theological Seminary was a separate institution from Princeton University, or New Brunswick seminary from Queen's College—later Rutgers University.

In addition, it was assumed that students would come to seminaries after their general liberal arts education at one of the historic (or other newly formed) colleges. Seminaries quickly instituted rules that required students to have completed their bachelor's studies before they applied to the seminary, even if they were never completely able to adhere to those rules. Seminaries made exceptions for those who had no previous education or proper preparation and continued to struggle with the ideal preeducational qualifications of their students.

In terms of sheer numbers, the divinity schools were a small percentage of the overall population of theology students at any given time. What made the creation of North American seminaries so important for the development of Protestantism in the United States was that they simply created "pastor factories" in which thousands of graduates were produced to meet the demand of the growing population of the country over the years. Whether the seminaries were successful in their mission is another topic for discussion. The creation of such a novel system in such a short period of time, however, demonstrates that there was a general desire for an educated clergy that met particular professional standards.

Sources

A wide variety of primary sources have been examined for this research. First, the seminary libraries have served as critical places of information. Each library supplied a treasure trove of records, including catalogues, annual bulletins, and rare books. Rare books were physically examined to ascertain their provenance and their use. Some libraries have also maintained a record of early accession lists and student borrowing records. This data provided information on what sources were available to students and whether they were actually checked out. Second, the annual catalogs of each school are replete with descriptions of faculty responsibilities and course listings. These published catalogs were indispensable for analyzing the curricula of the seminaries and where particular courses or lectures on Islam fit into the overall theological education. Third, the archives of the seminaries were also rich with collections of the syllabi, lectures, and letters of professors and missionaries who taught various aspects of Islam. The archives also included the records of the early student missionary societies formed during the early years of the seminaries. They provide an important perspective on the interests of students regarding foreign missions, the place of Islam in such missions, and student engagement (or lack thereof) with Islamic sources. While physical library research made up a most important part of this project, it also contributed to several research challenges, including their collections being locked up and physically inaccessible during the 2020–2022 COVID-19 pandemic. Thus, Internet Archive, HathiTrust, and Princeton's Theological Commons served as invaluable digital resources. Given all these resources, however, it is important to recognize that there are still gaps in the sources, and thus in the story.

Some of the information has either gone missing or was not accessible. Thus, we present the information as it has been available and uncovered.

Dates of the Research

This book examines the period from 1808 to 1910, roughly one hundred years. Andover seminary, the first official formal graduate seminary (as defined by Miller), opened its doors in 1808 and thus ushers in the history of North American graduate theological education as we know it.[26] There are several places where one could conclude such a study. The American Civil War provides a natural demarcation, as it catastrophically altered the infrastructure of the seminaries for some time. Students left the seminaries in large numbers either to serve in the armies of the North and the South, or to work as chaplains. Others returned home to be with their families during the trauma of the war. The seminaries under investigation, with the exception of Gettysburg seminary, were not physically impacted, primarily because of their being removed from the front lines of the war. Gettysburg, however, was the location of the deadliest battle of the Civil War, and the seminary building was used first as a command center for the Union Army and then as a hospital for months following the three-day battle in 1863. Another northern seminary that had to close because of the direct impact of occupation by troops was Mercersberg Seminary in central Pennsylvania. Philip Schaff, one of the two professors of that seminary, left Mercersberg and ended up in New York, eventually being called to Union seminary. His teaching plays an important role in the teaching of Islam, as we shall see.

However, the years following the Civil War proved to be an era of economic growth in the North. As the economy expanded through an industrial revolution, wealthy business owners became potential supporters for philanthropic causes. Presidents of the seminaries were able to take advantage of donations from prosperous industrialists and capitalists to expand campuses, faculty, and student living. From this period, known as Reconstruction, up to what is known as the Gilded Age, a period of immense prosperity for the upper echelon of American society, students began to enroll in the seminaries in larger numbers. It was during this period that the curricula of the seminaries became more intricate as American universities also began to develop into the institutions of higher learning that we would recognize today. In terms of the study of Islam, there was increased exposure to Islamic sources in the postbellum period. So, we find the last third of the nineteenth century to be the most active period of engagement with Islam in seminaries.

We complete the examination of seminary curricula in 1910, with the occasion of the Edinburgh World Missionary Conference. The conference, which brought together representatives of thousands of Protestant denominations from around Europe and North America, as well as missionaries and agents from around the world, was an unprecedented feat of organization. Participants included mission boards of the most prominent Protestant denominations, as well as freestanding voluntary mission associations. The conference addressed a wide variety of topics related to Protestant mission around the world, including specific sections on "Mohammedan Lands in the Near East" as well as a hearing on "Islam."[27] Several seminary graduates serving on the eight organizing commissions of the conference included James Dennis and Samuel Zwemer, American missionaries serving in the Near East, as well as Charles Watson, who grew up as the son of missionaries in Egypt and who would later serve as the first president of the American University in Cairo.

The significance of this world conference for the study of Islam in American seminaries was direct. The summit called for several missionary study centers to be created, particularly ones that would focus on the "Mohammedan" world. Following Edinburgh, Samuel Zwemer was asked to create a center in Cairo where he founded the *Moslem World* journal as a central mouthpiece for Christian missions to the Muslim world. Later it would become a journal for Christian reflection on Christian-Muslim dialogue at Hartford.[28] Because of the recommendations to found study centers, Zwemer would also be invited to Princeton Theological Seminary for various lectures on Islam. Later, in 1928, he was invited to take up a faculty post there. In addition, the conference also led to the establishment of the formal study of Islam at Hartford seminary and ultimately to the establishment of the Kennedy School of Missions there. The Edinburgh Missionary Conference of 1910 ushered in a new era wherein Protestant mission to Muslims became a focused reason to include Islam within the curricula of seminaries, as an object for research and study.[29] Because of the important impact that the Edinburgh conference had on Western Protestant missions to the Muslim-majority world, occasionally this book references events or writings that go beyond 1910. Nevertheless, the Edinburgh Missionary Conference had a direct impact on the teaching of Islam in seminaries and seems to be a good place to conclude this volume, allowing for further research in the future to analyze Islam in American seminaries in the post–World War I era.

Outline of the Book

While this is not a study of American seminaries, nor of their education in general, some orientation to the concept and purposes of theological education is necessary. Chapter 1 provides an overview of Protestant theological education in the late eighteenth and early nineteenth centuries to provide the background to the establishment of the American seminary system, especially the seven seminaries under investigation here.

Chapter 2 explores the library resources of the seminaries and what books were available for students to read. In some cases, various books on Islam were required reading or served as the basis for the lectures by the faculty. Several important books on Islam were present in all the seminary libraries during the nineteenth century, including various translations of the Qur'an. Thus, the Qur'an in English translation was relatively widely available for seminary students engaged in scriptural study. Early on, the most common books available were British Orientalist works, such as those by Edward Pococke and George Sale. However, from the 1830s onward, German scholarship began to predominate and show up in the libraries. American Protestants quickly viewed Germany as the leading country for theological and biblical research.

Chapter 3 reviews the image of Islam as represented in the prominent church history textbooks used across the seminary curricula. In many ways, these general church histories are the most important resources on how Islam was introduced and framed for American seminarians. Even if a student was not interested in learning about Islam or becoming a missionary, they nevertheless would have been exposed to the history of Islam as portrayed in these church history texts. Philip Schaff (1819–1905), the preeminent American church historian of this time, takes center stage as an important figure in the teaching of Islam. He was one of the longest-serving professors of theological education and taught thousands of seminary students throughout his fifty-year tenure as a professor, first at Mercersburg, then at Hartford, and finally at Union seminary. Even after his death his ecclesiastical histories were used by seminaries throughout the country as a resource until the first half of the twentieth century.

Chapter 4 explores how Arabic and the Qur'an became important components for teaching Hebrew to better understand the word of God in its original languages. It became common for seminaries to have at least one professor who taught Hebrew and "cognate biblical languages," usually Chaldean (the common name for Aramaic), Syriac, and Arabic. Charles Briggs at Union and John G. Lansing at New Brunswick taught numerous second- and third-year students that reading *ayat* (verses) from the Qur'an was often seen as an excellent way to help in interpreting the Hebrew.

Chapter 5 explores how Islam came to be studied not as a Christian heresy, a malicious off-shoot of Christianity created by Muhammad, but as a world religion that was an expression of the human desire for the religious life *homo religio*. Henry Preserved Smith of Union lectured, taught, and wrote about what he believed to be the development of Islam from its Semitic origins in the Jewish and Eastern Christian experience to its becoming a religious system in its own right. Smith utilized the work of the German scholar Max Müller to develop a comparative analysis of Christianity and Islam. This comparative religions perspective was fully on display during the Chicago World's Fair in 1893 when Union graduate John Barrow organized the first World Parliament of Religions. This area of comparative religions was the precursor of college and university religious studies.

Finally, chapter 6 examines how the role of Christian mission to Muslim-majority lands contributed to the teaching about Islam at seminaries, culminating in the decisions of the 1910 Edinburgh World Missionary Conference. Throughout the nineteenth and into the twentieth centuries, large numbers of seminary graduates became missionaries and went abroad. Often those who committed themselves to a lifetime of missionary service were the "cream of the crop" of the seminary classes. They were linguistically gifted and trained. A small number of these missionaries did go on to live as missionaries in Muslim-majority lands. As already noted, often these missionaries returned to their alma maters while on furlough to lecture and preach, and in some cases these missionaries came back to teach permanently. The public lectures provided important moments for other seminarians to ponder their own futures as missionaries in Muslim countries, or to instill in their own congregations the views of Islam that were disseminated by the missionaries. As a result of the 1910 Edinburgh conference, Princeton and Hartford seminaries became important missionary schools where Islam became a prominent field of study. While known for his work through the Kennedy School of Missions, prior to his direct involvement with training missionaries, Duncan Black Macdonald pioneered American Islamic studies some sixty years before the development of departments of Islamic studies at the major research universities in the United States.

It is during this early period in the development of seminary education, from 1808 to 1910, when denominations were defining themselves over and against other Protestant communities and seeking to gain new members from a growing American population, that Islam, Muhammad, and Arabic appeared regularly throughout seminary curricula. There were a wide variety of resources available for students to be exposed to and learn about Islam—from a Christian perspective. Some of these sources were required reading. Rarely, however, did they read Islamic sources, except for portions of the Qur'an. There were also various ways in which Islam was framed, but it was always seen as a foreign and culturally other entity. Orientalism, and American Orientalism in particular, were paradigms around which Islam was viewed as a foil for American progress.[30] Finally, as noted earlier, the Arabic language, even the Qur'an in Arabic, became an important part of biblical studies as Bible scholars examined the role of Arabic as a cognate biblical language. By the end of the nineteenth century, some professors even had students reading the Qur'an to help teach them how to better understand the Hebrew Bible. Before we examine the information that was available or taught in the seminaries, it is important to have a general understanding of the genesis of seminaries, as one of the earliest graduate schools in North America.

1

Early American Theological Education and American Seminaries

During the first half of the nineteenth century, American Protestant denominations developed a new system of theological education for the purpose of training clergy. Theological seminaries were created to provide an education that was distinct from the classical "arts and sciences" education of American colleges like Harvard, Yale, Dartmouth, and William & Mary. The interest in creating separate institutions from these colleges was born from a desire by the different Protestant churches to maintain what they believed to be orthodox Christian teaching in the midst of the Christian pluralism of the young American republic. For example, from its inception in 1636, Harvard College was considered the central institution of Calvinist doctrines for the Congregational churches of New England. The college taught not only the classics—Greek and Roman philosophy and history—but Calvinist biblical theology. However, throughout the eighteenth century, Unitarian theology gained in popularity at Harvard. The appointment of Henry Ware, who was a publicly professed Unitarian, as the Hollis professor of divinity in 1805, was the last straw for those pastors who adhered to Calvinist theology.

In 1808, a number of concerned Congregational pastors in New England took action to withdraw their support from the venerable institution and began sending the sons of their congregations to a newly formed theological academy originally known as Philips Academy, which eventually became incorporated as the Theological Seminary of Andover. Sixteen students enrolled the first year, a dramatic increase from the handful of candidates at Harvard who had been "reading theology" with a professor to prepare for ministry. Andover seminary was founded specifically to support "the training up of learned, orthodox and pious ministers of the gospel."[1] In a similar fashion, the Pastoral Union of Congregationalist clergy in the Connecticut River Valley took measures to found the Connecticut Theological Institute, later known as

Hartford Theological Seminary, as a place for "the defense and promotion of evangelical principles" and to counteract the theological "errors" being taught at Yale College. Fifteen students and two professors began their education together in the winter of 1834.[2] Disagreement over what ought to be understood as Christian orthodoxy and correct biblical interpretation has been part of the ongoing story of North American Protestant theological education to this day.

Prior to the establishment of Protestant seminaries, the Congregationalists of New England used the faculty resources of American colleges to assist in the education of their ministers. English-speaking colonists who felt a call to ministry could attend one of these few colleges, usually staffed by clergy, and "read theology" with the faculty member. Where there was no college, a preparatory academy established by a local clergyman would do for general theological instruction. These tutors were seasoned pastors who took students under their wing. When they were deemed ready, they would be examined by a committee of pastors and licensed to preach. Other Protestant communities had to rely on their churches in Europe to supply clergy. The Dutch and German Reformed and Lutheran immigrant communities appealed to the religious communities in their respective homelands to send pastors to the colonies. Those young men from these communities who were born in the Americas and felt a call to ministry would be sent to Europe to study theology and the confessions of their Reformation churches before being licensed and returning with their bona fides.

Anglicans provide a unique case among other Protestant communities in North America. Because of their belief in the historic episcopate of ecclesiastical authority, candidates for ministry were required to be trained and ordained under the supervision of a duly consecrated Anglican bishop. For a variety of reasons, including international and church politics, the Church of England failed to send a bishop to the North American colonies. This meant that Anglican priests needed to be ordained in England and then be appointed to posts in the colonies. It was not until 1784, after American independence, that Samuel Seabury (1729–1796) was consecrated a bishop to oversee the ministry of the Episcopal Church in America. A plan to organize a seminary for the training of clergy in the autonomous Episcopal Church in America did not take place until the second outbreak of hostilities with England in 1812.

The War of Independence was not only a political revolution but a social and religious one as well. After the war, the old models of reading theology at a few small, colony-sponsored colleges would no longer support the needs of a growing, diverse body of Protestants in a new America, for several reasons. The first was financial. Following independence from the English Crown, religious denominations were now under a new political reality, and it would take them some time to figure out how to organize and finance themselves. Under colonial rule, Anglican and Congregational churches and the salaries of their ministers were supported first by the colony and then by state taxes. After the ratification of the Constitution in 1787, it would take some time for any true separation of state and church to take place. Not only were there ecclesiastical structures to build separate from any state infrastructure, but the finances necessary to support church properties and ministers had to be sorted out. It was now up to individual denominations and churches to raise funds for the salaries of the clergy and upkeep of their properties, something that no one was truly ready for. All of this was taking place at a time when there was an expanding population of new citizens in North America for whom pastors wanted to provide pastoral care or to evangelize.

A second reason for the need to create a new model of theological education in the new United States was demographic. In 1700 the United States population stood at around 250,000. By 1800 it had expanded to 3,929,000 and showed no sign of stopping. There was no way the previous colonial model of ministerial education would suffice to support the growing number of congregations along the seaboard and for those citizens who desired to move inland into the frontier. Not only were there thousands of newly arriving immigrants who had belonged to Protestant churches in Europe, but there was a newfound experience of religious revivalism sweeping through the country known as the Second Great Awakening. This religious resurgence provided fertile soil for the proliferation of newly established religious communities and the need for more pastors and priests.

Finally, as noted above in the cases of Harvard and Yale, clergy had theological disagreements with what was being taught in the colleges. Theological disputation has been the heart of the Protestant Reformation. Ever since Martin Luther publicly contested some of the practices and theology of the medieval Catholic Church in 1517, Protestants have continually staked their claims to sound theology and "correct" biblical interpretation. Under a new political reality with no accountable state church, the young republic provided a unique opportunity for different religious communities to flex their social muscles and create new voluntary institutions. From the Calvinists in New England to the Methodists in the Carolinas, the many German sects in Pennsylvania, the Catholics in Maryland, and the Jewish communities in Rhode Island, Pennsylvania, and New York, the young American republic was a religiously plural land from its very beginning.[3] While some of the communities faced discrimination and prejudice, especially the Catholics and Jews, all voluntary religious communities were legally able to exist as part of the religious landscape of America, all except for enslaved Africans and Indigenous Americans, who had no rights whatsoever. Denominationalism in America required religious communities to distinguish themselves from others and teach their own doctrine in a marketplace of ideas and values, or, as Alexis de Tocqueville, the French visitor to America in 1835, labeled them—"democratic communities."[4]

As we have seen, feeling the need to establish their own schools to train American clergy, the various Protestant denominations took measures to create professional schools for the training of ministers separately where they would have more control than in the general college system. The Congregationalists, Episcopalians, Lutherans, Presbyterians, and Reformed began to require students to enroll in their own training schools for several years of postgraduate education under the supervision of professors who were duly recognized clergy, before the candidates were licensed or ordained to preach. Thus, seminaries became one of the first types of graduate schools of education in the United States.[5]

While this new seminary model was intended to educate substantial numbers of pastors more systematically and efficiently, it could not keep pace with the growth of the Baptists and Methodists. These denominations quickly made up half of the Protestant population of America. Initially, these denominations frowned on any kind of formal educational credentials for their clergy. Much to the chagrin of the Episcopalians and Presbyterians, Baptist and Methodist ministers without any formal training took advantage of the tent meeting revivals of the Second Great Awakening and the open expanse of the frontier. Their focus on individual responsibility before God wedded well to American frontier life. Those who were so moved by the Holy Spirit were free to take up their Bible and preach the Gospel wherever the Spirit led them. By the Civil War, Baptist and Methodist ministers, most of whom were not formally theologically trained in the seminaries, made up more than half of all American Protestant clergy.[6] Eventually, however, these denominations would establish their own seminaries to meet the growing needs of religious work.

Nevertheless, the established churches of the young republic continued to insist on an educated clergy centered on biblical and theological orientations of their own tradition. At Andover, the first newly created seminary, the principle as outlined by Ezra Stiles was simple: gather as many postbaccalaureate students as possible together in one place under at least three pastors who each taught one or two disciplines and provide them books to read from a common library. After three years a new cohort of graduates could be licensed and would be ready to serve any community that would have them.

The Andover model proved to be very successful, and other seminaries quickly followed suit. These seminaries were formed to meet specific denominational needs. In a new country with a free marketplace of religious ideas, or what Robert Baird called "the multiplication of sects," every denomination began to organize its own "pastor factories."[7] Students were required to be in residence with other students, attend lectures by faculty, and utilize the books that were collected in libraries. The earliest faculties of seminaries were well-respected clergy who were recruited by a board. These pastors taught the traditional fields of study: Bible and theology, along with the history of the church, specifically the history of their denominational heritage. As seminaries grew, the faculty expanded to include specialized areas, such as New Testament, Old Testament (usually referred to as "Oriental Languages and Biblical Literature"), preaching, and practical theology.

The original model assumed that students would come to the seminary after college. While the admission standards were rigorous on paper, they were not always strictly adhered to. Faculty quickly began to complain that their students were not adequately trained in the classical languages and they were wasting time bringing them up to speed. Yet, it was not always easy to insist on a complete college education before entrance to seminary. And, students often did not stay to complete a degree. It was almost a hundred years before any accreditation or degree standards were fully developed in the United States, and it was not uncommon for students to attend for only one or two years before moving on.

Seminary education was intended not only to provide information and knowledge about Christianity, the Bible, and doctrinal theology but to be a place of spiritual and social formation. Seminaries were communities that shaped and formed young ministers, socializing them into a new cohort of religious and community leaders for their denominations. They were also expected to provide spiritual and moral guidance in their civic community, speaking to the larger issues of national importance. These young men (as they were only men throughout most of the nineteenth century) were expected to be "learned gentlemen" of a new educated class in America.[8]

Creating a "Learned and Able Clergy"

Education and reading had been key elements of the Protestant Reformation. As a university professor, Martin Luther instilled the idea that education was a constitutive element of the Christian faith, not only for the clergy but for the family at home. The small Wittenberg university from which he taught and wrote set the expectation that it was not only clergy who were to take seriously their vocations as Christians. Luther's Small Catechism was to be used by the general population within the home. Parents were to read the Bible and the catechism daily with their children. Luther also advocated that political leaders "establish and maintain schools" in their towns, especially for girls.[9]

From the very foundation of English-speaking settlements in North America, literacy was an important part of civic life. A classical education, however defined, was not only a noble endeavor but an expectation of the professional class, whether one aspired to be a doctor, lawyer, or minister. As early as 1726, Cotton Mather, the Boston pastor, published his *Manuductio ad Ministerium*, in which he underlined the importance of a "learned and able" clergy who had access to knowledge of the liberal arts.[10] The denominations included in this study—Congregationalists, Episcopalians, Lutherans, and Presbyterians—have habitually required their clergy to be educated and credentialed. The level and quality of this theological education has always been fluid, but since the nineteenth century it has required a postbaccalaureate degree. These churches and their constituents have expected their clergy to have more than a basic understanding of the Bible and an ability to explain the major tenets of their faith and theological confessions, in addition to conducting pastoral care and preaching edifying sermons. Clergy were expected to be able to read the Bible in the original languages, Hebrew and Greek. In most cases, the churches also expected their clergy to be conversant with traditional classics of Western literature and history. Thus, they not only required a distinctly theological education but assumed a pre-theology classical education. This course of study was eventually called a bachelor of divinity. In the twentieth century this was upgraded to a master of divinity.

This desire for a learned clergy may have been a general expectation, but its execution was a perennial challenge. How much education was enough? Where were these future pastors to be educated? Who would teach them? And, most importantly, who was going to pay for their education? As previously noted, it was not uncommon for candidates for the ministry among the Dutch and German Reformed, as well as the Anglicans, to be sent back to Europe to attend university and then a theological college. However, this took too long and was very expensive. It also removed future pastors from the North American context in which they were going to serve. If there was no local candidate, communities wrote back to their home countries and pleaded for the church there to send pastors. Henry Melchior Mühlenberg (1711–1787) came to Pennsylvania at the request of German Lutheran settlers. He facilitated the emigration of many German clergy to North America to serve the German-speaking communities.

Prior to the establishment of the seminaries as postgraduate institutions of higher learning with a theological curriculum, Congregationalist and Presbyterian ministers were trained like all other professions in the colonies—through apprenticeships. Apprenticeships could happen in several ways: at the established colleges, through the local academies, or in the homes of pastors. Those who felt a call to ministry usually attended one of the early colonial colleges, specifically Harvard, William & Mary, or Yale. Harvard actually appointed a faculty member of divinity, the Hollis professor of divinity, whose responsibility was to guide these ministerial students. At Yale, President Timothy Dwight also personally guided students. Dwight and his divinity students attended Sunday services on campus, and the students actively listened to his sermons and "read" their own sermons to the cohort.[11] By the eighteenth century, new opportunities were available through the recently founded colleges of the University of Pennsylvania in Philadelphia, Brown in Rhode Island, King's College in New York, and Queen's College in New Jersey. Even further south, the colleges of Hampden-Sydney and Davidson were established by Presbyterians. Students might spend several months or up to three years reading with their mentors before being examined by the particular judicatory of their denomination and then licensed to preach in the churches of their denomination.

By the 1730s, however, a wave of religious fervor swept through the colonies. The Great Awakening supported new opportunities for pastors and evangelists who did not have access to a classical college education and who were not already part of an educated class. The Spirit was moving in the tent revivals and no amount of church order was going to squash the fervor of religiosity. In the interior of the country, pastors began to organize small academies to provide rudimentary education that focused on Bible study. The precursor to the College of New Jersey, or Princeton, was the "Log College," created by Gilbert Tennent, a Scottish Presbyterian preacher, in 1735 in Neshaminy, Pennsylvania. Newbury Academy in North Carolina and Liberty Hall Academy in Virginia provided rudimentary levels of education for aspiring pastoral students.[12] The oldest Lutheran theological academy in North America was Hartwick Seminary. A seminary in name only, Hartwick was literally willed into existence through the resolve of John Christopher Hartwick (1714–1796), whose legal will required his land and monies be used to establish a Lutheran seminary. The school officially opened its doors in New York City in 1797 under the leadership of pastor John Kunze. When a campus and building were established in Otsego County in upstate New York in 1815, the seminary welcomed some nineteen students. However, the seminary was in essence a preparatory school, teaching children as young as seven years old. Its curriculum included literature, history, math, and science. The theology students had to attend the additional meetings of the "Theological Society" under the tutelage of the pastor.[13] In essence, this was the pattern at the colleges, but only at a more rudimentary level of education.

Regardless of whether a student began attending a formal college or a local academy to read theology, many decided to seek out and serve as an apprentice under another pastor.[14] This apprenticeship model is what Norman Kansfield has called "parsonage education."[15] Popular and well-respected pastors took in students as their apprentices. Many of the students moved into the parsonage and lived with the family. Students would be instructed by the pastor, much in the same way as they would be instructed by private tutors. They were required to read the theology and spiritual classics from the pastor's personal library and were given assignments to write sermons on various topics. Often the pastoral tutor would pose a series of theological questions in response to which the students were required to draft essays that would lay out their own views on the various topics. Students were also required to follow their mentor on visits and activities throughout the afternoons and evenings. These apprenticeships provided the students with experience in practical ministerial work. When they were judged by their mentor as having sufficient knowledge or experience, they were then examined and licensed.

The apprenticeship method, however, was time consuming and draining for the pastor's family and spouse, who may have had several students in their household at any time. (This may also explain why so many pastors' daughters married aspiring young pastors!) The model also lacked any formal regulation. Popular preachers attracted more students, creating further demand and a drain on them. They became victims of their own success.

In the end, there were several ways to demonstrate one's fitness for ministry, either by "reading theology" at a college, attending an academy, or serving as a pastoral apprentice, or a combination of these, but all demanded approval by a judicatory.[16] Normally, this required an examination before a committee of pastors from the denomination. All in all, each year the colleges and the pastoral apprenticeships created only a handful of students who were prepared for ministry. However, the growing population of America with the increasing number of denominations and the religious fervor of the Great Awakening led to the need for a greater number of clergy who could be trained more efficiently. This is the context that led to the opening of the doors of Andover seminary in 1808, after which denominational seminaries became the standard expectation of theological education up until today.

Against the "Manufactured Pastors"

As we have previously stated, not all American Protestant churches were in favor of this movement toward the formal theological education of the clergy. Some felt that it stifled the work of the Holy Spirit among those who were truly called to preach the Gospel. In fact, theological education could be seen as counterproductive to letting God's spirit flow through the gifts and graces of spirit-led pastors. Hollifield calls this a debate between "professionalism" and "populism," a debate that is still very much alive and well among Christian denominations and traditions in the United States.[17]

The Second Great Awakening, which swept through New England, upstate New York, and then the frontier of the young republic, provided ample proof that clergy could function well—perhaps even better—if they were not held back by the constraints of a European-style classical education. In fact, critics of the seminary system argued that pulling ministerial candidates out of their context and having them read with scholars in colleges or pastors in their homes kept them from truly learning what God was doing in the rural church. Rather, the "church itself was the place of worship, the agent of mission, and the location of theological education."[18]

The Methodists were effective in evangelizing North America very quickly because of their circuit riders, who traveled throughout the rural communities bringing a message of individual repentance and salvation not mediated by the church. These Methodist preachers focused not on correct translation of the original languages of scripture or on confessional theology set during the Reformation, or even sound knowledge of doctrine, but on personal conversion and conviction. The Methodist Church wanted preachers who could "warm the hearts" of their hearers. Formal theological education in their view was at best not necessary, and at worst it was destructive to the emotive opportunities of the Spirit. The Methodists believed that the Presbyterians and Congregationalists "manufactured preachers" rather than allowing the Holy Spirit to naturally work through them.[19] Rather, a Methodist candidate simply apprenticed with a minister for two to four years in the field before they were deemed ready to preach on their own. The student was not to be educated in books but to be "a 'man of the people,' whose primary role was to save souls through preaching."[20]

The Methodists were not the only ones who held this general rule of theological education. The Baptists, too, held a similar view. Their ministers were, by and large, free from oversight of a denomination that required one to demonstrate "correct" theological views and relied solely on individual reading of the Bible for their interpretation. They did not even require an established church building or structured congregational constitution, but rather used the tent revival meetings in the countryside to great effect. By the mid-nineteenth century, Methodist ministers made up 40 percent and Baptists nearly 30 percent of all clergy in the United States.[21]

Ultimately, the need for clerical accountability in rural areas was too strong for this understanding of the ministerial call. As the frontier became settled and the circuits included growing villages and towns in need of organized congregations, the wandering preachers had to meet the needs of their settled citizens. These communities required schools for their children and then colleges for their young adults. With their heavy emphasis on Sunday School education for children, the Methodists eventually realized that an educated clergy was necessary. By the middle of the twentieth century, Methodists required a master of divinity, and even the Southern Baptists encouraged theological education to sharpen the skills of called ministers even if such formal education came after they were preaching.

Organizing Theological Education

The Great Awakening had challenged the authority of the established church structures of the Congregationalists and Anglicans. Nonconformist churches scattered throughout the massive territory of the young United States, and the rise of Enlightenment, Deist, and antireligious thinking created an atmosphere of a free marketplace of religious ideas that defied stolid Calvinist theology in its Congregational and Presbyterian forms. However, it was the American War of Independence that brought a decisive end to the colonial Christian education system. During the war, many of the theological academies were closed, and their students either enlisted in the war effort or moved to safer environs in the cities.

Prior to the war, Anglican priests and Scottish Presbyterian pastors originally received their training in England and Scotland. The American colonies were under the authority of the Crown through colonial governors who provided charters for congregations. And the vast majority of Anglican clergy received their funding through the Society for the Propagation of the Gospel, the Anglican missionary society specifically set up to support Anglican mission in the Americas. After the War of Independence, however, the society withdrew its funding from the rebellious colonies. The American Episcopal Church found itself at an existential crossroads, organizationally and financially. In addition, the Dutch and German Reformed communities scattered throughout New York and Pennsylvania had always relied on their consistories and synods back in the Old Country to provide pastors who were already trained. However, relying on pastors from Europe was never an easy or efficient method. Indeed, between 1648 and 1747 there were just eight ordinations of Dutch pastors approved by the Classis of Amsterdam to serve in the colonies.[22]

During and after the war, churches could no longer count on a supply of religious leadership from across the pond. Not only did the new United States need to develop its own system of government, but its diverse religious communities needed to create new structures to become self-governing, self-supporting, and self-propagating. American denominations needed to find ways to re-create systems to educate their clergy. Throughout the nineteenth century and into the early part of the twentieth century, they provided the leading role of formalized postgraduate education with a three-year curriculum and a faculty of different teachers. The first year of study focused on scripture, the second on theology, and the third on history. In many ways, the three-year seminary curriculum would remain the standard up to the second decade of the twenty-first century.

The move toward an "assembly line" of theological education was an instant success However, to be fair, the New England clergy were not the only ones contemplating such a new educational method. The Dutch Reformed had begun working toward the goal of creating a seminary in New York as early as 1784. However, due to disagreements over ownership, leadership, faculty, and location, the General Synod of the Dutch Reformed Church did not establish the New Brunswick seminary until 1812. It was then that it had an established board, three faculty, a building, a small library, and students.[23] The Presbyterians had begun voting in their presbyteries on a plan for a national church seminary in 1810, and by 1812 the General Assembly successfully incorporated Princeton seminary with a board, three faculty (divinity, Oriental and biblical literature, and ecclesiastical history and church government), a building with books, and only three students. However, by 1828 they had managed to enroll one hundred students.[24] Other denominations or local judicatories also made plans to "upgrade" their academies to provide a formal curriculum for ministerial candidates with more than one pastor providing the pedagogical oversight.

While this new method of theological education was simple, it did require substantial resources and an ongoing financial investment. Seminaries as separate institutions required founding boards of like-minded supporters who could gather regularly to plan and raise funds. The seminary required lecture halls or classrooms, and a library room for the books. There was the need for a building or campus that could support not only the educational needs but the daily needs of students who would now live together as a community. It also required a staff of faculty who were to be paid regularly (which did not always happen). Most of all, the seminary required students who were responsible to, or affiliated with, the particular denomination in which they sought ordination or licensure to preach.

Denominational Authority

For the Dutch and Germans, seminaries became not only a way to educate clergy for their churches but an opportunity to raise up culturally aware ministers who could preach and lead worship in their own languages, as well as their own denominational confessions. Not only was seminary training about educating seminarians to serve as apologists and defenders of particular Protestant theological truths, but it also shaped and formed their communal identities. Dutch, German, Swedish, and Norwegian congregations required pastors who could speak their traditional languages to serve among the rural settled communities throughout the country. However, as the second and third generations of immigrant communities became settled, many found that they wanted their clergy to assimilate and become Anglicized to be effective. Even if their communities continued to worship in old world languages, pastors needed to be fully fluent in English and function in a dominant Anglo culture. In fact, this was the initial purpose for the founding of Gettysburg seminary. Samuel Schmucker wanted to create a curriculum in English that would help German Lutheran clergy to become part of the larger Anglo Protestant culture of the young republic.

To some extent, the Anglicans were in the same predicament regarding the need to train their clergy. Anglican priests had to walk a fine line between maintaining the traditions of the Anglican Church, whose head was the king of England, and being fully engaged in American civic life. There were lingering questions and suspicions about Anglican clergy. Robert Baird notes that some Anglican parishioners abandoned the Church of England because their priests spent most of their time engaged in "fox hunting and other sports, in company with the most dissolute of their parishioners."[25] This jab at imagined aristocratic lifestyles aside, there was a general feeling of uncertainty that Anglican clergy might still harbor sympathy to the Crown due to their previous special status as state-employed and -paid civil servants. Nevertheless, because their priests and bishops were White and part of the dominant Anglo-American culture, they were able to prove their Americanness much more easily and more quickly than Dutch and German colleagues.

American seminaries were both a product of and a contributing factor to the social and religious pluralism of American Protestantism. With the disestablishment of religious institutions from state finances, and the growing number of immigrants from various nationalities and religious communities, America was becoming a "land of sects," as Philip Schaff put it. "It is a fact," he stated to his German colleagues on a visit to his homeland in 1854, "that the civil equality of all churches and sects in America, and the voluntary system inseparable from it, have aroused and are sustaining a great mass of individual activity and self-denial for religious purposes, and an uncommon rivalry."[26]

As we have seen, Andover and Hartford seminaries were organized by New England clergy who were horrified at what they perceived to be the unorthodox views of Unitarianism and liberal Calvinism at Harvard and Yale, respectively. In this regard, the trustees of the seminaries defined the direction of the school. Seminary boards, originally made up of clergy of a particular denomination, set the rules of engagement for these new institutions, and in some cases required the faculty to adhere to or even sign a statement of faith. They not only oversaw the fiduciary responsibilities, but they also reserved the right to approve or veto the appointment of faculty and to set the examinations for graduates. While academic freedom is a bedrock of higher learning, seminary boards originally served as the gatekeepers of the orthodoxy for their schools. The board of General seminary, for example, which was made up of the bishops and representatives from each of the dioceses of the Episcopal Church, approved the reading list for the curriculum. In fact, General's origins stemmed from a debate over precisely what diocese or bishop had the right to educate their own candidates for ministry.[27] It was eventually agreed that the Episcopal Church needed at least one seminary that was beholden to the whole denomination, that is, all of the bishops! Thus, the board was in essence a function of the General Convention of the Episcopal Church. Likewise, Princeton seminary was instituted as a seminary of the whole denomination. Unlike Union seminary in New York, which desired to be open to any and all candidates within the region of New York City, or other Presbyterian seminaries like Lane and Auburn, Princeton was an institution of the whole church.

This board structure inevitably led to questions over the appointment of professors and their theological views and scholarship. For example, Lane Seminary, founded in Cincinnati, Ohio, in 1829, was thrust into a heresy trial only six years into its new life. Lyman Beecher was brought up on charges for supporting revivalist preaching and individual conversion, which ran counter to traditional Presbyterian teachings. In 1886, the board of Andover seminary charged five faculty with heresy: Egbert Smyth, William J. Tucker, J. W. Churchill, George Harris, and E. V. Hincks.[28] In 1892 at Union seminary, which was then under the authority of the General Assembly of the Presbyterian Church, Henry Preserved Smith and Charles Augustus Briggs were both accused of heresy regarding their views of the Bible. This would happen again in 1897 when the Presbytery of New York brought Arthur McGiffert, the future president of Union Theological Seminary, up on charges. While McGiffert was exonerated through a complicated presbytery review process, both Smith and Briggs were defrocked. Ultimately, these events led to a legal battle in the courts in which the board of Union won its right to establish the school freely, separate from control of the denomination.

The orthodoxy of Gettysburg seminary was continually under fire from supporting Lutheran synods. Its first president, Samuel Schmucker, was a staunch supporter of an American Lutheran Church that was fully assimilated into English American society. The debate over the Germanness and the Lutheran confessional orthodoxy of the seminary led synods to withdraw their support or, if they maintained it, to press for the removal of certain faculty members if they were not believed to be upholding the traditions of the German Lutheran confessions. The faculty themselves were at odds over their understanding of Lutheran confessionalism. Charles Frederick Schaeffer held to a traditional German view of the confessions over against Schmucker, with Charles Philip Krauth caught in the middle. Eventually, this led to a split in 1863 when some of the faculty left to create the Lutheran Seminary in Germantown, Philadelphia.[29]

These challenges to the academic freedom of the faculty led to the independence of the seminary boards from denominational control, or to the proliferation of more seminaries as faculty broke away to establish their own institutions. For the most part, however, seminaries continued to provide annual reports to and sought financial support from the denominations from which they drew their students and with whom their alumni served. But they eventually maintained a legal separation. Faculty could teach what and how they wanted, as long as they were supported by their presidents and boards, and not by the denomination to which they were sending their students. Thus, there has always been an uneasy alliance between Protestant seminaries and the denominations or traditions with which they are affiliated. Their raison d'être was to train religious leaders for ministry in particular Protestant traditions. Even so, highly skilled professors who spent their lives engaged in academic research were not content to simply have their students accept doctrine and dogma, but wanted them to question and explore. There was also an uneasy conflict between seminary professors and established pastors over who had the authority to interpret the tradition. The history of American Protestant seminaries is a story of the struggle between confessional instruction and academic freedom. The twentieth century is also replete with examples of theological crises between the denominations and the seminaries: Princeton in the 1920s, Concordia Seminary in the 1970s, and Southwest Baptist and Baylor seminaries in the early 1980s. While universities established religion departments that were completely free from any ecclesiastical oversight, it is not the case that seminaries abandoned critical biblical and theological scholarship in the face of "scientific inquiry." Rather, some faculty simply moved to those seminaries that embraced the move toward higher criticism and the historical critical method or further scientific inquiry. Progressive or liberal seminaries have continued to utilize higher criticism as an important tool in biblical hermeneutics. In addition, graduates from these seminaries often went on to teach in the religion departments of private liberal arts church colleges well into the end of the twentieth century.[30]

German Educational Influence

While the earliest seminaries were modeled after the English college system and relied on the availability of English and Latin theological works for their libraries, German scholarship quickly became critical for American seminary education. This was important for the development of critical biblical scholarship in America in general, but it was also important for the availability of German Orientalist works on Islam.

German biblical and theological scholarship was important for nineteenth-century American theological education for several reasons. First, German scholarship, especially biblical scholarship, was highly respected, and the university system in Germany was hitting its stride as American seminaries were starting up. So, many Americans went to study in German universities, including seminary professors who wanted to prepare themselves for their own teaching responsibilities. They went to study in Berlin, Halle, Bonn, and Göttingen, where the theological faculties were held in high esteem. Professors like Schleiermacher, Tholuck, Neander, and Geiseler were considered the ideal "Christian gentleman" as well as scholars.[31] Young professors like Moses Stuart and Edward Robinson at Andover, as well as Charles Hodge at Princeton, were not only impressed by these theological giants but brought back with them to America a love of German scholarship, which they began to emulate in their own seminaries.[32]

The second reason German scholarship was important for American seminaries was that many of the German pastors, missionaries, or scholars who emigrated to the United States brought with them their German training. The most famous example here is that of Philip Schaff, who emigrated in 1843 to teach at Mercersburg Seminary until 1870, when he moved to Union Theological Seminary.[33] Paul Haupt, a young scholar from the University of Göttingen, became the inaugural professor of Semitic languages at Johns Hopkins University in 1883. R. J. H. Gottheil, of German descent but born in England and educated at Berlin, began teaching Semitic languages at Columbia University in 1889. As we will see, philological studies were an important discipline for the study of Islam, even in American seminaries.

Finally, because German biblical and theological scholarship was coveted, German works were translated into English for wider consumption. For example, the British publishing house of T&T Clark translated major German works in biblical studies. The Foreign Theological Library series ended up comprising a total of forty-three volumes that were made available in American seminary libraries.[34] Those Americans who had studied in Germany also began to translate German works. Charles Hodge's review of German books in the Princeton seminary journal *Biblical Repertory* and Edward Robinson's description of the values of German theological education in *Biblical Repository* demonstrate that German scholarship was esteemed and would be utilized for several generations to come—at least until World War I.

This American admiration of German scholarship is important for the focus of this book. Not only did German biblical and theological scholarship find its way into the libraries and lecture halls of American Protestant seminaries, but German Orientalist scholarship on Islam did as well. German scholarship on Islam arose out of the History of Religions School of thought in biblical scholarship. Translations of the Qur'an and the biography of the Prophet were an extension of this German textual scholarship of the Near East. And, as we will see, this learning affected the way American seminary professors began to engage and interpret Islamic sources.

Postbellum Theological Education

As has been discussed, the Civil War and subsequent Reconstruction period disrupted antebellum American higher education, including seminary education. Enrollments dropped as young men joined the armies or became involved in the war efforts of both the South and the North. Others who would have gone to study at a seminary were simply unable to travel or leave their homes and families during these tumultuous years. Gettysburg seminary was dramatically impacted, of course, its campus being the site of that most important battle and its building used as a hospital for the wounded for months after the fighting was over. Mercersburg Seminary in central Pennsylvania also closed its doors during the war. It would relocate to Lancaster on the campus of Franklin and Marshall College. Southern seminaries were in many instances simply destroyed. Other seminaries limped along and then tried to recover after the war. Ironically, however, as enrollments dropped, the war created the need for the profession of the military chaplain. About 10 percent of all clergy in America served as chaplains in the armies of the North and the South.[35] Thus, at a time when the armies needed chaplains, there were not enough graduates from the seminaries to supply the front lines.

Most significantly, the war resulted in the official splitting of denominations, creating northern and southern branches of each church. The Presbyterian Church in the Confederate States of America separated from its parent denomination, the Presbyterian Church in the United States of America. Similarly with the Methodists and the Baptists. Even Lutherans and Episcopalians found themselves on different sides of the conflict. They were not only caught up in the national debates and disagreements over slavery and the identity of White American culture, but their churches ended up in different de facto countries. The effect was the withdrawal of resources, including students, from the existing denominational seminaries and the creation of new entities or the reordering of existing seminaries in the South.

The most important and long-lasting effect of the war on seminary education was the opportunity for the creation of Black denominations, church colleges, and seminaries. In 1892, what was ultimately to be called Payne Theological Seminary was created to serve the African Methodist Episcopal Church, a denomination that had been in existence since 1816. Like other university divinity schools, Howard University Divinity School was created as a department of theology within the larger university in 1870 within the Congregationalist and Reformed branches of the African American church.[36]

The disruption of the war to church college and seminary life ultimately created new opportunities in higher education in America. It was during the Reconstruction era that the American university took root. The period from 1865 to 1910 has been noted as the "age of the American university."[37] Prior to the war, the church college was the mainstay of higher education. Originally, many colleges were founded by particular religious denominations to support the educational needs of their own communities, including the training of their clergy. Modeled after the British college system, they were more often than not secondary boarding schools, like the Hartwick Seminary and College or the Philips Academy. These colleges developed into the residential liberal arts schools well known in the twentieth century.

However, it was also throughout this postbellum period that American universities began to take shape as places of research with specialized departments. This shift brought with it an interest, a need, and public funding for not only classical liberal arts education but training for new professions as well—particularly in the areas of agriculture and the sciences. The Land Grant act of 1862 created a new opportunity for a different kind of higher education that was not limited to developing the upper class to become "learned gentlemen" but included the training of new professionals in every field imaginable. The church college had to make way for and compete with the scientific university, both private and public. And yet, this did not lead to a simple and clean break of the secular university from the religious church college. The relationship between the two was much more complicated and nuanced.

Seminaries have always had a symbiotic relationship with a local church college. While the institutions grew to support very different missions, relationships have always remained—even if tenuous. Sometimes the seminary was created first and an academy or college followed, and sometimes vice versa. The College of New Jersey, which became Princeton University, was created with a divinity school in mind. Princeton seminary grew out of the Princeton college. Gettysburg College, on the other hand, grew up as the preparatory school after the creation of the seminary. Queen's College, which later became Rutgers University, was attached directly to New Brunswick seminary originally as the preparatory school for the seminary. And in New York, King's College, or Columbia College, was tied up in the founding of General seminary. However, it would later establish a working relationship with Union seminary when it moved to its current location on the Upper West Side of Manhattan. This was a common story of the original church colleges and later universities, and seminaries. The professors of the seminary felt that they needed to prepare students with some classical education before they could undertake theological studies. In many cases, the faculty of the seminaries taught in or even led the colleges as their presidents.

Even the founders of the new secular universities—Cornell (1865), Johns Hopkins (1876), Chicago (1890), and the University of Michigan (1837)—held to particular Protestant perspectives. The creators of early American higher education embraced a new world of scientific knowledge with a sense of Christian humanism. Natural laws and orders of creation were seen as part of a divine plan or mystery to be discovered and mastered. George Marsden has provided a helpful description of the changing roles of education in an industrializing Gilded Age of America: "The values, assumptions, economic pressures and national aspirations of middle-class capitalist and enlightened America were reshaping Protestant outlooks at least as much as distinctly Christian concerns were infusing American growth. The two sorts of influences were, indeed, so intertwined, or perhaps one might say, like tares sowed among the wheat, that they were impossible to sort out clearly."[38] The church colleges, as varied as their American denominations, responded differently, but they could not escape the transformation of public knowledge about science and technology. For their part, progressive church colleges and seminaries embraced the cultural changes and the growth of scientific thought and sought ways to train their clergy to provide ethical and moral leadership for a new middle-class, urbanizing America. Debates between science and religion, between evolution and creationism, captured the nation's attention in the 1920s, and this ultimately led to the 1929 breakup of the Princeton seminary faculty, which was divided between "fundamentalists" and "modernists." However, such results were not a given in the 1870s, nor would they be the end result for other seminaries at the turn of the twentieth century. Some embraced the "Darwinian canopy." Some church colleges and seminaries incorporated the critical study of religion while sustaining their faith commitments, holding both in tension, while others fought against it.

Interestingly, as religious studies departments in church colleges and universities developed throughout the twentieth century, they became more diverse, many of them trying to shed their historic denominational and religious heritages. And yet, as they did so, hiring new non-Christian practitioners as faculty, they still had to deal with debates about the critical study of religion versus the teaching of religion. The case of teaching Islam in colleges is especially pertinent. There has developed a similar pattern to the study of Islam versus the teaching of Islam in colleges that happened with Christianity in Christian colleges. The hiring of Muslim faculty at traditional church colleges or university religious studies departments at the end of the twentieth and into the twenty-first century has provided new opportunities for the teaching and framing of Islam by both scholars of religion who happen to self-identify as Muslim and those who are Muslim religious leaders or practitioners who teach Islam. Islamic studies in American higher education has experienced some of the same complexities that traditional church colleges faced one hundred years ago regarding teaching about Christianity versus the teaching of Christianity.[39]

The Professionalization of Seminaries

The period between the end of the Civil War until the turn of the twentieth century, known as the Reconstruction era and the Gilded Age, was driven by industrialization and advances in just about every field imaginable—transportation, business, medicine, and the various disciplines of scientific research. The war effort had provided opportunities for many entrepreneurs to create and supply new inventions and innovations. The telegraph, the train, and the steamship used effectively during the war were then utilized for civilian purposes to move people, goods, and services around the country. The postbellum period was also a time of dramatic social change in American society. People began moving to the cities to find work in the new factories and businesses. Formerly enslaved African Americans began their Great Migration to the cities of the North. At the end of the Civil War the country was still predominantly rural. However, by 1910 the Northeast and the Midwest had the majority of its population living in urban spaces.

The technological advancements created a desire and need for specialized methods of education to meet the demands of a rapidly modernizing economy, and there were wealthy philanthropists willing to invest in new models of education to meet the needs. Between 1889 and 1892, a number of well-funded private universities were founded: Clark, Stanford, the University of Chicago, and Johns Hopkins.[40] Along with the new universities came a revolution in the pedagogy of higher education. The classical recitation of the British system and even the lecture style of the German lecture hall gave way to the creation of seminars and laboratory research. The classical curriculum of the college system gave way to elective courses that allowed students the opportunity to delve into fields of inquiry that interested them and allowed them to develop their interests. In addition, professional schools took on shape and form and began to regulate themselves.[41] Medical schools, law schools, and engineering programs began to organize their own standards of education. It was now possible to become a professional, trained in any number of specialized areas. The seminary, which had existed for some time, was slow to catch up with the changes in secular professional graduate schools.

This vision of the university by American educational reformers dramatically affected seminaries. Seminaries had been among the first postgraduate schools to organize and to create standards of education for their graduates. While the quality of that postgraduate training was often lacking, from the very beginning seminarians had to be college graduates to begin their seminary training. In the antebellum nation, clergy were usually the most well-educated people in the rural communities they served. They had been a product of the church college and seminary system that was expected to create an educated elite well versed in the classics and the finer debates of confessional theology who would become public leaders. In the postbellum world, however, there was an interest in using higher education to advance scientific knowledge, techniques, and discoveries. Administration, organization, powers of persuasion, and efficiency were skills that were more valuable than the knowledge of Latin declensions.

In the same way that secular professions were becoming specialized, so was the Christian ministry. Seminaries began to attract different kinds of individuals. While there was still a large portion of seminarians who would go and serve in rural parishes throughout the country, seminary training began to take on its own professionalization. Students might no longer be the elite of the East Coast colleges. They were men—and now women—interested in various kinds of ministry, working in urban spaces, developing Christian educational material, working for social justice, or promoting temperance or Christian missions.[42] The dramatic changes in urban society prompted a pastoral response toward the "Social Gospel" movement, which put pressure on the traditional theology of individual repentance and conversion.[43] Seminary students would experience a faculty who also began to become more specialized in their own fields of study. It was no longer sufficient to have one faculty member teaching Bible. There needed to be at least one Old Testament and one New Testament faculty member, if not more. The advances in psychology and sociology prompted the hiring of faculty who were not just pastors but had training in or at least had read up on the latest innovations in social theories.

Seminary faculty were now expected to be well-educated specialists who would spend a lifetime researching and passing on their knowledge to be implemented by skilled professionals. As Miller notes, "Both the academic study of Christianity and the development of important insights into the church's place in contemporary culture continued, as did the attempt to systematize ministerial practice. Seminary catalogues and curricula increasingly contained long lists of courses, more or less organized under departments that were occasionally related to larger fields. More and more continued to be known, thought, and done. Knowledge of the whole was rapidly losing place to knowledge of the parts."[44] Seminary curricula were restructured, departments were created, and specialized elective courses were offered for advanced-level students. Libraries became more complex and required specialized staff to care for them, rather than simply junior faculty assigned to guard the books. Administration and fundraising became the job of a president of the institution rather than the faculty.[45]

No one embraced these changes more than Chester Hartranft, president of Hartford seminary from 1889 to 1903. Hartranft was a graduate of New Brunswick in 1864, and a pastor of the Dutch Reformed Church. He was called to Hartford in 1879 and served several positions in church history and biblical studies until he was elected by the faculty to serve as the president in 1889. During his tenure he expanded the faculty by hiring young scholars who had expertise in various fields rather than the traditional well-respected, long-serving pastors. He created specific departments in which the professors taught. He also supported and developed the library of the seminary. At his inaugural address as president, Hartranft underlined the importance of research, teaching, and publication as the object of the seminary faculty. It was only by providing support for the faculty to engage in a life of research in their chosen fields that the church would be able to educate pastors and religious educators who could respond to the challenges and opportunities of the modern age.[46]

Seminaries were a novel way to educate a larger number of pastors more efficiently than the previous apprenticeship model. The primary focus of this version of theological education was to teach how to read and exegete the Bible for the spiritual edification of one's community, not only the congregation but the local civic community as well. Reading the Bible in its original languages (Hebrew, Greek, and Latin) was considered a necessity to understand God's Word. But, students also learned how to interpret the Bible through the orthodox teachings of their denominational tradition: Calvinist, Lutheran, Anglican, etc. Thus, theology went hand in hand with biblical interpretation. From these two disciplines—biblical studies and theology—students then learned about the history of the Christian faith, from their particular denominational and American historical perspectives. Many nineteenth-century theologians believed that America was a theological continuation of the story of salvation history from scripture. It was seen as the "new Zion" or the "city on a hill." Thus, it behooved an American theologian to know where the nation fit into the larger picture of the ongoing triumph of Christianity, through its many reformations.

Once these disciplines were engaged, then seminary students were taught how to "be" ministers—how to preach, counsel members, and instruct their congregation. But, in the rapidly changing and industrializing country of the Reconstruction era, the arts of ministry became more complicated and detailed. There were skills that needed to be learned in administration and governance, as well as fundraising and organizing. As new immigrants arrived and as more and more people relocated into the cities, seminaries were challenged to produce clergy to meet the changing needs of American society. Preaching, Bible reading, praying, singing, and the exhortation of the flocks were not enough. Pastors were now expected to gather their constituents, organize them into communities that were self-sustaining, and then support not only the spiritual well-being of their members but their social and civic life, including addressing growing economic injustices. This was no small task.

Within the context of the dramatic changes in American society throughout the nineteenth century—from the dawn of the early republic to the dawn of the twentieth century—and the changes within seminary theological education, Islam, perhaps surprisingly, figured persistently throughout the curricula of seminary education in interesting and important ways. It is to this engagement with learning about Islam within the seminary curricula that we now turn. First, we examine the primary vehicle that professors used to teach and students used to learn—books.

2

Seminary Libraries and Islamic Sources

Reading the Bible for devotional and spiritual purposes is a central element of Protestant Christian spirituality. Martin Luther's determination
to make the Bible available for everyone to read for themselves meant
that reading and belief went hand in hand. Reflection on the written
word of the biblical text and commentaries on scripture became an
expected part of Protestant piety. And, reading the Bible in its original
languages—Hebrew and Greek—has traditionally been considered a
necessary skill for Protestant clergy. Thus, gathering ministerial students
together with books and a tutor was the central focus of early American
seminary education. Yet, acquiring a sufficient number of books for a
solid education was a challenge in the early years. However, by the turn
of the twentieth century, several of the seminaries had the largest specialized libraries in the country.

During his first visit to Germany for further advanced studies in 1831,
the American biblical scholar Edward Robinson detailed the resources
of the German universities and libraries. Writing to his American colleagues about the library of Göttingen, he opined,

The library of Göttingen is one of the largest, and for practical uses the
best, on the continent. . . . The number of books is often said to be near
300,000. . . . The arrangement of the manuscript alphabetical catalogue
is such, that it occupies 150 folio volumes. For the increase of the library
the government appropriates 3000 dollars annually; though in particular
cases they are permitted to exceed that sum. The library is open every
day for reading and consultation; and the students are allowed to take
out books on the usual terms. The interior of the library in Göttingen,
particularly the hall of history, is one of the most interesting spots for a
scholar that the old world presents. Other libraries have a more splendid
location; but there is here so much neatness and simplicity, such perfect order and utility of arrangement, such an adaptation of the means of

learning to facilitate the acquisition of it, that the mind of the beholder receives a deep impression, and loves to recur in idea to these ancient and venerable halls, long after the traces left by literary pomp or princely grandeur have faded from the memory.[1]

Robinson's American colleagues at Andover were most likely beside themselves with envy as he described what was for them the luxurious resources of European university libraries. These libraries were not only bigger, with more books and folios, but they were open all week, were neat, and had a library staff. American seminary libraries, on the contrary, were small, often open only one hour a week, and staffed by junior faculty or even students. Robinson, who served as the librarian at Andover, edited the library catalog in 1833. At that point there were thirty-two hundred volumes listed: just over 1 percent of the total volumes said to be housed at Göttingen.

In addition to the university libraries, visiting American students were also astounded at the size of the private libraries of their professors. These private collections often dwarfed the meager theology libraries of American seminaries. As a result of their experiences, American seminary professors who studied in Europe were committed to building up their specialized libraries and pressed their boards for funds to purchase as many books as possible. Robinson took it upon himself to make a number of large purchases for Andover and, later, Union seminaries. In 1838, he purchased the Lander Van Ess personal library of 13,500 volumes for Union seminary, dramatically increasing its holdings.

Unaided by state funds, seminary boards struggled to raise money on their own to purchase the necessary books. And yet, within a hundred years, several seminaries boasted some of the best libraries in religion in the United States. While the primary focus of seminary libraries was biblical studies and Protestant theology, Western sources on Islam also became widely available, from basic encyclopedias to translations of the Qur'an. And, by the beginning of the twentieth century, Hartford would boast one of the best collections in Islamic material in North America. This chapter examines the development of American seminary libraries, and more specifically the books on Islam that were collected, used by seminary professors in their classes, and often read by students

Early Seminary Libraries

Books and the Protestant Reformation go hand in hand. As noted previously, learning to read and study the Bible led the Reformers and their followers to write all manner of theological treatises and Bible commentaries. The exploitation of the printing press during the early modern period made it possible to support and widely disseminate this religious knowledge production. The expectation that Protestant clergy were to be educated to read and study the Bible was built into the very DNA of Protestant Christianity.

Up until the growth of American colleges and universities following World War II, clergy were often the most formally educated members of their communities, especially in rural areas. Reflecting on the importance of theological education at the dedication of the Robert E. Speer Library at Princeton seminary in 1957, Nathan Pusey, president of Harvard University, remarked that the Presbyterian Church had always had an "an overriding concern that the Church's ministry should be a learned one." Originally, a Protestant minister was *the* professional scholar of each community, stated Pusey. However, by 1957, because the Protestant minister was now only one professional among many in their community, a sound theological education was needed even more. Pusey reflected, "Faced by the necessity of preparing for such a complex and demanding role, a minister is ever to become, or remain, a learned interpreter of the faith."[2] Pusey's remarks highlighted that the training of an educated clergy required a teacher, a student, and books.

When the various Protestant communities in the young republic of the United States began to organize their theological colleges and seminaries, the boards not only hired professors but also worked to collect a library. The initial covenant among the Dutch communities in New York to establish a seminary in New Brunswick in 1807 required funds to be set aside both for a professor and for a library to be built.[3] The synod established a fund of one hundred dollars to be raised from among the supporting Dutch Reformed congregations each year to purchase books for the library.[4] However, while a commitment and declaration were one thing, execution was quite another. Due to the slow pace of fundraising, the New Brunswick library was not finished until forty years later. It was not until 1847 that arrangements were made for a room for the seminary in Van Nest Hall at Queen's College (later Rutgers College). The seminary, which met on the college campus, had its own small library installed. One of the senior students was appointed as the librarian to care for the books.[5] Soon after its dedication, however, the library room was needed as a lecture hall. This meant that the books were often disturbed by students coming and going to their classes and were left in an unorganized state. The books began to deteriorate without proper oversight and care. Finally, in 1856 the seminary built its own building separate from the college and moved its library holdings into one room of the newly built Hertzog Hall. The initial collection included some two thousand volumes and was available to students only at certain hours of the week.[6]

It was not uncommon for seminaries to open their doors to their first students without a library at all.[7] Prior to having their own library room, the earliest seminary libraries were in the homes of the pastor-mentors and then professors. Archibald Alexander served as the president and librarian at Princeton from 1812 until 1851 (when the first full-time librarian was hired). He made his personal library available to students. By 1822, he had about two thousand volumes that needed to be moved into the newly acquired library room in Alexander Hall. The first library building built on campus, however, was not completed until 1843. Named after the philanthropist and financier James Lenox, the new library was "the most inspiring space in all of Princeton."[8]

This was the common path for the establishment of seminary libraries. The private libraries of professors were used in their homes, then a room of the main lecture hall was set aside to house books, and finally a library building was built to house the collection. The trustees were responsible for the long and arduous process of fundraising for a building. And, once that did happen, it did not take long for the boards to propose plans for additional costly fireproof buildings. Ultimately, the expense of the library buildings siphoned money away from purchasing books. Professors complained continually to the boards that in addition to impressive buildings, libraries needed good books!

Even when the seminaries had a dedicated space and a core collection of books, there was often a less than suitable method to organize and systematically make them available to the students. The books were organized according to the scheme developed by the faculty member who was appointed as the responsible librarian at any given time. In

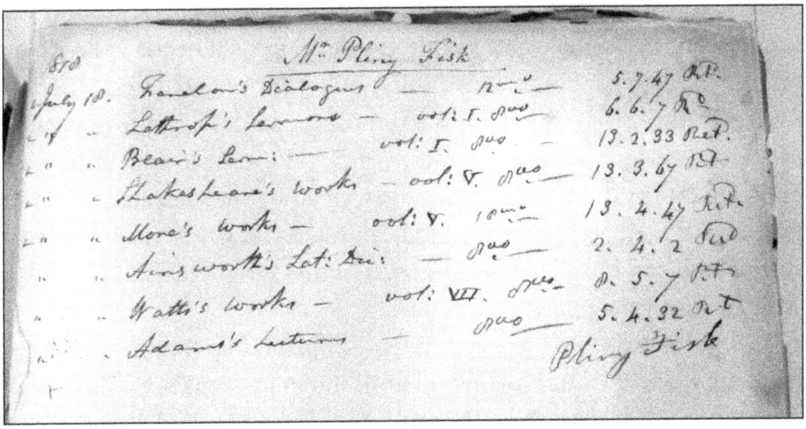

Figure 2.1. Andover student library record of Pliny Fisk, 1810, Yale Divinity School Library Archives. Photo by David D. Grafton.

order to take a book out, students were required to sign out their books on a written ledger only when the faculty member was present. It was not until the 1840s that seminary libraries began to develop systems for collecting, organizing, and cataloging their books.[9]

The Acquisition of Personal Libraries

Professor A. C. Thompson at Hartford lamented the insufficient library resources, and that the board "seemed to regard a few thousand volumes, chiefly as could be spared from a pastor's study, as sufficient" for seminary education.[10] Moses Stuart at Andover complained continuously to the board about the need for suitable books, even Bibles. Thus, it was necessary to "kick start" the collections through the acquisition of several private libraries of retired or deceased clergy, or by donations of patrons. For example, Edward Everett, professor of Greek at Harvard, and a supporter of the Andover seminary, was authorized by the board to purchase books for the seminary when he traveled to Europe in 1815.

In 1826, Edward Robinson, the newly appointed professor at Andover, traveled to Germany to spend two years studying in Halle and at the new university in Berlin. In addition to studying the latest German techniques in biblical studies and theology, he was authorized to purchase books from private libraries. There he acquired more than one hundred dollars' worth of books. According to the catalog records, Robinson's acquisitions had a major impact on the development of the library. The original catalog of 1819 included thirty-two hundred volumes. After his return from Europe the library more than doubled. The 1838 catalog included twelve thousand volumes.[11] Some of these recently purchased books included the translation of the Qur'an by the German Lutheran pastor Abraham Hinkelmann and Silvestre De Sacy's *Christomathie Arab*. Robinson more than likely acquired these when he studied Arabic with De Sacy while he was in France.[12]

In 1837, Union seminary appointed Robinson its professor of sacred languages, and he once again had an immediate impact on the development of the library there. When hired, Robinson had already been planning a research trip to the Near East. As part of his agreement with Union, he was granted a leave after only one semester of teaching to complete his travels. Robinson's journey to Egypt, Palestine, and Syria led to one of the most important American contributions to biblical studies in the nineteenth century, *Biblical Researches in Palestine, Mount Sinai, and Arabia Petraea: A Journal of Travels in the Year 1838*.[13] While he was in Europe on his way to Egypt, he had the opportunity to procure part of the library of the retired German Catholic scholar Leander Van Ess (1772–1847). Robinson convinced the board of Union seminary to borrow money during the economic recession of 1837 to purchase the Van Ess collection, which became the core of the Union seminary library at the time. The seminary acquired between thirteen and fourteen thousand volumes at the cost of a little more than five thousand dollars.[14] The decision by the board to purchase the library was a demonstration of its commitment to reading and research as a constitutive part of seminary education. Forty years later, the library boasted over 33,500 volumes and was undoubtedly the largest theological library in America and certainly larger than many colleges of the time.[15] Most of the works from the Van Ess collection focused on biblical studies or Reformation church history. However, there were several important English Orientalist sources on Islam.

We can see that Robinson had an important role in the early acquisitions of books at both Andover and Union seminaries. His research interests included biblical texts and ancient Near Eastern geography and culture. While he served as the librarian for Andover from 1830 to 1833,

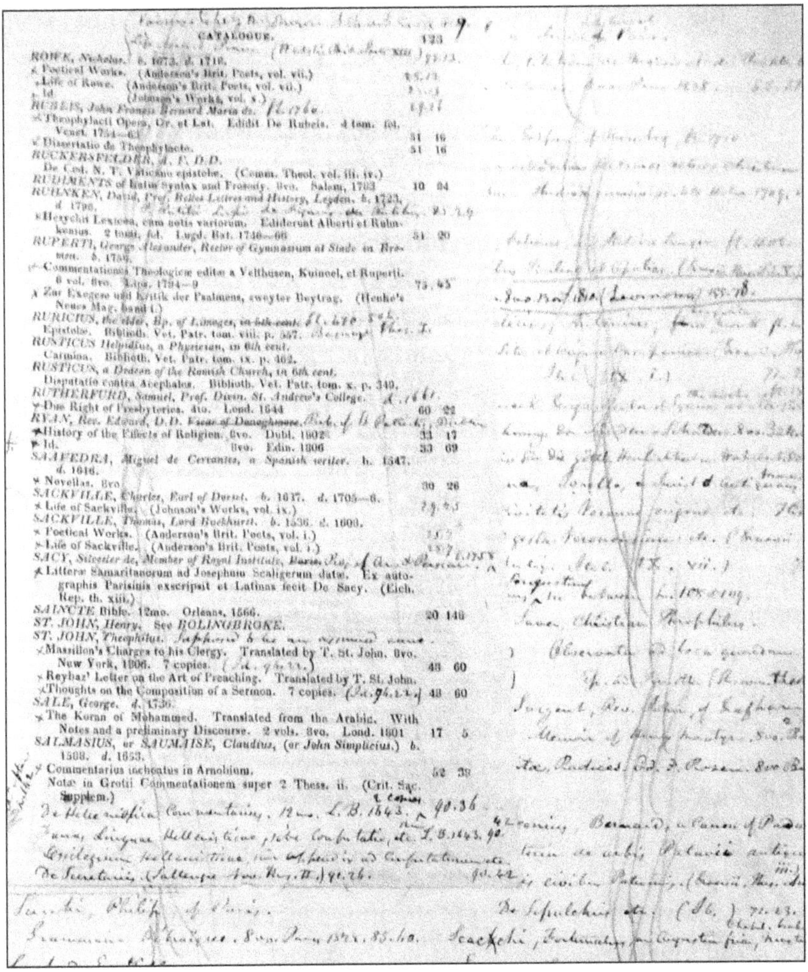
CATALOGUE. 123

ROWE, Nicholas. b. 1673. d. 1718.
Poetical Works. (Anderson's Brit. Poets, vol. vii.)
Life of Rowe. (Anderson's Brit. Poets, vol. vii.)
Id. (Johnson's Works, vol. x.)
RUBEIS, John Francis Bernard Maria de.
Theophylacti Opera, Gr. et Lat. Edidit De Rubeis. 4 tom. fol. Venet. 1754—63
Dissertatio de Theophylacto. 51 16
RUCKERSFELDER, A. F. D.D.
De Cod. N. T. Vaticano epistolæ. (Comm. Theol. vol. iii. iv.)
RUDIMENTS of Latin Syntax and Prosody. 8vo. Salem, 1793 10 94
RUHNKEN, David, Prof. Belles Lettres and History, Leyden. b. 1723. d. 1798.
Hesychii Lexicon, cum notis variorum. Ediderunt Alberti et Ruhnkenius. 2 tom. fol. Lugd. Bat. 1746—66 51 20
RUPERTI, George Alexander, Rector of Gymnasium at Stade in Bremen. b. 1758.
Commentationes Theologicæ editæ a Velthusen, Kuinoel, et Ruperti. 6 vol. 8vo. Lips. 1794—9
Zur Exegese und Kritik der Psalmens, zweyter Beytrag. (Henke's Neues Mag. band i.)
RURICIUS, the elder, Bp. of Limoges, in 5th cent.
Epistolæ. Biblioth. Vet. Patr. tom. viii. p. 567.
RUSTICUS Helpidius, a Physician, in 6th cent.
Carmina. Biblioth. Vet. Patr. tom. ix. p. 462.
RUSTICUS, a Deacon of the Romish Church, in 6th cent.
Disputatio contra Acephalos. Biblioth. Vet. Patr. tom. x. p. 349.
RUTHERFURD, Samuel, Prof. Divin. St. Andrew's College.
Due Right of Presbyteries. 4to. Lond. 1644 60 22
RYAN, Rev. Edward, D.D. Vicar of Donaghmore.
History of the Effects of Religion. 8vo. Dubl. 1802 33 17
Id. 8vo. Edin. 1806 33 69
SAAVEDRA, Miguel de Cervantes, a Spanish writer. b. 1547. d. 1616.
Novellas. 8vo. 30 26
SACKVILLE, Charles, Earl of Dorset. b. 1637. d. 1705—6.
Life of Sackville. (Johnson's Works, vol. ix.)
SACKVILLE, Thomas, Lord Buckhurst. b. 1536. d. 1608.
Poetical Works. (Anderson's Brit. Poets, vol. i.)
Life of Sackville. (Anderson's Brit. Poets, vol. i.)
SACY, Silvestre de, Member of Royal Institute,
Litteræ Samaritanorum ad Josephum Scaligerum datæ. Ex autographis Parisiis exscripsit et Latinas fecit De Sacy. (Eich. Rep. th. xiii.)
SAINCTE Bible. 12mo. Orleans, 1566. 20 140
ST. JOHN, Henry. See BOLINGBROKE.
ST. JOHN, Theophilus.
Massillon's Charges to his Clergy. Translated by T. St. John. 8vo. New York, 1806. 7 copies. 48 60
Reybaz' Letter on the Art of Preaching. Translated by T. St. John.
Thoughts on the Composition of a Sermon. 7 copies. 48 60
SALE, George. d. 1736.
The Koran of Mohammed. Translated from the Arabic. With Notes and a preliminary Discourse. 2 vols. 8vo. Lond. 1801 17 5
SALMASIUS, or SAUMAISE, Claudius, (or John Simplicius.) b. 1588. d. 1653.
Commentarius inchoatus in Arnobium. 52 39
Notæ in Grotii Commentationem super 2 Thess. ii. (Crit. Sac. Supplem.)

Figure 2.2. Edits and additions by Edward Robinson to the 1819 Andover Library Catalog. Photo by David D. Grafton

a number of Arabic texts were added to the library, including Silvestre De Sacy's *Chirstomathie Arabe* (1806), Gustav Freytag's *Lexicon Arabico-Latinum* (1830), and Thomas Erpenius's *Arabische Grammatick* and *Arabische Christomathie* (both 1777).[16] An important addition to the Union seminary library that Robinson secured was the German Lutheran Orientalist Theodore Hackspan's *Fides et leges Mohammaedis* (1646). In the first part of *Fides* Hackspan notes the importance of Arabic for the study of the Bible, about which Robinson would certainly have been interested. The second part of the book is a theological analysis of the Qur'an, where Hackspan refutes several passages related to the denial of Jesus' divinity.[17]

The use of Arabic texts, including the Qur'an, figured prominently in late-nineteenth-century Protestant biblical study. Arabic was considered a cognate biblical language to Hebrew and students were encouraged to learn it, to better understand many of the hapax legomenon, words that only appear once in the text that have uncertain meanings, of the Hebrew Masoretic text. Thus, it is not surprising that a variety of translations of the Qur'an would be acquired by the seminaries as part of their collections. The Arabic text was seen as a potential aid in understanding the biblical Hebrew.

Union was not the only seminary to seek out books in Europe. For example, Gettysburg seminary sent a representative to Germany seeking financial support among German churches and books for its new library. The Reverend Benjamin Kurtz, a pastor in Hagerstown, Maryland, and supporter of the Lutheran seminary, spent twenty-two months in Europe. His efforts were somewhat successful, as he brought back approximately five thousand donated books for the library, mostly in German. Samuel Schmucker, the president of Gettysburg, had also appealed to American congregations and pastors for funds and donations for books, collecting over a thousand volumes himself. By 1869, there were some ten thousand volumes in the library.[18]

Gettysburg's library collection at the time focused primarily on German works in Lutheran and Reformed history, confessional theology, and biblical studies. Its distinctive collection was determined by the ongoing debate among German Lutherans as to whether the seminary would support a German- or English-speaking church. Samuel Schmucker had visions of an Anglicized Lutheran Church that would participate in the broader Protestant cultural landscape. However, others wanted to hold onto the German language and traditions as an important part of their Protestant identity. This debate was not settled until after World War I, when German American Christians abandoned the German language as a sign of public loyalty to demonstrate their support of American ideals and culture.

At other seminaries, patrons or board members were significant benefactors and donated monies for their collections. For example,

John Pintard, an important businessman and civic leader in New York City, helped to support the first library of General Theological Seminary.[19] Pintard almost single-handedly built the library, purchasing books from dealers in New York and England. Two of the initial purchases by Pintard were the earliest collection of the writings of the Church Fathers, *Sacra Bibliotheca Sanctorum Patrum*, originally published in Paris in eight volumes in 1851 by the French Catholic scholar Marguerin de la Migne, and numerous volumes of the Erelangen edition of *Luther's Works* that were still being published at the time.[20] He was also responsible for procuring the Complutensian, Paris, and London polyglot Bibles, the first, second, and third editions of Erasmus's New Testament, and a Guttenberg Bible.[21] These were major additions to General's collection.

In the 1830s, Rev. John McVickar, who taught economics at Columbia College, also assisted in collecting donations for the General seminary library. By 1837 the library had more than six thousand volumes.[22] With regard to Latin and English Orientalist books related to the study of Islam, we find several important works reflected in the 1824 library catalog, including Prideaux's *True Nature of Imposture* (1697), an English translation of Henri de Bougainvilliers' biography of Muhammad (1731), Adrian Reland's *De religione Mohammedica libri duo* (1717), and a then recent publication of Hugo Grotius' *Truth of the Christian Religion* (1808). However, General's overall collection focused almost exclusively on church history and doctrinal works of the early and medieval church.

In 1826, the trustees of the New Brunswick seminary purchased the personal library of Dr. Selah Woodhull, and in 1832 the library of Dr. John De Witt. Both had been professors of ecclesiastical history at the seminary. De Witt's library was estimated to be worth over two thousand dollars at the time.[23] The purchase of De Witt's library led the seminary to create its first official catalog of library holdings, and to appoint a faculty member as the librarian to oversee the library collection. But it was not until 1863 that the library began to expand to a size that would truly meet the needs of the students.[24] The seminary received a bequest of thirty-five hundred volumes from the library of the Reverend George W. Bethune, a pastor of the Dutch Reformed Church.[25] The acquisition of this personal library prompted the need to move the library from one room into an actual building. It would take another ten years, however, before the Gardner Sage Library was erected through the donations of Colonel Gardner A. Sage, a member of the seminary board. By 1888, the library had amassed forty thousand volumes. The collection included a wide variety of liberal arts works in English, Italian, German, and Dutch, also intended to assist in the general education of students at the college. Given the history of the seminary of the Dutch Church, it is not surprising that it had the largest collection of Dutch writings, both religious and secular works, in the United States at the time.

Bibles and biblical exegesis made up the largest section of the seminary library. There were printed versions of the Bible in Greek, Hebrew, Latin, Coptic, Arabic, and Syriac, and large volumes of the London, Paris, and Complutensian polyglot Bibles. After this there was a strong collection of German and Dutch Reformation works, including many books by German theologians. When John G. Lansing came to teach at New Brunswick in the late 1880s, having grown up in Egypt, he brought with him "a goodly array of Arabic books" to add to the library. According to John Van Dyke, the librarian, "Many of them deal with the Kuran in commentaries and with the history of Mahomet; many treat of Sufism and the Sufic poets, the legends of Tamerlane, and Arabic astronomy; many again are histories of various tribes, accounts of manners and customs, volumes of poetry and stories."[26]

Hartford seminary's board struggled to provide enough library resources for its students. By May 1837, there were 3,528 volumes, mostly due to donations and the gift from a large estate by a benefactor who had been previously unknown to the seminary, Samuel Stone. Monies from this estate were used by a board member to travel to Europe to secure additional books, primarily in the area of church history.[27] Yet by 1860, there were still only 7,194 volumes. This was the case primarily because there was still no dedicated library building to house a collection at its Windsor Hill location. When the seminary moved to its Prospect Street property in downtown Hartford in 1865, there was still no one room that could hold all the books. So, the collection was split up and placed in four separate rooms. This made it difficult for the faculty member who was the librarian to keep track of books. In addition, one of the rooms was in the basement and would flood during heavy rains, necessitating that the books be relocated. The only place to be found for these endangered books was in shelves in the main hallway of the building. By 1878 there were only twelve thousand volumes. This was certainly due to the lack of space and a concerted effort to budget for more books.[28]

In 1880, the seminary moved into a newly designed building on Broad Street. A board member and an important publisher in Hartford, Mr. Newton Case, began to regularly donate funds for the purchasing of books. However, the library room itself was still not sufficient to meet the growing needs. So, he eventually also gave a gift to build a separate library annex that was attached to the main building. The Case Memorial Library was completed and dedicated in 1893. With this new addition, ongoing financial support, and the concerted leadership of President Hartranft, who had previously served as the librarian, the library began to grow. When the Case Memorial Library opened there were approximately fifty-two thousand volumes.[29]

One of the collections that was purchased for Hartford in 1894 was that of the German Orientalist scholar August Mueller, who was professor of philology at the University of Königsberg. The Mueller Semitic Library, as it came to be recorded, contained 2,367 books and 353 pamphlets, many of them in Arabic, Syriac, or Persian.[30] The library contained Qur'anic commentaries of al-Baydawī, many Islamic histories (including the *Annals* of al-Ṭabarī), and Arabic poetry. This collection was used extensively by the newly arrived professor of Hebrew, Duncan Black Macdonald. The collection provided an incredible opportunity for Hartford to become known as a center for Arabic and Islamic studies under Macdonald shortly after his arrival.

The acquisition of these personal libraries, however, was not always helpful or desired by the library staff. Donations were often duplicate copies of what the seminary library already had. These gifts often placed a burden on the staff to find places for the donated books in an already crowded library space. For example, in 1879, the Episcopal Diocese of Maryland received the library of its previous bishop, William Whittingham, who had also been the professor of theology and librarian at General seminary from 1836 to 1840. His personal library included nearly twenty thousand volumes.[31] The estate required that the books not be broken up but be maintained intact as a whole collection. So, finding separate space for the complete collections in the small libraries was impossible. The Maryland diocesan librarian pleaded with the Episcopal Library Committee of the diocese that there was not sufficient room to

56 | SEMINARY LIBRARIES AND ISLAMIC SOURCES

adequately house and care for the books. The collection was then accepted on loan by the Peabody Institute of Johns Hopkins University and housed there until 1966, when the books were finally moved to General seminary, though at the time of transfer to General, the librarian at General indicated that they still did not have sufficient room or funds to adequately house the collection. On a visit to the seminary in 1974, the archivist of the Maryland Diocese noted that many of the boxes of the Whittingham collection had simply been stacked up in the middle of a room in the basement and were deteriorating. After much legal wrangling about the original intent of the will, the library was ultimately sold to the Pitts Theological Library of Emory University in Atlanta, Georgia, in the 1990s, some eighty years after its donation.[32]

While the donation of this personal library did not find its way to General until the 1960s, the individual books within the collection do help us to better understand what books were available to pastors and seminary teachers during the middle years of the seminary's existence. Bishop Whittingham's library and the Van Ess collection at Union are particularly beneficial in this regard. The Whittingham library includes the 1649 English translation of the Qur'an by Alexander Ross and Fluegel's 1834 Arabic edition of the Qur'an (although there is no indication that Whittingham was able to read Arabic). Whittingham's library also included a 1708 edition of Humphrey Prideaux's *True Nature of Imposture*, Abraham Geiger's 1833 original publication of *Was hat Mohammed aus dem Judenthume aufgenommen,* and editions of Gustav Weil's *Geschichte der chalifen* from 1851. These personal libraries demonstrate that many pastors who ended up teaching in the seminaries had a variety of Orientalist and Islamic resources at their disposal.

English Orientalist Works and Latin Translations of Oriental Sources

The earliest collections of books in the seminary libraries focused primarily on biblical studies. Because the Bible was central to the spiritual and ethical life of the Protestants, it is not surprising that the earliest books collected for student use in the library were Bibles not only in English but in Hebrew, Greek, and polyglot editions, especially the London Polyglot Bible, as well as grammars to assist in the reading and translation of the primary languages. Theology and early church history books rounded out the collections. However, we also find a core of English and Latin Orientalist works on the Near East and Islam. By the 1830s, these were supplemented by German Orientalist studies on the life of the Prophet and various translations of the Qur'an. As Nabil Matar has demonstrated, the earliest Europeans to begin reading Islamic texts and translating them into Latin were clergy. These books proliferated in their libraries during the seventeenth century.[33] Many of these publications eventually found their way into the private libraries of American clergy in the eighteenth and nineteenth centuries and were then donated to the seminaries as a bequest or via acquisition at an estate sale. The most common of these was Hugo Grotius' seventeenth-century *De Veritate Religions Christianae*.

During the sixteenth century, Europeans encountered new peoples who had previously not been part of their worldview. Prior to traveling westward across the Atlantic, Europeans categorized the peoples of Asia or Africa on the basis of assumptions about their biblical origins. They were identified as the descendants of individuals and tribes referenced in the Bible, such as Noah's sons Shem and Ham. Muslims and Jews were likewise grafted into the biblical history through Ishmael and Isaac, respectively. Thus, it was a novel idea that Hugo Grotius' famous *De Veritate Religions Christianae*, originally written in Dutch, then translated into Latin and finally into English as *The Truth of the Christian Religion* (1631), categorized the world into four groups of peoples—Christians, Jews, "Turkes" (i.e., Muslims), and Pagans. Grotius' book was intended to be an evangelical manual for sailors who were navigating the world. He wanted them to be able to demonstrate the reasonableness of the Christian faith to any and all with whom the explorers might come into contact. Grotius' fourfold worldview became common by the eighteenth century. The English edition was found in all the seminary collections from the 1820s onward.

Grotius places the coming of Islam in the context of what he describes as the bitter theological debates between Eastern bishops during the first few centuries of Christianity. Thus, he saw Islam as a punishment on Christendom for its infidelities, especially those of the Catholic Church. In his book, Grotius also interprets Muslim prayer life and the importance of legal resources. He avers that Islam was a legalistic religion, much like that of the Catholic Church. (This was a common Protestant view, held by Luther as early as 1518.)[34] Thus, Grotius positions Protestantism as "the truth" of the Christian religion. Grotius's primary critique of Islam was that it was advanced by war, by those "calculated for Bloodshed" compared to the "God fearing" apostles who were martyred for their faith. Grotius notes that Jesus had foretold the coming of false prophets (in Matthew 7:15), "Mahomet" among them.

Grotius' primary sources for his sections on Islam were several polemical Christian writings. The first was *Confutatio Alcorani*, by the medieval Dominican missionary Riccoldo da Monte di Croce (1243–1320). The second was Theodore Bibliander's *Machumetis Saracenorum principis*, a collection of medieval literature about Islam originally written in Spain in the twelfth century, known as the "Toledan collection." Bibliander's compendium included Robert of Ketton's 1143 Latin translation of the Qur'an. It is from these medieval works that Grotius based his understanding of Islam during the "age of exploration," especially for Dutch expansion in southeast Asia.[35]

Another popular work that was commonly in the seminary libraries was Alexander Ross's *Pansebeia; or, A View of All the Religions of the World* (1655). Ross was most famously known for his translation of the Qur'an into English in 1649 from a French version by Alexander Du Ryer. *Pansebeia* sets out to describe the known religions of the world and all of the known Christian heresies. He argues that Christianity, Anglican Christianity at that, was the true religion and all others were false. And yet, he maintains that even false religions provide spiritual guidance and cohesiveness for communities. They are part of the innate human nature to seek the divine, whereas atheism is more destructive than false religion. Critics of revealed religion, such as the Deists, were seen as a real threat to not only religion but European society. Thus, Ross adds a fifth category to Grotius's fourfold designation of religions: atheism. In this way, Jews and "Turkes" (i.e., Muslims) were distinct not only from Christians but even from the pagans and atheists.

Pansebeia reflects the expanding worldview of Europeans during the beginning of imperialism as Portugal, Spain, and the Dutch were establishing their colonies in the transatlantic world. For example, Ross describes the supposed newly "discovered" religions in Africa and the Americas. His depictions of the religions of Asia, however, focus only on the Near Eastern religions of antiquity: the Babylonians, Phoenicians, and Egyptians, as well as the "idolatrous" religions of India. Using Greco-Roman and medieval Latin European sources, Ross does not seem to have any knowledge of Buddhism or the expressions of Brahmanism, what we now call Hinduism. Judaism is illustrated in its Levitical form from the Old Testament and the Second Temple period through Christian sources. He does not reference the Mishnah or Talmud, which indicates his lack of knowledge of rabbinical Judaism. Most importantly for the purposes of this book, the "religion of the Mahometans" is depicted as "one of the prevalent" religions of Europe, alongside Christianity.[36] For early modern Europeans Islam was most notably experienced through its contentious relations with the Ottoman Empire in eastern Europe. In fact, Turkish expansion into eastern Europe reached its apex during Ross's life. It was only with the final and failed siege of Vienna in 1683 that the Ottomans began to lose territory, ceding their lands to the Hapsburg and Russian empires. Prior to this, the Ottomans had been a prominent fixture in English and German literature as a threat to Christianity.[37] Because of Ross's popularity as an author, *Pansebeia* and his English translation of the Qur'an were important sources of information for English readers on both sides of the Atlantic. His writings found their way into the libraries of early American clergymen, which were eventually donated to the early seminary libraries, including General, New Brunswick, and Princeton seminaries.

General seminary's original collection of reference material, which was approved by the Episcopal bishops, originally only included information on Islam in various dictionaries or encyclopedias, such as Ross's *Pansebeia*, William Turner's *History of All Religions in the World* (1695), Samuel Burder's *Oriental Customs: Applied to the Illustration of the Sacred Scriptures* (1807), and William Hurd's *History of All Religions* (1815). These books placed Islam and Muslims within the larger framework of the phenomenon of religion found among all the recently "discovered" peoples of the world.[38]

A prominent encyclopedia that was available at Andover, Princeton, and Hartford was Barthélemy d'Herbelot's *Bibliothèque Orientale*. Originally completed in French in 1697, it was reprinted in an expanded version in 1777, and a German translation was made in 1785, which was purchased for the Gettysburg and Union libraries. According to one reviewer, this work can be considered the first encyclopedia of the Qur'an that was available to Western readers.[39] *Bibliothèque* is based on a wide collection of medieval and early modern Islamic sources, primarily anthologies and compendiums. It is, as one reviewer noted, a "bouquet of bouquets," having brought together a wide variety of Arabic, Turkish, and Persian sources into one encyclopedic format.[40] While other Orientalists of his day may have criticized its organization and the structure of the work, for American seminaries, it was a one-stop shop for quick information. The first generation of American seminary professors did not have sufficient knowledge of the Orientalist literature on Islam to be able to assess or critique this work, as may have been done by European Orientalists. Given that few students would have been able to read French, it was probably not used by students. The German edition was most likely the one to be used. The book was laid out in much the same way as other Bible dictionaries and provided a quick and easy reference regarding Islamic terms and concepts.[41] Edward Robinson had published and edited previous European Bible dictionaries for American audiences, and it seems likely that he had a hand in acquiring this encyclopedia for both seminaries, although we have no evidence for this.[42]

One interesting source located at Andover and Union was the seventeenth-century *Fides et leges Mohammaedis* (1646) by Theodore Hackspan. Hackspan supported the study of Arabic and Islam at a time when most Christian clergy in Europe still had negative views about the topic. Hackspan provides a Lutheran confessional perspective in responding to the theological perspectives put forward in the Qur'an. In particular, he was interested in the Qur'anic perspectives on Jesus and the Trinity, primarily to refute them and put forward Christian responses.[43] The fact that *Fides et leges Mohammaedis* was only at Andover and Union, and not Gettysburg—the Lutheran seminary—indicates that, again, both were probably obtained by Edward Robinson in his acquisitions for Andover and Union during his European trips.

Finally, two books found in each of the seven libraries, providing very different arguments about Islam and the life of the Prophet, were Humphrey Prideaux's *True Nature of Imposture Fully Display'd in the Life of Mahomet* and Edward Gibbon's *Decline and Fall of the Roman Empire*. Gibbon's first volume was published in 1776, and the sixth and final volume was completed in 1788. Because of the American Revolution, it

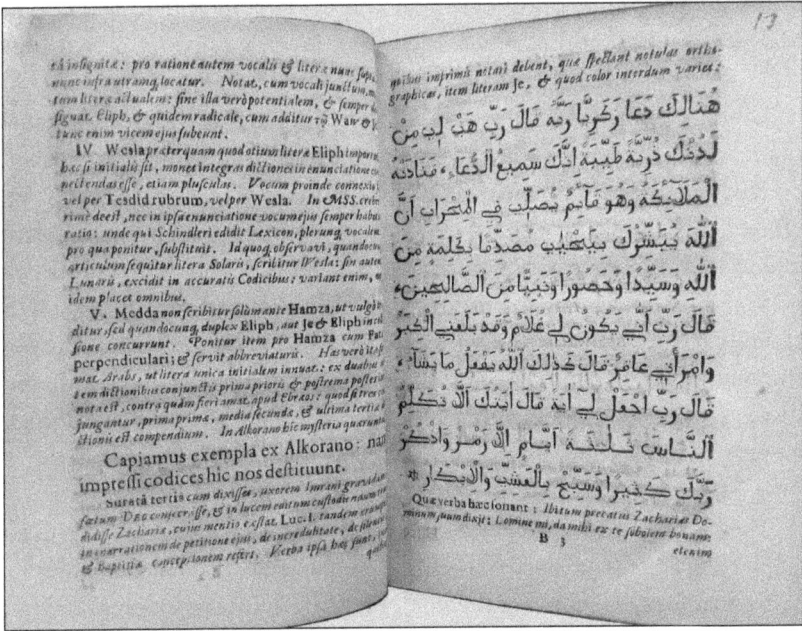

Figure 2.3. Theodore Hackspan, *Fides et leges Mohammaedis* (1646), Burke Library, Union Theological Seminary. Photo by David D. Grafton.

became difficult to import books from England. It was not until 1804, when the work was published by William Y. Birch & Abraham Small in Philadelphia, that it began to appear in American libraries.

Gibbon's history was written during the height of the Enlightenment, when religion—especially Christianity—was exposed to a vast array of critiques. While Christians began examining the roots of Oriental religions and cultures, the Deists and other secular thinkers examined the roots of Christianity in the same manner as they looked at any other ancient religion. Edward Gibbon's imposing *Decline and Fall of the Roman Empire* subjected Christianity to the same scrutiny he applied to Islam. Gibbon had a relatively positive view of Islam and saw Muhammad as a contributor to the development of world civilization. He intimated that of the two religions, Islam was more rational than Christianity, with its focus on the divinity and miracles of Jesus. As a result, Gibbon was heavily criticized by English clergy but was very popular among Deists and Enlightenment thinkers.[44] In chapters 50 to 52 of volume 3 he reviews the biography of Muhammad and the period of the *rashidun*, or the early caliphs, and concludes his volume with a history of Muslims and the Crusades in chapters 58 to 60.

Gibbon is infamously remembered for his description of Muhammad, who, "with the sword in one hand and the Koran in the other, erected his throne on the ruins of Christianity and of Rome."[45] And yet, while this phrase has been oft quoted by many to point out the negative effects and influences of Muhammad, ultimately Gibbon has a positive view of Muhammad. The Prophet was a leader who brought order and stability to the Arabs, creating a world empire. Gibbon debunks many of the medieval Christian legends about Muhammad's life and death and disparages the Christian sources for their calumny toward him. Rather, he remarks how the Muslim sources recall a very different Prophet:

> They applauded his commanding presence, his majestic aspect, his piercing eye, his gracious smile, his flowing beard, his countenance that painted every sensation of the soul, and his gestures that enforced each expression of the tongue. In the familiar offices of life he scrupulously adhered to the grave and ceremonious politeness of his country: his respectful attention to the rich and powerful was dignified by his condescension and affability to the poorest citizens of Mecca: the frankness of his manner concealed the artifice of his views; and the habits of courtesy were imputed to personal friendship or universal benevolence. His memory was capacious and retentive, his wit easy and social, his imagination sublime, his judgment clear, rapid, and decisive. He possessed the courage both of thought and action; and, although his designs might gradually expand with his success, the first idea which he entertained of his divine mission bears the stamp of an original and superior genius.[46]

From Gibbon readers are introduced to a world leader who contributed to the downfall of Rome by erecting a new civilization in its eastern provinces and into Europe, but not a deceitful and lecherous villain as represented in much of the Latin medieval material.[47]

However, the most ubiquitous work on Islam available first and foremost through the private libraries of educated clergy in the American colonies and then purchased for the seminary libraries was Humphrey Prideaux's *True Nature of Imposture Fully Display'd in the Life of Ma-*

homet, originally published in 1697. As prominently as Muhammad figures in the title, Prideaux's primary concern was not the danger of Islam posed by Turkish incursions into Europe but Deism and atheism during the age of the Enlightenment. The first part of the book is a biting critique of Islam while the second half focuses on Deism. Prideaux argues that Christianity serves as the basis of an enlightened Europe while Islam holds the East in darkness and immorality. He warns his European readers that if Europe is not careful, without Christianity as the moral glue of society, they too might sink into oblivion. As Nabil Matar has noted, "Prideaux used Islam as a cudgel with which to beat the deists because he believed that as Islam/Muḥammad had destroyed the Eastern Church so, too, would deists (along with Quakers and Socinians) destroy Christianity."[48] *The True Nature of Imposture* was one of the most prominent eighteenth-century works whose ideas were repeated and referenced ad nauseam by other American pastors and theologians, the most prominent being Archibald Alexander, the first professor of Princeton seminary.

Archibald Alexander, later the venerable president of Princeton seminary, utilized several English Orientalist works in his own response to Deist charges against orthodox Christianity. His *Brief Outline of the Evidences of the Christian Religion* originated as a sermon preached by Alexander at a chapel service of Princeton College in 1823. He wanted to respond to the ongoing debate among students about the role of reason versus revelation among philosophers such as David Hume, whom he calls one of "the enemies of revelation."[49] Alexander wanted to demonstrate the reasonableness of Christianity in the face of popular secularist and Deist critiques. As was common in the day, he published the sermon. Alexander's popularity as one of the most important reformed American theologians of the early nineteenth century ensured that his work would be circulated and read by many, and it would find its way to the libraries of the American seminaries.[50] By 1836, the year in which Alexander published an expanded version of the book, he also taught a course at Princeton called "Evidences of Natural and Revealed Religion." Although we have no extant text of his lectures, only notes from his students, including Hodge and Schmucker, we can safely assume that Alexander included his book for the course, as it would have been common for the students to recite the assigned text with their instructor.

As a part of the expanded work, Alexander rehearses the arguments against Islam originally put forward in Prideaux's *True Nature of Imposture Fully Display'd in the Life of Mahomet*. Like Prideaux, Alexander's diversion into the topic of Islam was related to the Deist debate, as the Deists had often argued that while Christianity was a religion founded on superstition and irrational beliefs, Islam supported the natural belief in a human prophet who guided communities toward upholding social laws and mores.[51] However, Alexander sought to demonstrate that Islam was deficient and morally backwards when compared to Christianity. He makes a comparison between what he saw as defective religious systems around the world contrasted with an enlightened Protestant Christianity in America.

> Over the rich and salubrious regions, possessed by Muhammad, we hold a wide spread desolation. The fairest portions of the globe where arts, literature of refinement formerly flourished, are now blighted. Every noble institution has sunk into oblivion. Despotism extends its iron scepter over these ill fated countries, and all the tranquility ever enjoyed, is the dead calm of ignorance and slavery. Useful learning is discouraged; free inquiry is proscribed, and servile submission required of all. Justice is perverted or disregarded. No man has any security for life or prosperity; and as to liberty it is utterly lost, wherever the Mohammedan religion prevails.[52]

Alexander then goes on to provide a point-by-point argument for what he views as the inadequacies of Islam compared with Christianity. First, Muhammad peformed no miracles, unlike Moses or Jesus. Second, in comparing Jesus to Muhammad, he notes that Muhammad was "ambitious, licentious, cruel, and unjust" while Jesus was "the most perfect example of disinterested zeal, pure benevolence, and unaffected humility."[53] Third, unlike the Bible, the Qur'an is a "confused and incongruous heap, of sublime sentiments, moral precepts, positive institutions, extravagant and ridiculous stories, and manifest lies and contradictions."[54] Alexander's comments about the Qur'an imply that he had read it. (This would have been more than likely from George Sale's translation of the Qur'an, which we will examine further below.) Fourth, compared to Jesus, who spread his message successfully through preaching, Muhammad required propagation "by the sword."[55] Finally, the effects of each religion are clear. Christianity produces profitable and "happy" countries with liberty and "security of life" whereas Islam produces despotic ones.[56]

Alexander draws on several sources for *Evidences*. His primary source is Prideaux, whom he quotes directly. The second source Alexander draws on is the work of the English Anglican priest William Paley (1743–1805), whose *View of the Evidences of Christianity* was another popular work found in the seminary libraries. Originally published in 1794 in England, Paley's book was extremely popular among clergy in colonial North America. It was republished in the United States by 1826, and then continuously after that. It became a commonly used text in seminary. Like Alexander after him, Paley was primarily interested in providing an apology for Christianity in the face of the Deists and the Enlightenment philosophers, especially David Hume and Edward Gibbon.[57] For Paley, the "success" of Christianity in Europe was due to the moral and ethical persuasion of Jesus and his followers, as opposed to Muhammad, who used the threat of violence and power. Here, Paley also draws directly from George Sale's "preliminary discourse" appended to his translation of the Qur'an.[58]

While Prideaux's and Paley's writings were part of an evangelical Christian response to the secular philosophy of the day, which was of primary concern for these prominent clergy, we should not lose sight of the general tenor of American feelings toward the Ottoman Empire and the Barbary states of North Africa. Alexander's work reflects early American animosity and frustration toward the corsairs from North Africa, who preyed on American merchant vessels and enslaved American sailors for ransom from the late eighteenth to the early part of the nineteenth century.[59] This scourge of international piracy ultimately led to the creation of a federal navy and the United States' first war as an independent nation with the North African states from 1801 to 1815.

Alexander and other clergy also had access to the letters of American missionaries in the Ottoman Empire published in the newsletter of the American Board of Commissioners of Foreign Missions (ABCFM), the *Missionary Herald*. The *Herald* letters from missionaries provided Alexander and other clergy with information about Islam and the possibilities of Protestant evangelization in the Holy Lands.[60] For Alexander, the

American experience of the North African pirates and the obstacles put in the way of the early American missionaries to the Ottoman Empire were evidence of foreign despotism seeking to undermine American Christian prosperity. During this period, the Ottomans and their vassal states had been referred to by some, including Jonathan Edwards, as the "locusts of the abyss" from Revelation 9:3.

In a similar vein to Alexander, Samuel Van Vranken (1792–1861), the professor of didactic and polemic theology at New Brunswick seminary from 1841 to 1861, introduced all his students to Islam through his lectures on "Religion in General."[61] For Van Vranken, as humans were created in the image of God, they all have the ability to perceive true and false religion. True religion draws from just principles. False religion, however, is that "where the true God is not the object of worship," and there are four forms of false religion: Paganism (which includes Hinduism and Buddhism), Judaism, nominal Christianity (that is, Catholicism and Deism), and "Mohammedanism." Through the handwritten notes from his students, we can get a general sense of Van Vranken's views on Islam, and only a general idea of his sources.[62]

For twenty years, the students at New Brunswick were introduced to Islam through Van Vranken's lectures on didactic theology. He provided them a general overview of the life of Muhammad, the Qur'an, and the basic tenets of Islamic belief. The precepts he highlighted were the unity of God, and the belief that "Jesus the son of Mary is an apostle" but not the Son of God. Muhammad taught the "doctrines of providence and predestination," and that salvation comes through "good works . . . prayers, purifications, and alms-giving." It is most likely that Van Vranken used George Sale's "Preliminary Discourse," that was prefixed to his translation of the Qur'an, which was available in the library. There are also direct references to Prideaux and Edward Gibbon's *Decline and Fall of the Roman Empire* in the lecture notes, as noted by his comments that refer to Muhammad as an "extraordinary man" and yet an "imposture."

According to Van Vranken, Muhammed developed his "system" by combining aspects of Judaism, Paganism, and Christianity, which was and is a common view among Christian historians. In the same manner as Archibald Alexander, Van Vranken highlighted Muhammad's "gratifications of the carnal propensities of his followers." While he forbade wine, he did allow sexual debauchery through the support of polygamy and "his celestial paradise was no more than a Haram." The Qur'an "contains the pretend revelations of the Impostor" and is a "magazine of rhapsodies thrown together" (a reference to the Qur'an by Gibbon). It takes many "facts and sentiments" from the Bible that are scattered throughout, and they are "incongruous, extravagant, ridiculous & false." As an example, Van Vranken describes Muhammad's night journey from Mecca to Jerusalem and then his ascension to heaven "in the twinkling of an eye" as an "extravagant and ridiculous" story.

Thus, we can see that early on, faculty drew upon the resources of English Orientalist works that were in their seminary libraries. These books would have been used by the faculty for lessons with their students as well as for their own lectures, providing students with access to the information they propagated about Islam. In addition to these sources, the faculty and students also had access to translations of the Qur'an.

Translations of the Qur'an

Translations of the Qur'an were quite prevalent in the American seminary libraries at Andover, Union, Princeton, and Gettysburg in the 1820s. A translation was not found in the General seminary library at this time, however. Given that the required material was approved and assigned by the bishops of the Episcopal Church, it is not surprising that we do not find a Qur'an present. The focus of the acquired books in that library were in the areas of early church history and dogmatic theology.

When the seminaries began acquiring books from Europe to establish their libraries, an early translation of the Qur'an usually included in collections was that of Ludovico Marracci. Marracci was an Italian Catholic scholar who produced a two-volume translation in 1691 and 1698. The first volume, *Prodromus ad refutationem Alcorani*, was an introduction to the organization and structure of the Qur'an, as well as an overview of the life of Muhammad.[63] The second volume, *Refutatio Alcorani*, was the actual translation of the Qur'an from Arabic into Latin. Marracci's title of his work alludes to his polemical approach to what was commonly thought of as "Muhammad's Qur'an." While Marracci's translation was available in the seminary libraries, it was not very useful. Many colleges in the United States required or taught Latin in undergraduate study, but the seminaries never officially required it. It was assumed in the 1820s that students would have had Latin in grammar school, so entering students were only required to demonstrate that they were spiritually fit, were in good standing with a church, and had completed a "regular course of education."[64] The focus of the early curriculum in seminary was on the original languages of the Protestant Bible—Hebrew and Greek—except for General seminary, where Latin was associated with the Latin Vulgate Bible. Thus, the English translations of the Qur'an proved to be more valuable in seminary libraries.

Throughout the nineteenth century, numerous different translations of the Qur'an proliferated. However, the most ubiquitous version of the Qur'an that appeared in all the libraries was George Sale's *Koran, Commonly Called the Alcoran of Mohammed*. Professors not only used Sale's translation to read Qur'anic passages, but his "Preliminary Discourse," which provides an overview of Islamic history and the beliefs and practices of Islam from Muslim sources, was also consulted by professors to prepare lectures. Sale's *Koran* was readily available in multiple editions in colonial and republican North America. Andover had at least one edition listed in its collection in the early 1819 catalog, in addition to Hinkelmann's Arabic translation of 1644, noted previously. Throughout the years, further editions of Sale's translation were donated or purchased by each of the seminaries. The 1852 library catalogue of Princeton lists an 1801 edition of Sale's translation. Princeton also acquired an 1825 edition from Professor Joseph A. Alexander after his death in 1860.[65] The 1862 accession list of books at Gettysburg seminary included an 1835 edition. Gettysburg also has a 1764 edition that was donated from a private library, although it is unclear exactly when the seminary acquired it.

Sale's translation had long been available in the colonies of North America. Denise Spellberg has recounted the story of Thomas Jefferson's acquisition of not one but two copies of Sale's translation (the second after one was lost in a fire at his home).[66] Like other Enlightenment aristocrats of his day, Jefferson saw Muhammad as a ruler and legislator, and the Qur'an as a law book, rather than as a revealed spiritual text. Because it was published in Philadelphia, it did not have to be imported from England and was relatively cheap to acquire. Thus, Sale's version was widely disseminated.[67]

As noted above, it was not only Sale's English translation that was valuable to readers, but Sale's "Preliminary Discourse" also included a

THE

KORAN,

COMMONLY CALLED

The Alcoran *of* MOHAMMED,

Tranflated into ENGLISH immediately from
the Original ARABIC;

WITH

EXPLANATORY NOTES,

TAKEN FROM THE MOST

APPROVED COMMENTATORS,

TO WHICH IS PREFIXED,

A Preliminary Difcourfe.

VOL. I.

By GEORGE SALE, Gent.

Nulla falfa doctrina eft, quæ non aliquid veri permifceat.
Auguftin. Quæft. Evang. l. ii. c. xl.

LONDON,

Printed for L. HAWES, W. CLARKE, and R. COLLINS, at the
Red Lion in Pater Nofter Row; and T. WILCOX, at Virgil's
Head, overagainft the New Church, in the Strand.

M DCC LXIV.

1764

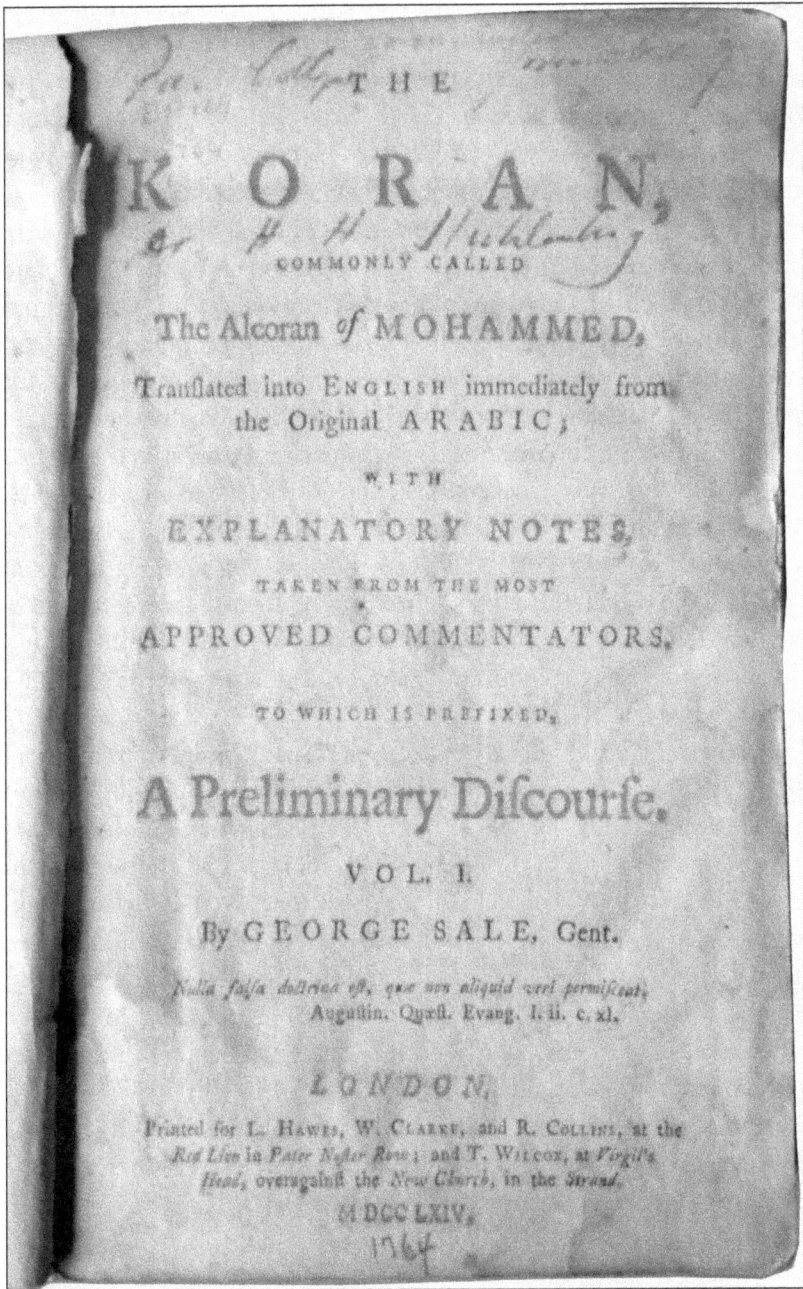

Figure 2.4. 1764 edition of Sale's Qur'an from Wentz Library, Gettysburg Theological Seminary. Photo by David D. Grafton.

biography of the Prophet and a history of the compilation of the Qur'an. Overall, Sale has a positive view of Muhammad and his role as an Arab and religious leader. Sale had worked with the Anglican Society for Promoting Christian Knowledge (SPCK) by providing other translations for their work in promoting Christianity. He was not a Deist nor an antireligious Enlightenment thinker. Rather, he was interested in promoting Christianity among Muslims through a fair and reasoned approach. Thus, he wanted to provide accurate information about the Qur'an and Muhammad's life in a balanced manner. He even specifically calls out Humphrey Prideaux for spreading lies about the Prophet. Because of this, the translation was met with severe criticism in England after its publication. Sale was even accused by his critics of having converted to Islam.[68] However, the work never became controversial in the United States. It was the only English translation available to many up until the 1840s. The translation was also used by E. M. Wherry in his commentary on the Qur'an in 1882, which cemented reliance on this translation well into the twentieth century. Wherry's commentary was intended to be used by missionaries living and working in Muslim countries and still continues to be a common reference work among some Christian missionaries.[69]

The 1886 Princeton library catalog lists nine different translations of the Qur'an available in the library (not including the various editions of Sale's translation). Two other important English translations that appeared on the shelves of the libraries were those of J. M. Rodwell in 1861 and E. H. Palmer in 1880. Palmer, the professor of Arabic at Cambridge, contributed his translation to volumes 6 and 9 of Max Müller's *Sacred Books of the East*, and it was used well into the twentieth century as a standard reference work in seminary libraries. Arabic editions of the Qur'an began to appear as early as 1836. Princeton acquired Gustav Fluegel's Arabic edition, originally published in Germany in 1834.[70] This rendering became important when Union, New Brunswick, and Hartford began to teach Arabic and use the Qur'an as a text. While the Arabic versions were not common, they were available.

Biographies of the Prophet

The final resources on Islam that the seminaries collected throughout the nineteenth century were biographies or histories of the Prophet. Throughout the century, the seminary libraries acquired a surprising number of studies on the life of Muhammad. These resources became important for two professors in particular, Duncan Black Macdonald at Hartford and John G. Lansing at New Brunswick. Both used these sources as a part of their regular teaching beginning in the 1880s.[71]

However, as early as 1833 the library catalog of Andover lists translations of two prominent Orientalist sources on the life of Muhammad; the first is a copy of *Chronicum Syriacum*. This medieval history, written by the thirteenth-century Syrian monk Bar Hebreaus, reviews the history of the Arabs, the life of Muhammad, and the history of the Qur'an.[72] The second source is *De vita et rebus gestis Mohammedism* by Jean Gagnier (1670–1740), published in 1723. This biography of Muhammad was primarily a translation of the fourteenth-century Syrian Abu al-Fida"s *al-Mukhtaṣar*. However, Gagnier expanded Abu al-Fida"s work by including other, later Hadith sources that include prominent episodes in the life of the Prophet.[73] While *al-Mukhtaṣar* was itself a late biography and included many later traditions of Muhammad's life compared to the numerous other earlier and more reputable Muslim biographies, nevertheless, this was the first truly Muslim source made available in Europe and North America.[74] Gagnier's publication was the primary source used by Washington Irving in his biography of Muhammad in 1859.[75]

Interestingly, and perhaps not surprisingly, all of the seminary libraries acquired the first American biography of Muhammad, written by the Presbyterian minister George Bush (1796–1859) in 1830. *The Life of Mohammed: Founder of the Religion of Islam, and of the Empire of the Saracens* was Bush's first published book. Originally from Vermont, Bush was a graduate of Princeton and served a Presbyterian congregation on the frontier in Indiana before moving to New York City, where he taught Hebrew at New York University and worked for the American Bible Society.

At some point during his time in New York, he became interested in the life and thinking of Emmanuel Swedenborg, who claimed that he had received spiritual messages directly from Jesus and taught that the Millennium, or the End Times, had already begun. Bush became a prominent member of Swedenborg's New Jerusalem Church. As a result, he was kicked out of the Presbyterian Church. Nevertheless, while Bush became known for his unusual beliefs on mesmerism and spiritualism, his biography on Muhammad became a bestseller. The biography lined the shelves of the seminaries,[76] though as we will see, Bush's narrative of Muhammad would be directly refuted by Duncan Black Macdonald in his *Religious Attitude and Life in Islam* (1909).

We can see how *The Life of Mohammed* contributed to Bush's belief in the Millennium. He ascribes several apocalyptic passages from the books of Daniel and Revelation to Muhammad's life. Thus, Muhammad's role and life, and the coming of Islam, were part of "the great scheme of the Divine administration of the world."[77] *The Life of Mohammed*, however, is not a unique perspective on the biography of the Prophet. Bush did not use any original sources and relied on many of the other Orientalist works already available in the libraries, such as Sale's "Preliminary Discourse" and translation of the Qur'an, Edward Gibbon's *Decline and Fall of the Roman Empire*, Simon Ockley's *History of the Saracens* (1708), D'Herbelot's *Bibliothèque Orientale* (1697), Paul Rycaut's *Present State of the Ottoman Empire* (1686), and, most importantly, Humphrey Prideaux's *True Nature of Imposture* (1697). In this regard, Bush simply rehashes Prideaux's argument, summarizing that Muhammad's life was one of "fanaticism, ambition, and lust."[78] He was an "imposture." An additional important source Bush used was the recently published travelogues of John Lewis Burckhardt's journeys to the Levant, Upper Egypt, and Arabia. Bush highlighted these recent "eyewitness" descriptions of Mecca and Medina to support his view that Islam was one of the signs of the End Times.

Around midcentury, a number of English Orientalist works became widely available, including William Muir's *Life of Mahomet*, published in 1858. William Muir was a lieutenant governor of the northwest provinces of India during British occupation of India and served there during the Indian Mutiny of 1857. Muir's *Mohammedan Controversy*, which included a retelling of the debate between the missionary Karl Pfander and the Indian Muslim scholar Rahmatullah Kairanawi in 1854, was an extremely popular work for those Christian students considering missionary work in Muslim-majority countries.[79]

German Orientalist scholarship on the life of Muhammad became important to the understanding of Islam for many of the seminary professors in antebellum America. As we have seen, many early American seminary professors spent time studying in Germany and brought back many German resources. Thus, the seminaries acquired not a few German publications. These works were used by faculty to prepare lectures, which was becoming a new technique in graduate teaching and learning. An important German source on the life of Muhammad was Abraham Geiger's *Was hat Mohammed aus dem Judentume aufgenommen?* Published in 1833, it was frequently cited by biblical studies professors in their critical studies of the Hebrew Bible. Gustav Weil's *Mohammed der Prophet* and *Biblische Legenden der Muselmänner*, published in 1843 and 1845, respectively, were widely read in Europe. *Biblische Legenden* was translated into English as early as 1846 as *The Bible, the Koran, and the Talmud; or, Biblical Legends of the Mussulmans, Compiled from Arabic Sources, and Compared with Jewish Traditions*. *The Bible, the Koran, and the Talmud* was an extremely popular work that contributed to the generally accepted knowledge of Islam as part of the larger frame of the Near Eastern cultural and religious milieu. It transformed the understanding of Islam as a Christian heresy (as reflected in early Christian literature) to that of a Near Eastern Semitic religion. Both books appear in the Andover and Union seminary catalogs by 1863 but appear more widely in other catalogs in the 1880s. As we will see, Weil's work was used by both biblical scholars and comparative theologians throughout the curricula of several seminaries.

The most important contributions to the development of Western Islamic studies were those of Theodor Nöldeke (1836–1930) and Ignaz Goldziher (1850–1921). In 1860, Nöldeke published *Geschichte des Qorâns*, which has become the standard work for historical research on the Qur'an in Western Islamic studies. Nöldeke's research was groundbreaking. Approaching the Qu'ran as he did the Hebrew Bible and other Near Eastern texts, he engaged in form critical analysis and the historical origins of the structure of the Qur'an. While the techniques that Nöldeke applied were similar to those applied to other ancient religious texts, the content and argument were specifically focused on the history and structure of the Qur'an. *Geschichte des Qorâns* does not appear in several of the seminaries discussed in this book until 1890 at the earliest. We find record of it in Princeton, Hartford, and New Brunswick, but not the others. By the 1890s, only Hartford maintained any interest in Islamic studies through the scholarship of Duncan Black Macdonald. By this time, secular universities were beginning to organize their own departments of Near Eastern studies and copies could be found there.

Additionally, what is most notable in the library collections is the almost complete absence of Ignaz Goldziher's scholarship, including his seminal work, *Muḥammadenische Studien*, published in 1890. This work is considered the origin of modern Western Islamic studies. Only Duncan Black Macdonald at Hartford seminary referenced and actually used Goldziher's work in his teaching and writing. Goldziher's research focused on the history of Hadith collections and their role in the classical Muslim interpretations of the Qur'an. It is technical in its outlook and method and required familiarity with Islamic sources. An English translation of *Muhammedanische Studien* did not appear in the United States until 1961.

It is very possible that the absence of Goldziher's work in the American Protestant seminaries reflects a broader anti-Jewish bias in American biblical scholarship at the time. The challenges and pressures that Jewish Orientalist scholars faced in Europe in the nineteenth century have been well documented. Many were required to convert to Christianity to secure their positions.[80] The role of anti-Judaism in nineteenth-century biblical scholarship is now under intense scrutiny.[81] Given that Jewish scholars like Geiger and Weil saw commonalities between medieval Judaism and Islam, this may have been sufficient for Protestant scholars to support a biblical supercessionist view of true Protestant Christianity over Judaism and Islam as inferior monotheistic religions. However, it is also important to note that the work of Nöldeke, who was not Jewish, does not appear in the libraries of Princeton or Hartford until very late—1890 and 1891, as well.

By the end of the nineteenth century, fewer theology students traveled to Germany for advanced theological education. And, fewer theology students continued learning German. In the non-Lutheran or Reformed seminaries, reading German became relegated only to a minority of students undertaking advanced-level theological or biblical studies. German scholarship needed to be translated into English to make its way into American seminary classrooms.[82] Perhaps the American Civil War may explain a drop in interest in German. Fewer students were able to travel to Germany during the war, and fewer German textbooks were brought back during the war and in the following decades. Or, perhaps the rise of American university departments of Near Eastern studies in the 1870s and 1880s drew away from seminaries those students who were purely interested in Near Eastern texts. Nevertheless, it is clear that Nöldeke and Goldziher were not widely available or read in the seminaries except at Hartford during this period.

At the end of the day, a library is only as valuable as the patrons who use it. Having a curated collection of theological works to serve students means nothing if the books are not used or read. Norman Kansfield has examined circulation records from New Brunswick seminary from 1825 through 1855 and noted that students borrowed on average only ten books throughout the tenure of their three years of seminary education![83] A comparison with the circulation lists at Andover demonstrates that most students there took out only a handful of books as well—Edward Robinson's student borrowing record being an important exception. His handwritten library record spans numerous pages, indicating his voluminous reading as a student. While a sample of student records at one seminary cannot be considered definitive for other times or other seminaries, nevertheless, the point is well taken. Library books do not read themselves. The use or disuse of library resources was and continues to be dependent upon curricular requirements or individual student research interests.

Yet, student circulation records aside, many of these books on Islam were used by faculty in their preparation of lessons, lectures, or recitations with students. The content about Islam was well in circulation among the faculty first, and then among their students. In the early years of seminary education, the recitation of books and then faculty lectures served as the primary pedagogical method of instruction. Students were dependent on the interest of the instructor. And, in this vein, by the middle of the nineteenth century, American seminary professors had a wide variety of Western resources available on Islam from which to draw. Interpretations of Islam varied greatly in the accessible sources. Biographies of Muhammad represented the anti-Muslim polemics of Prideaux and Bush, as well as the more congenial sources of Irving and Gibbon.

The sources one chose to read would frame the perspective of Muhammad's intentions and identity either as an "impostor" or an Arab hero. However, there was no debate in the overall assumption that the arc of history tilted westward toward American Protestantism as the pinnacle of God's intentions for humanity, overshadowing Islam as a scourge found in scripture. Early references to Muslims as the "locusts" of Revelation or Muhammad as the "horns" of the beast in Daniel were very rare and limited to the early comments by Mather, Edwards, and then Bush. The focus was rather on contemporary experiences and examples of Ottoman or North African "despotism." In the following chapter we will examine how Muhammad and Islam were portrayed specifically within church history textbooks assigned to students, to see what students were required to read about Islam.

3

Islam in American Church History

One of the most common ways Islam was introduced to seminary students in the nineteenth century was through lectures and required reading in church history courses. From medieval Latin sources on Islam that had been translated by European Orientalists to the sweeping histories of the church compiled by German historians and then translated into English, seminary students were broadly introduced to Islam in its relation to the church. Islam was portrayed as an external danger to Christianity. However, it was not set apart as a distinctive nemesis or singled out as "the" spiritual danger, and Muhammad was not portrayed as the "anti-Christ," as was common in Latin and early modern Christian literature. Islam was presented like many other heretical movements or cruel invaders of Europe, another obstacle for orthodox Christianity to overcome.

By the time that Philip Schaff began to publish his own church histories in the 1870s, he was able to use more recently published biographies of the Prophet Muhammad as well as to draw from his own experience of traveling to the Near East. Schaff shifted the image of Muhammad from that of a religious nemesis or "impostor" to that of a Bedouin Arab leader who guided the Arabs out of the dark ages, even if he finally succumbed to the temptations of power. For Schaff, Muhammad's attempts to reform a Jewish religion for his Arab compatriots was commendable, but eventually he could not overcome the crude nature of the Near East. Even those students who had no interest in missionary work would have encountered references to Islam from Schaff's various writings in their required church history lectures and reading material. His works became ubiquitous in American seminaries. This chapter examines how Islam was portrayed in the historical works used by seminaries from their inception into the twentieth century.

American Church History

From the earliest days of the seminary system, the faculty normally consisted of a professor of scripture (or sacred literature), theology (often called didactic, and later systematic or apologetic theology), and ecclesiastical history. While the triumvirate of positions was considered standard and necessary, in reality church history positions were often the last filled and regularly combined with other titles or areas of responsibility. For example, even though it had been in the plan from its inception, it took Union fourteen years to finally hire a church history professor. Princeton did hire one right away in 1813, Samuel Miller, but his chair was that of a "professor of ecclesiastical history *and* church government."[1] For all the plans to create a complete faculty, scripture and theology were still the foundations from which seminary boards built their institutions. Church history was a distant third. As Elizabeth Clark has noted, history as a discipline was slow to develop in American higher education. By 1884, Princeton College only had one professor of history, who also taught political science. If the dearth of historians was true for the budding American higher education system, it was especially true in seminaries, which often ran short of their goals in raising funds for faculty chairs.[2]

Perhaps one of the reasons why history as a discipline never received its full respect in the curriculum was the pedagogical methods being used at the time. In the early nineteenth century, teachers merely had students "recite" or read aloud chapters of books. Reading Greek and Roman classics, such as Tacitus and Cicero, was an important part of early American classical education. It was assumed that knowing Greek and Latin was important to demonstrate learning. And, as we have seen previously, it was assumed by seminary faculty that entering students had such knowledge, which was often an incorrect assumption. Thus, an instructor could not count on the whole class of students being able to "recite" a history text together. Recitations were eventually supplanted by professors who required their students to read textbooks but added their own perspectives in a lecture from which students were required to take notes. And, naturally, some instructors were better at lecturing than others. Clark, in *Founding the Fathers*, provides an excellent overview of the methods several seminary professors used during this period by analyzing student notes from their classes. For example, Clark remarks that Henry Smith at Union was particularly engaging and thought provoking for his students while Samuel Smith never changed his lectures throughout the years.[3]

By the time American seminaries were founded, there were several church history texts written in German and translated into English. Students were required to read the German historical compendiums of Mosheim, Geiseler, and Neander, whose volumes were available in all the seminary libraries reviewed here.[4] It was not until the last third of the century when seminars became a popular method through which students could engage in deeper research on a specific historical or theological topic from their library books.

As was common with other disciplines, Americans relied heavily on German scholarship in this field. Henry Boynton Smith (1815–1877), professor of church history at Union from 1850 to 1855, studied under August Tholuck in Halle from 1838 to 1840. Smith brought back with him a German method of understanding history as he gleaned it from Tholuck's lectures on "Theological Encyclopedia," that is, the systematic definition of terms and categories to be used in the field.[5] This method of engaging church history was then continued by Smith's successor at Union, Roswell Hitchcock (1817–1877), cementing a German method of historical analysis at Union for several generations of students.

As American seminary professors traveled to Germany for their advanced theological education, they were introduced to the German concept of *Wissenschaft*, an approach to the world that combined ideas and culture with empirical scientific experience, what Americans called the "arts and sciences" of education.[6] German historians began not only to read the past for a record of political events or for the biographies of famous individuals but to make connections between events and theories.[7] "History" came to be understood not only as facts of the past but as a way of interpreting the past constructed through ideas. German church historians viewed ecclesiastical history as a "history of dogma," or historical theology, and not just a record of the names of people, popes, and bishops.[8] American theology students who studied in Germany gleaned this new perspective of history.

One of the clearest examples of how the German outlook on history at that time affected American theological education comes from the pen of Roswell Hitchcock. A graduate of Andover, he became the Washburn professor of church history at Union seminary in 1855, and later was the president from 1880 to 1887. Like so many others of his day, he spent time in Halle and Berlin, studying with August Tholuck. Hitchcock absorbed the idea that the history of the church was part of God's salvation history being worked out in the world. Through this view, Hitchcock saw the United States as part of this salvific plan. For Hitchcock, among others, there had been a shift away from Europe to North America, which was now "in charge of the final theatre and the final problems of history."[9] Philip Schaff, a German immigrant to the United States, was also attracted to this idea. For Schaff, there was an organic development of history rather than a determined Hegelian style of progress.[10] Schaff believed that America and American Protestant Christianity were part of God's divine providence. And, as we will see, a consistent theme that appears among the faculty in these seminaries throughout the nineteenth century is a firm belief that human societies and cultures progressed to become more moral, ethical, and spiritually pure. They held, essentially, to a religious Darwinism. And in the context of the field of comparative religions, White Protestant Christianity—in its North American form—was seen as the pinnacle of human spiritual aspirations and achievements.

Our interest in this chapter, however, is not the historiography of church history in general but rather those historical sources that provided information on Islam that were used in seminary education, both the resources faculty drew upon for their lectures and writing and those sources that students read. As we have seen, there were a wide variety of different sources available in the libraries. Of particular note for us are those that provided information about Islam in the church history classroom. As the lecture method became popular, instructors used the library (their own or the seminary's) to address various topics, but also required students to read the newly translated German compendiums of history.

Lecture Notes on Islam

John DeWitt was professor of biblical literature and ecclesiastical history at New Brunswick seminary from 1823 to 1831. His lectures on the history of the church provide a helpful example of how medieval and even Reformation sources were used for teaching about Islam during the early years of seminary education. He taught during a time when the lecture format was coming into vogue but prior to the availability of the large church history compendiums.

DeWitt was a classically trained pastor. He graduated from Princeton College and went on to study law. However, he had a conversionary experience, and then went into the ministry. He apprenticed under the Reverend Dr. Porter, a Presbyterian pastor in Catskill, New York. At Princeton he would have read Greek and Latin classics, and under Porter he would have recited the New Testament in Greek. When DeWitt came to New Jersey, he was called to teach both at the New Brunswick seminary and Queen's College, later Rutgers College.[11] During this period the library resources were at a minimum, even deplorable. Thus, most of what he used to develop his class material came from his own personal library. In his lectures on "A System of Sacred Interpretation," DeWitt used a Reformation history, the *Magdeburg Centuries*, published between 1559 and 1574, which drew on early medieval Christian texts.

DeWitt's lectures focused on the theme of church history as a continuation of the story of the early New Testament church. For DeWitt, history provides an important continuity of divine providence. It follows the establishment of the church at Pentecost, the development of the orthodox creeds and councils, the correctives of the true faith during the Reformation, and the role of the North American church as part of God's plans. In his lectures, DeWitt includes only a small amount of material referring to the "non-Christian religions."[12] His references to Islam come from the 1559 Latin Reformation record, the *Magdeburg Centuries* of Flacius Illyricus. Flacius himself draws on some of the Latin and Greek histories of the eighth through the ninth centuries, including Venerable Bede's *Ecclesiastical History of the English People* (ca. 731), Theophylact Simocatta, a Byzantine historian from around 630, and Theophanes the Confessor (760–818), whose *Chronicle* from 602 to 813 was one of the most widely used Christian sources in reference to Islam.

Using Flacius's history as a base for his information, DeWitt remarks that the Persian Empire was destroyed by the "Saracens," a

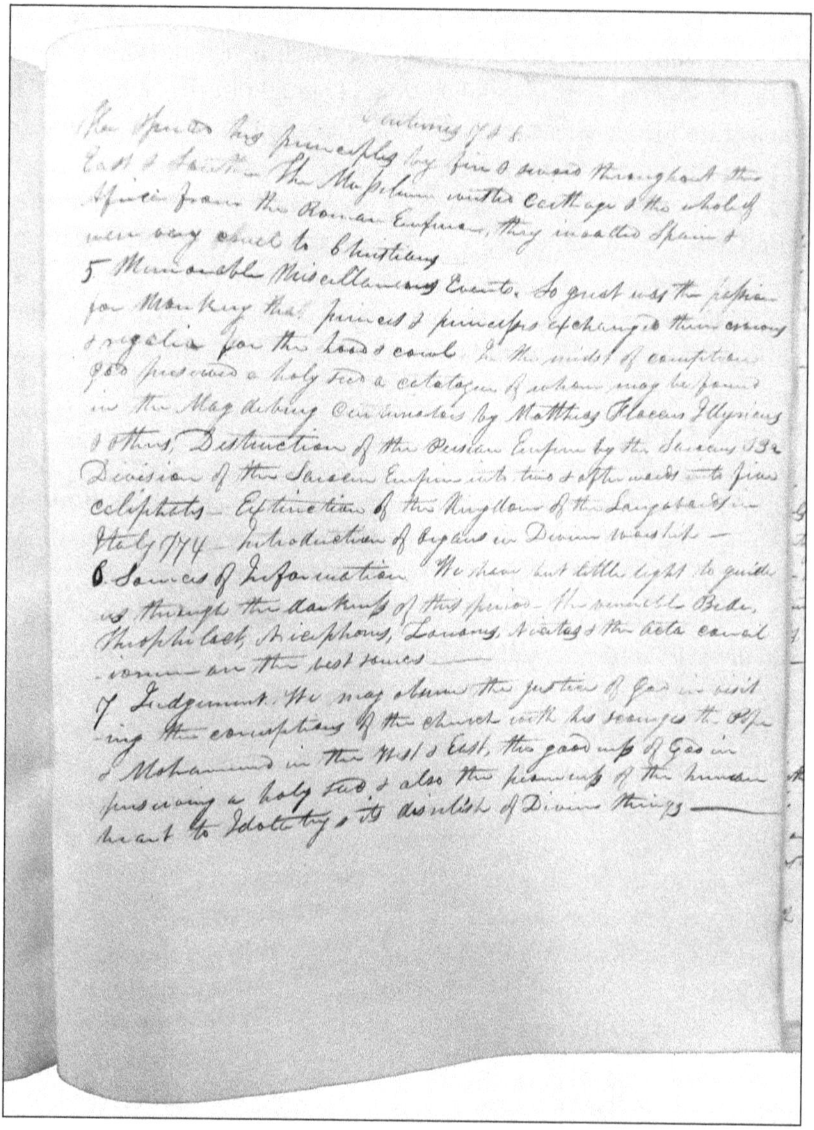

Figure 3.1. John DeWitt's Lecture on "A System of Sacred Interpretation," New Brunswick Theological Seminary Archives, Sage Library. Photo by David D. Grafton.

common term used by Latin Christians in referring to Muslims.[13] Flacius then remarks that the "Saracen Empire" eventually split into two caliphates, a reference to the Sunni and Shi'a branches of Islam, which he does not properly identify or expound on. While Bede and Theophylact provide general comments about the "Saracens," it is Theophanes in his *Chronographia* who presents the most information about the life of Muhammad and extensive references to the life of Christians under the Arab Muslim empires. For his part, to piece together his information on Islam, Theophanes relied on the Syriac history of Theophilus of Edessa (d. 785) that had been translated into Greek. (Theophilus's work, unfortunately, is no longer extant.) Theophanes was able to relay important information about the Christians, churches, and monasteries under the Umayyads and 'Abbasids that would not be accessible to a Byzantine.[14]

Theophanes interprets the coming of Islam and the defeat of the Byzantines within theological categories, attesting that "success and failure [of empires] are associated with orthodoxy and heresy."[15] For example, when the Byzantine emperor Heraclius asserted the theological compromise of Monothelitism, which later became labeled as a heresy, Theophanes claims the emperor was punished by God and overrun by the "Saracens." When Leo III introduced his iconoclastic rules forbidding the standard practice of the use of icons in Christian worship, Theophanes remarks that Leo was possessed by a "Saracen mentality" (*sarakēnophrōn*) and punished by God.

Theophanes is the first Western Christian source who makes the claim that Muhammad suffered from epilepsy. It had been commonly known among Muslim commentators and from the biographies of the Prophet that when Muhammad received revelations from God, he would go into trances, often having sweats. According to some Muslim accounts, at first Muhammad thought he was being overcome by a demon, but it was later revealed to him that such episodes were the coming of the Angel Gabriel who was reciting to him the Qur'an. Theophanes and later Christians interpreted these incidents in Muslim sources as a sign of weakness and maligned Muhammad's physical and mental abilities. Theophanes also makes the claim that Muhammad was descended from Ishmael's descendant Nizaros, who was "the father of all Arabs."[16] The connection to Ishmael also became a commonly repeated Christian accusation of Muhammad in reference to the "blessing" of Ishmael in Genesis 16:12: "He shall be a wild ass of a man; his hand shall be against every man, and every man's hand against him." Later Christians incorporated Theophanes's claim, which often appears in apocalyptic Christian traditions.

The writings of Theophanes the Confessor were ultimately collected, compiled, and included in a massive collection of Christian primary sources in the nineteenth century. The French priest Jacques-Paul Migne (1800–1875) created one of the most important assemblies of patristic writings to this day. The collections of the Greek and Latin church fathers, *Patrologia Graeca* and *Patrologia Latina*, include an incredible 169 and 218 volumes, respectively. The collections were published between 1844 and 1857. While Migne did not provide critical editions of these primary sources, and he relied on dubious or inadequate manuscripts, nevertheless, his collection provided many seminary professors and students with direct access to early and medieval church writings.[17] At the time of DeWitt's tenure, Migne's collection had not been published. Given the challenges that New Brunswick had in developing its library, it is most certain that DeWitt owned his own copy of the *Centuries*. His lectures demonstrate the importance of the personal library of the early seminary professors.

Fifty years after DeWitt taught church history at New Brunswick, his successor Samuel M. Woodbridge (1819–1905), professor of pastoral theology, ecclesiastical history, and church government, organized his own lectures in much the same way as DeWitt. Woodbridge was one of the longest-serving professors of New Brunswick, serving on the faculty for forty–eight years, from 1857 to 1905. In his "Lectures on Church History," which are available in the New Brunswick archives, Woodbridge has very little to say about Islam. He draws his comments on Islam primarily from Edward Gibbon, *The Decline and Fall of the Roman Empire*, as well as Edward Pococke's *Specimen historiae arabum*.

Woodbridge introduces Islam and the life of Muhammad to his students under the title of the "Mohammedan Persecution." He provides a basic outline of the life of Muhammad that is fairly accurate, although the dating is a bit off in places, noting Muhammad's death, for example, as occurring in 622 rather than 632. This indicates that he was reading Theophanes, probably through the published edition of Migne, who makes the same claim. Woodbridge also provides some basic information about the followers of Muhammad expanding their empire into Africa and Egypt and subjecting their enemies to "slavery and other frightful calamities." Muhammad's successors then split into two great empires, a reference to the Sunni and Shi'i split noted in Theophanes. Woodbridge, however, also mentions in some detail the burning of the library of Alexandria by Amr ibn al-'As as recorded by the twelfth-century Syriac historian Gregory Bar Hebraeus. Bar Hebraeus, as noted earlier, was transmitted to English audiences through the English Arabist Edward Pococke's *Specimen historiae arabum*. Pococke's work was located in the Gardner Sage Library of New Brunswick.[18]

According to Bar Hebraeus, when the Arabs conquered Alexandria, they wrote back to the caliph Umar ibn al-Khattab to ask for advice on what to do with the ancient library of Alexandria. According to the tradition, Umar responded, "If these writings of the Greeks agree with the book of God, they are useless, and need not be preserved: if they disagree, they are pernicious, and ought to be destroyed." The library was then burned.[19] However, Edward Gibbon, in *Decline and Fall*, doubts the authenticity of this tradition. Gibbon comments that the library may just as well have been burned by Julius Caesar during his taking of Alexandria in 47 BCE, or by the Christians themselves during their expunging of Alexandria from the influences of the Ptolemaic cults and their destruction of the great temple of Serapis in the fourth century. Gibbon correctly notes that there were no other references to the burning of the library in other contemporary histories of the Arab invasion. And libraries all over the world have been burned by invading armies through general wanton destruction. Gibbon simply sets aside the "repugnant" tradition as spurious. Nevertheless, Woodbridge continued to teach this tradition from the Christian sources and laid the groundwork for negative perceptions of Islam among his students. "The injury the Mohammedans did . . . is almost inconceivable," Woodbridge lectured. "They destroyed wherever they came—including literature and libraries, the Alexandria library among them. Those who live under them were allowed a 'miserable existence.'"[20]

Woodbridge had a profound impact on the students whom he taught. In fact, one of his students, Samuel Zwemer, would go on to be the most prominent Protestant "missionary to Islam" in the twentieth century. An examination of Zwemer's copy of Woodbridge's theology textbook, *Analysis of Systematic Theology*, published in 1883, demonstrates the importance of Woodbridge's impact on Zwemer's theology. Page after page of Zwemer's book is littered with marginalia in which he translates Woodbridge's English terminology of Calvinist theology into Arabic. It is unclear whether Zwemer made these notes while he was at New Brunswick, or later when he was a missionary. Zwemer did learn some Arabic at seminary under John Lansing, who grew up as the son of American Presbyterian missionaries in Egypt; however, the notes indicate a more advanced understanding of Arabic terms and ability to translate the Calvinist concepts into Arabic.[21] Thus, the notes may have been written by him during his time in the Arabian Gulf (1890–1906) or perhaps even as late as his time in Egypt (1906–1928).[22]

Another example of how church history professors recycled medieval Christian sources through later Orientalist translations is found in the work of Milo Mahan (1819–1870), professor of ecclesiastical history at General seminary from 1851 to 1864. Mahan was in the process of organizing his lectures on church history into a textbook when he died in 1870. A publisher eventually edited Mahan's lectures and published them posthumously as *A Church History of the First Seven Centuries*. The first edition came out in 1873 and a second edition in 1878. Mahan's general overview of church history covered the major ecumenical councils up to the fourth century, which all Episcopal seminary students were required to study. Mahan's manuscript, however, also examined the seventh century and Christian engagement with Islam. Mahan wrote in his draft preface that he assumed students would read his textbook along with the fourth-century historian Eusebius and Johan Karl Ludwig Gieseler's church history textbook. This was more than likely his teaching method in his classes—combining primary and secondary source material with his lectures. Within the 560 pages of *A Church History*, references to Islam amount to only two paragraphs, citing two prominent eighteenth-century English works, Edward Gibbon's and Simon Ockley's *History of the Saracens*.

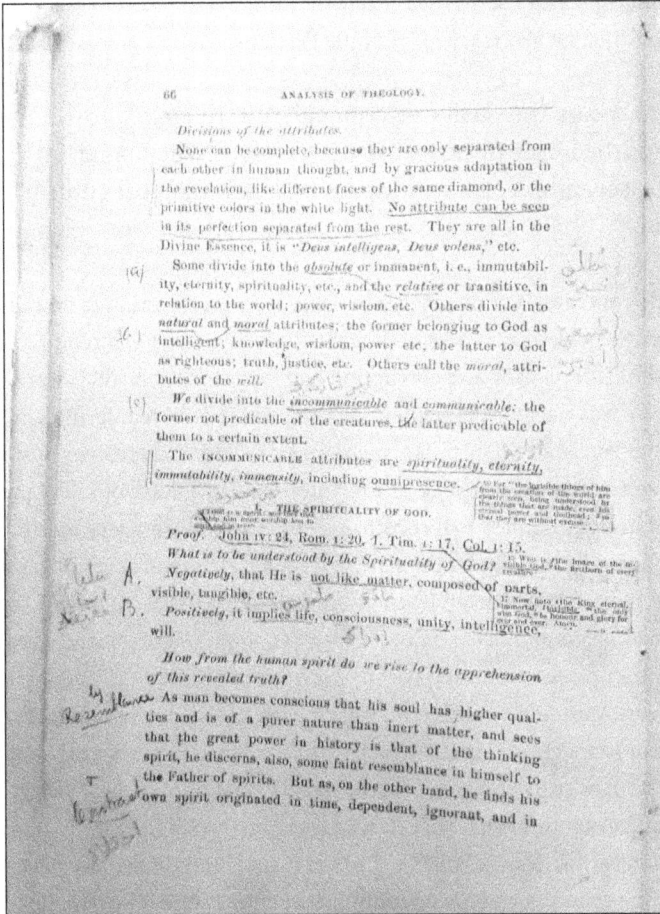

Figure 3.2. Samuel Zwemer's handwritten notes in Samuel Woodbridge's *Analysis of Systematic Theology*. New Brunswick Theological Seminary Archives, Sage Library. Photo by David D. Grafton.

For it was in the latter days of Heraclius that the "little horn" appeared in a corner of his dominions, which was destined ere long to threaten the whole world. [Quoting Gibbon, he writes,] "While the Emperor triumphed at Constantinople or Jerusalem, an obscure town on the confines of Syria was pillaged by the Saracens, and they cut in pieces some troops who advanced to its relief: an ordinary and trifling occurrence, had it not been the prelude of a mighty revolution. These robbers were the apostles of Mohammed: their fanatic valor had emerged from the desert; and in

the last eight years of his reign, Heraclius lost to the Arabs the same provinces which he had rescued from the Persians."[23]

Mahan repeats the well-worn apocalyptic reference to Muhammad
as one of the horns of the beast in Daniel 7.[24] Then, after introducing
the mid-seventh-century Monothelite Christological controversy, he
continues:

> While controversy thus raged, the Saracens were wresting from the em-
> perors the fairest provinces of their dominions: or rather, it required little
> wresting; for tyranny and corruption had long since done their work, and
> the tree was no sooner touched than the rotten fruit fell. Jerusalem, un-
> der the Patriarch Sophronius, maintained its old character for obstinate
> resistance: but after a siege of four months, in which not a day passed
> without fighting, it was forced to submit to a yoke heavier than it had
> ever borne before. Under the same yoke it has continued ever since; apart
> from eighty-eight years of Latin occupation during the Crusades. Damas-
> cus had fallen four years before Jerusalem, Tyre, Caesarea, and number-
> less other places submitted within a few years after. By the middle of the
> century, Alexandria and Egypt, with the isle of Cyprus, passed under the
> yoke of Islam. The Empire, in fact, was threatened in every part, and had
> little to oppose the invader, save the passive resistance of mere weight and
> bulk. Constantinople, however, was saved by the strength of its walls, by
> the courage of despair, and by the timely invention of the terrible Greek
> fire. The conquerors were not only checked for awhile, but were forced to
> do homage for their possessions in Syria and Egypt, by the payment of a
> nominal tribute.[25]

Given that Mahan's lectures, along with Geiseler's history, were required
reading of all first- and second-year seminary students at General seminary, the students would have had only a cursory introduction to Islam.
Islam was introduced as a disruptive force during a period of Eastern
Christian heretical debates, a view of Islam that holds prominence even
into the early twenty-first century. This perspective of Islam was consistently expressed at General through the period of our study. We see
an even clearer view of the violence of Islam as expressed in the lectures of Frederick Joseph Kinsman (1868–1944), the St. Mark's Church

in-the-Bowery professor of ecclesiastical history from 1903 to 1908. Kinsman was more well versed in the history and theology of Eastern Christianity than his predecessors. He was an Anglo-Catholic who eventually left General in 1908 when he was elected as the Episcopal bishop of Delaware. He ultimately converted to Catholicism in 1919.

Kinsman gave a lecture on "Mohammedanism and Its Effects upon Eastern Christianity" for second-year students. This lecture would ultimately become a chapter of his *Outlines of the History of the Church*, titled "Mohammedanism and the Crusades."[26] Here, Islam is introduced as a military foil to the rise of Catholicism. Muhammad is described as the one who proclaimed "himself as the one true prophet of the One God, the foe of all idols, the predestined leader in a Holy War which should subjugate the world to his faith. Before he died, he had effected the conquest of Arabia, and had collected and trained an army of ruthless zealots."[27] Once Arabia was subjugated, then followed the conquest of North Africa, into France, and the "repeated attacks on Constantinople." For Kinsman, Islam is driven to warfare, invasion, and fanaticism: "The morals of the Koran are very different from those of the Bible. Mohammed imposed a standard of morals which his followers found it easy to adopt. He required scrupulous observance of certain religious forms and willingness to fight; but he allowed full gratification of sexual impulses, and entire freedom in the ferocities of warfare. Hence, the position of women is a degraded one and a narrow and ferocious fanaticism is encouraged in spreading the system of Mohammed, one of the great missionary faiths of the world."[28] In contrast to the Muslims' atrocious acts, however, Kinsman praises the popes of the Catholic Church, who provided true spiritual leadership in a time of crisis. "There is no more striking example of the place and influence of the mediaeval Popes than in their relation to the Crusades. Above the rivalries of individual princes and peoples, they exercised a spiritual sway recognized by all the West, and were able to moderate between contending factions, and often to dictate terms for settlement of disputes. . . . Never did the Popes use their position of leadership more obviously than in calling on kings and princes to lead their followers against the Infidel."[29] However, Kinsman has little to say about Islamic belief or practice or the role of Islamic cultures. In fact, the information he passes on to his students is simply not accurate. For example, he remarks that the creed of Mohammedanism is "Allah is great; there is no God but Allah." Here he conflates the *takbir*, the extolling of God as the greatest, with the first half of the *shahada*, the creed of Islam that states, "There is no God but God, and Muhammad is the Prophet of God." While he does note that the Qur'an is like the "Wisdom literature of the Old Testament," he does not introduce any readings or examples from it. He also seems to have no knowledge of Hadith, the history of Islamic exegesis of the Qur'an (*tafsir*), or the science of interpreting Islamic law (*fiqh*).

Islam was thus introduced into church history classes as a dangerous interruption to the flow of Western Christian history. The coming of Islam was interpreted by most church history professors as due to either the negligence or the infidelity of the church. The one exception is Kinsman, who lauds the Latin church for its responses to the threat of Islam. Given his ultimate conversion to Catholicism, it is not a surprise that he would have a generous reading of Latin church history. Nevertheless, there was no interest in Islam as a religion or theology, nor certainly was there a use of Islamic sources, including readings from the Qur'an. Rather, the instructors reviewed here used a variety of sources, including translations of Eastern church histories. In the case of DeWitt, he owned a Latin copy of a Reformation text that used a Greek source. The rest of the professors used Orientalist works that translated and framed the earlier histories.

Church History Texts

As we have seen, Islam showed up only in a cursory manner in church history lectures, and when it did it was simply to recall the Saracen invasions as recorded by Christian sources. These histories were recycled by European Orientalists, such as Pococke, d'Herbelot, Ockley, and Gibbon, then read by their nineteenth-century American Protestant seminary professors and passed on to their students. The medieval Christian authors were usually not mentioned by name in the lectures (with the exception perhaps of Theophanes), which took these European sources at face value, as the content on the Saracens was dropped into the lectures only in passing.

These oral references to Islam in lectures often went hand in hand with textual sources read by students—the multivolume church history textbooks that were required reading. As noted above, Milo Mahan required his students to read the three-volume church history by Johan Geiseler (1793–1854), *A Textbook of Church History*. Geiseler's history became available in an American edition in 1836, and was subsequently reissued in 1855 and 1868, demonstrating its high demand. As is common in these midcentury compendiums, Islam fits into the overall history of the church as almost a side story and an imposition. Geiseler's first volume of 576 pages contains only one chapter of two and a half pages of information on Islam, including references on the personality of the Prophet. Another arguably more important German church history work, available in English by 1832, was that that of Johan Mosheim (1697–1755). Mosheim's work was translated by James Murdock, the church history professor at Andover seminary from 1821 to 1828.

Murdock was trained at Harvard, having been trained in a classical education that required reading Latin and Greek sources. He then went to Andover seminary for his ministerial preparation. After he served as a pastor in Massachusetts for a short period, he returned to Harvard to receive his doctorate. Murdock taught at the University of Vermont and then Dartmouth before he was called to Andover in 1821 as the professor of sacred rhetoric and then the Brown professor of ecclesiastical history. During his doctoral studies at Harvard, Murdock also learned Syriac. He would use his linguistic skills to create a modern translation of the New Testament in Syriac after he retired from Andover. During his retirement, he also began to teach himself Arabic to read the Old Testament in that language. His interest and linguistic training point to a common pedagogy among some seminary professors, that is, the study of Arabic as a Semitic language for the purpose of interpreting and understanding the Bible. Murdock was a founding member of the American Oriental Society, and his connections with the many seminary professors who were also fellow society members ensured that his American edition of Mosheim's textbook would be used at many of the seminaries and its updated editions purchased for their libraries.

Johann Lorenz Mosheim (1694–1755)

Born in Lubeck, Germany, in 1694, Johann Mosheim was a much sought after and respected Lutheran scholar. Having written exegetical studies on the New Testament and investigations into the early church, he was eventually invited to Göttingen to help set up its new university in 1734, and ultimately became its first chancellor. Mosheim's *Institutiones Historiae Ecclesiasticae Antiquae et Recentioris*, published in 1755, was widely read throughout Europe and North America. It was quickly translated into French, English, and German. The first English edition, *An Ecclesiastical History: Ancient and Modern*, was translated and edited by the Englishman Archibald Maclaine. Maclaine's original translation was heavily criticized as being stilted and dry, and taking great liberties with Mosheim's original. James Murdock, however, prepared the first American edition in 1832, retranslating Mosheim but keeping Maclaine's notes and adding his own "copious additional notes" to Mosheim's text. Thus, Murdock's edition is not a critical edition of Mosheim but a retranslation and reworking for an American audience, entitled *Institutes of Ecclesiastical History*. Murdock took the original Latin four-volume compendium and edited it down to three volumes, having to repaginate the original document but maintaining Mosheim's organizational structure. A second revised American edition was prepared and published in 1839. Without any copyright regulations or requirements, twenty other editions were released by different publishers between 1841 and 1944, demonstrating the demand for this large church history reference.[30]

Mosheim organized his sweeping history by centuries according to two categories, an "internal history" and an "external history" of the church. The "internal history" examines the development of the church's structures, organization, doctrines, and theology. The "external history" explores all those events that have "befallen on this sacred society."[31] Each of these categories then includes a section that describes the *prosperous* and the *calamitous* events that occurred, inside and outside the church. Islam is introduced in numerous centuries throughout the history, but always as part of the *calamitous* "external history" of the church. Thus, structurally, the readers understand that Islam posed an external threat to the progress and well-being of the church. It is introduced as a "clash" of rival forces.

For example, the first encounter of the church with Islam is introduced in the "external history" of the seventh century of volume 2 as that "most powerful adversary of the Church."[32] Mosheim describes the

"Turks'" assault on the Byzantine territories in the East and the "Saracens'" invasion of Spain by this "warlike people" who were able to "exterminate the Christian faith."[33] When it comes to the fourteenth century, Mosheim narrates the terror of the Mongols, Tamerlane's conversion to Islam, and the subjugation of the Christians of the East. He avers that this brought on a particularly dark period for Christianity.

> And this religion [of Islam], though somewhat corrupted, was embraced by that most potent emperor of the Tartars Timur Beg, or as he is commonly called Tamerlane. Having subjugated the greatest part of Asia by his arms, and even conquered the Turkish sultan Bajazet, and moreover caused the terrors of his name to pervade Europe, his mere nod was sufficient to cause vast multitudes to abandon Christianity. But he also employed violence and the sword. For being persuaded, as the most credible historians of his life inform us, that it was the duty of every true disciple of Muhammed to make war upon Christians, and that those who should compel many of them to embrace the religion of the Koran might expect high rewards from God, he inflicted numberless evils on persevering Christians, cruelly butchering some, and dooming others to perpetual slavery.[34]

The description of the Turkish capture of Constantinople in the fifteenth century remarks that "the Greek church was at an end; nor had the Christians any protection against the daily oppressions and wrongs of their victors, or any means of resisting the torrent of ignorance and barbarism that rushed in upon them."[35] Mosheim clarifies here, however, that Christians were not forcibly converted at this time and were able to maintain their Christian faith and practices after they had submitted to Islamic imperial rule, even if their liberty to practice their religion was confined and narrowed by later rulers.

There is a clear theme that the events brought on by the "Saracens," "Tartars," "Mameluks," and "Turks" are part of the *calamitous* story of the church.[36] However, unlike previous Latin Christian histories, Mosheim does not use these terms for Muslims interchangeably or as pejorative monikers. He is aware that Muslims are of different ethnic origins and span various cultures. They belong to different schools of thought. Mosheim demonstrates insights and nuance in discussing the adversarial relationship that had escaped many previous Latin Christian historians.

It is also important to note that while the Muslims were clearly seen as adversaries in the West and East, they were not the only enemies of the church that brought about "calamitous events." There were plenty of "internal challenges" that affected the prosperity of the church throughout its history, including individual bishops, schismatic communities, and heresies. In fact, Mosheim's overarching theme throughout his narrative is that even in the face of many different external and internal threats, the church continued to overcome its challenges and succeed, bringing enlightenment to those nations that accepted the faith. Thus, Islam is never set apart as the only nemesis of the church but is positioned as one of many challenges.

Mosheim does not provide a biography of Muhammad but focuses on the political impact of Islam on the Christians of the Near East. References to the biography and even to the descriptions of the Qur'an are relegated to footnotes supplemented by Murdock in 1832. However, Mosheim does venture to offer his explanation as to what he believes to be the sincerity of Muhammad. At the time when Mosheim was writing his history, there had been an ongoing debate about the personality of the Prophet. Humphrey Prideaux's ubiquitous label of Muhammad as the great "impostor" followed the lead of those Orientalists like Barthélemy d'Herbelot, whose *Bibliothèque orientale* (1697) was a scathing rebuke of the Prophet. These authors followed in a long line of medieval Latin Catholic writings. Others, like Simon Ockley and especially Henri de Boulainvilliers, took an opposite approach. Boulainvilliers' *La vie de Mahomed* (1722) portrayed Muhammad in a positive light and as a great Arab leader. Mosheim, however, takes a middle path:

> No one can at this day form a perfect judgment of the entire character, views, and designs of Mohammed. For we cannot safely rely on the Greek writers, who made no hesitation to load their enemy with slanders and falsehoods; nor can we trust to the Arabians, who are the very worst historians, who conceal all his vices and crimes, and depict him as altogether a divine person. Besides, a very considerable part of his life, and that too from which the motives and secret springs of his conduct would best appear, lies concealed from us. It is very probable, however,

... that he really believed, that he was divinely commissioned to reform the religion of the Arabs, and to reinstate among them the worship of the one true God. But it is also certain, that afterwards, when he saw his attempts going into successful operation, he deluded the fickle and credulous multitude with impious tricks and impositions, in order to strengthen his cause; and even feigned divine revelations, whenever occasion seemed to require it or any great difficulty occurred. Nor was this fraud inconsistent with his being a fanatic; for most fanatics look upon the deception, which seems necessary to their success, to be holy and approved by God.[37]

Mosheim argues that it is not unreasonable to consider that Muhammad believed he was truly a prophet, called to challenge the idolatry of his people. He was no impostor, though he was a "fanatic." Being successful, Mosheim writes, Muhammad was overcome with the realization that he could press his advantage over people and rationalized his use of power. The obstinacy of his own people and the negative responses from the Jews and Christians in the end forced him to do things he would not have otherwise chosen to do given different circumstances. These choices and actions are not unique to the life of Muhammad, according to Mosheim, but represent the challenges and choices that world leaders always face. Overall, Mosheim has a fairly positive view of Muhammad. Muhammad was an "Arab nobleman" and "naturally eloquent possessing great acuteness of mind."[38]

The brilliance of Muhammad for Mosheim was that his religion was truly of the East; it was part of the culture of the Near East and, thus, easily accepted by the Arabs. They accepted Islam not only because of force of arms, as was often the argument, but because there were originally few religious requirements or strict laws to follow. Islam fit into the local worldview. Furthermore, he writes, it was the "consummate ignorance" of the Arabs, Syrians, and Persians that gave him "easy control of the minds of immense numbers."[39] In addition to the proactive expansion of the Arab empire, Mosheim notes that the fractured state of the various Christian communities of the East at that time contributed to the collapse of the Byzantine Empire. Following the argument from Ockley's *History of the Saracens*, he opines that the success of Islam after the death of Muhammad was the result of the "furious fanaticism" of his successors and assistance from the non-Chalcedonian Christian communities, rather than the villainous nature of Muhammad.

It is Murdock, in 1832, who added a significant section on the biography of Muhammad into the main text. Murdock obviously felt that Muhammad's life was significant enough to insert a gloss of two pages into Mosheim's original text. He points to the very same Western sources that Mosheim had used: Gagnier, Herblot's translation of Abulfida, Prideaux, and Sale. Murdock, however, relies heavily upon Gibbon and even uses George Bush's biography, the latter offering a negative biblical critique of the Prophet. In his additional notes, Murdock highlights Muhammad's experience at the cave on Mt. Hira, his early family converts, the oppression by the Meccans, and his eventual flight to Medina. It is in the expanded version of the history where Murdock states that Muhammad "pretended to have a command from God to propagate the truth and to suppress all false religions by the power of the sword."[40] To be conquered by Muhammad was to submit to the law of Islam. To disobey the law was treason and death. The final effect for American readers was a lengthy introduction to the life of Muhammad, who becomes the primary antagonist against not only the church but civilization, whereas for Mosheim, Islam was only one example of a natural and general flow of empires that created external adversity for the church. This expansive narrative of internal and external challenges to the church provided a rather dry and static presentation of history. This led most church history professors to abandon Mosheim in favor of the works of Geiseler and especially Neander.[41]

Johan Karl Ludwig Geiseler (1793–1854)

Johan Geiseler was the son and grandson of Lutheran pastors in Westphalia, Germany. He was educated at Halle and went on to teach theology at the University of Bonn and then, like Mosheim, he moved to Göttingen University. Having worked on the history of the canonical Gospels and the early church, Geiseler turned his energies to what became a larger, six-volume project on the history of the church, which was a product of his own lectures. The first volume was originally published in 1823, followed by the second and third volumes. Unfortunately, he died before he could complete the project. Volumes 4, 5, and 6 were published posthumously.[42] The whole of the history was originally translated into English by Samuel Davidson in England, and the American edition of Geiseler's first volume, *A Textbook of Church History*, was published in 1836 in Philadelphia. It became a popular item for T&T Clark, a prominent New York publishing house that made Christian theology and biblical studies accessible for American audiences. Henry Smith at Union undertook a new English translation of Geiseler's work, which was eventually completed posthumously in 1880, showing its use as textbook for more than fifty years, even though it was widely regarded as dry and unimaginative.[43]

Geiseler includes one short chapter of only three pages on the origins of Islam, covering the years from 622 to 726. After describing the Persian-Byzantine wars, Geiseler writes, "In the meantime, a far more dangerous enemy of the Church had appeared in Arabia. . . . [Muhammad] extended his dominion and his doctrines thence, prince and prophet in one person, till they spread far into Arabia; at length conquered Mecca (630); consecrated the Caaba as the chief temple of Islamism; and bequeathed to his successors (Chalifs) [*sic*] Arabia, as a country completely subject to their faith and their dominion."[44] In a brief comment, Geiseler mentions the Koran as the holy book that contains Muhammad's teachings, compiled by the first caliph, Abu Bakr. He does not indicate, however, what is in the Qur'an or what Muhammad taught. He only expounds a religious worldview of "absolute dependence of man on God." This dependence, however, was not based on any sense of morality but "by making it a religious duty to wage war on unbelievers, by its fatalism, and its sensual promises, it excited among the rude and powerful people of the Arabs so unconquerable a spirit for war, and so wild a desire for conquest . . ."[45]

In an additional note inserted by Samuel Davidson (and included in the American edition), Davidson remarks that Jews and Christians were originally tolerated by Muhammad and the Arabs, having only to pay a "poll-tax." They were not required to convert to Islam once conquered, even though many Christians were attracted to the particular social and political advantages that came with such conversion.[46] However, Davidson argues that while Muhammed may have originally been tolerant of Christians, surahs 9 and 67 shows that Muhammad changed his mind. Muhammad then carried out a "religious war" against them to exterminate them.[47] Like many other Christian authors, Davidson assumes that Muhammad wrote the Qur'an as circumstances arose, and that he changed his mind about things if need be.

The compendium provides scattered references to the "Saracens" and their invasion of and continued wars with Europe. Of particular interest is the very brief discussion of the Christian martyrs of Cordoba from the ninth century. Between 850 and 856 at least forty-nine Christians were martyred by Muslim rulers in Spain in response to the Christian insistence on publicly blaspheming against the Prophet Muhammad. This story had been recounted by the firsthand witnesses of Eulogius of Cordoba in his *Memoriale sanctorum* and *Liber apologeticus martyrum* and Paul Alvarus in *Vita Eulogii*.[48] Eulogius encouraged Christians to publicly defame Muhammad and to seek martyrdom. His encouragement brought about the willing death of these Christians, some of whom insisted on the death penalty even when offered clemency by the ruling Muslim jurist. The martyrdom movement created a controversy among Spanish Christians, the majority of whom disagreed with the concept of provoking the Muslim rulers to seek death. While this event has long been debated by historians, Geiseler merely brushes away the sordid affair with a simple but unexplained, "Gradually, however, a calmer state of things returned."[49]

Geiseler relied on many of the available sources on Islam found among the early Orientalists, including Pococke and the Dutch philologist Joseph Scaliger. He drew on a German edition of Jean Gagnier's 1723 *De vita et rebus gestis Mohammedism*, as well as Gustav Weil's most recent study on the life of Muhammad, *Mohammed der Prophet* from 1843. Geiseler also indicates his access to various translations or expositions of the Qur'an, including a 1783 edition of Maracci's Latin translation, Dettinger's *Beiträge zu einer Theologie des Korans* from 1831, and C. F. Gerock's *Darstellang der Christologie des Koran* from 1839. Thus, we see that Geiseler had at his disposal some important Orientalist references to Islam. And yet, the extent of his knowledge and interest in Islam is minimal. It is from Geiseler that many of the American church history lectures provided an underlying view of Islam as the product of fanatical Saracen barbarians who oppressed the Jews and Christians of the East, but he provides no substance as to their beliefs and practices, no examination of the theology of the Qur'an, nor even of the Western debate of Muhammad as either a prophet or a villain.

Augustus Neander (1759–1850)

Augustus Neander is the most celebrated German ecclesiastical historian of the nineteenth century. He taught theology and church history for almost forty years, from 1811 until his death in 1850. A former student of Frederick Schleiermacher, Neander received great approval from his former teacher as well as accolades from his student, Philip Schaff.[50] As we will see, Schaff would go on to become an important Neander devotee and the most important American church historian of the last half of the nineteenth and first half of the twentieth century. Thus, Neander not only developed a prominent reputation in Europe but had a great impact in North America. Neander studied at the Pietist seminary at Halle under Schleiermacher. He passed his examinations for Lutheran ministry but decided to take up an academic life rather than ministerial pursuits. He taught first at Heidelberg, then went on to the Prussian university of Berlin until his death.

Neander was most renowned for his nine-volume *Allgemeine Geschichte der christlichen Religion und Kirche*, which was published between 1825 and 1852. He released a second edition of his first two volumes in 1842 even while he was carrying on with writing later volumes. The first English translation, *The General History of the Christian Religion and Church*, was published in 1831 by Joseph Torrey, professor at the University of Vermont and an alumnus of Andover seminary. The English translations of all Neander's volumes were eventually repackaged as part of T&T Clark's Foreign Theological Library series and reprinted up until 1896, which ensured their accessibility in England and North America. The English edition, and in some cases the German second edition, were available in all the libraries included in this study, denoting its importance in the education of American seminarians. Volume 5 of the English edition, which first appeared in 1854, introduces the history of Islam. Neander frames this section as part of the "new dangers" of the Persian invasion of Palestine and Egypt in 616, which destroyed many churches and monasteries. Although Emperor Heraclius managed to regain this territory from the Persians, it was quickly lost by the swift advance of Muhammad and his Arab tribes.

Unlike the previous church histories that focused primarily on the political events of the Arab and subsequent Muslim empires, Neander

provides a more thorough analysis of the theology of Islam as he interpreted it not only through the ancient Christian sources but also through
a reading of Marracci's Latin edition of the Qur'an and the more recent
studies on Muhammad by the likes of Abraham Geiger. Gone is the pejorative and demeaning language about the Prophet that was common
in the Latin medieval stories of his life and the mechanical record of
invasions of the "Saracens," as in Geiseler. Rather, Neander grounds his
assessment of Muhammad and "his religion" as part of the Near Eastern
origins of Judaism and Eastern Christianity, a "simple monotheism" that
grew from the "primitive religion" of the Arabs. In this regard, Neander
is directly indebted to the arguments of Abraham Geiger, whose study
of Muhammad had only just come out in 1833.

According to Neander, Muhammad lived within a cultural and religious milieu of polytheistic Arabs, Jews, and Eastern Christians. His
eventual success among the Arab tribes confirmed to him that he was
part of the Jewish prophetic tradition. But he ultimately claimed to be a
prophet not only for the polytheistic Arabs of Arabia but for all people.
He then thoroughly imbibed the legalized character of Judaism (whatever that may have been at the time, Neander does not tell us). Neander
writes that Muhammad's religion was "a Judaism degraded to the level
of natural religion," leaving aside the most significant role of prophet-
hood in Judaism, that of the Messiah.[51] Muhammad saw himself as the
culmination of all previous prophets but not the Messiah. According
to Neander, his success in gaining the support and fealty of other Arab
tribes and the ultimate refusal of the Jews and Christians to accept him
as a prophet resulted in his blind ambitions taking over the better part
of his moral nature.

Neander does not so much provide a critique of the personality of
Muhammad as offer what he sees as Muhammad's unfortunate misunderstanding of the true nature of God. Muhammad's view of God developed from a combination of Arab Judaism and apocryphal forms of
the Christian tradition mediated through Gnosticism. Muhammad was
not an impostor or a trickster. Rather, Muhammad had a genuine heart
to reform his people from idolatry to worship the one true God. But his
Arab cultural "primitive religion" created the belief in a capricious God
that required "servile submission" as opposed to ethical living.[52] Neander does not suggest that Muhammad picked from Judaism or Chris-

tianity those traditions he saw fit to choose in order to create a new religion, which was another common Christian critique. Instead, Neander proposes that Muhammad's spirituality was endowed with a genuine desire to eradicate idolatry and introduce radical submission to the one God. He writes that "in a man possessed of the lively temper and fiery imagination of Mohammed, the awakened consciousness of God would lead to a reaction against the idolatry in which he had been nurtured, and by which he was surrounded—a reaction, however, which would be disturbed by the sensuous element so predominant in the national character of his people."[53] Muhammad failed to capture the relational implications of belief in God, maintains Neander. This was due to the general belief among the Arabs in the great chasm between the creator and each human being. "The sense of God's exaltation above all created things, of the infinite distance between the Creator and his works; the sense of utter dependence on the Almighty and Incomprehensible— this one element of the knowledge of God—constituted the predominant ground-tone of his religious character; whilst the other element which belongs to the complete unfolding of the consciousness of God, the sense of relationship and communion with God, was, in his case, wholly suppressed."[54] It is here that Neander finds fault with Muhammad. As was common among many Pietist Protestants of the nineteenth century, belief in God had a moral component that was understood to lead to an ethical life. This is what was absent in Muhammad's religious view, says Neander. The relationship of creator and created is overpowered by God's determinism, which ultimately led to fatalism and a lack of moral accountability.

Neander was fully aware of the previous Christian responses to Islam of John of Damascus and Theodore Abu Qurra through the Latin collections known as the *Bibliotheca veterum patrum antiquorumque scriptorum ecclesiasticorum Graeco-Latina* of André Galland (1709–1779) and the *Bibliotecha Orientalis* of the Maronite Giuseppe Simone Assemani (1687–1768). Neander also had access to the Latin translation of the fifteenth-century history of Egypt by al-Maqrizi, *Historia Coptorum Christianorum in Aegypto Arabice*, edited by Jacob Wetzer in 1828. These are sources that escape the other two previous German histories and set Neander apart as the most notable historian of his day. What is particularly important about Neander's use of Maqrizi is his acceptance of

Maqrizi's claim that Coptic Christians had been oppressed by Byzantine imperial forces because of their non-Chalcedonian views, and so supported the invading Arab Muslims to help them overthrow the Byzantines.[55] In this Neander provides a distinction between the Western Byzantine church and Eastern Christian communities.

One particular episode in the history of Christian-Muslim relations that Neander covers much more extensively than Geiseler is the story of the Cordoba martyrs. Neander spends nine pages examining the debate among the Christians of the time about the efficacy of such martyrdom. He asserts that Eulogius encouraged the public denouncement of Islam and Muhammad because he believed he was merely following the faithful path of the apostles who had been martyred by the Jews. Neander provides a summary of the counterargument by bishops who denounced these witnesses for provoking martyrdom, which they maintained went against Christ's teachings.[56] Neander ultimately concludes that the bishops rightly argued, as Romans 13 requires, that Christians should be subservient to the ruling authorities. Neander concludes that when more thoughtful bishops doused the flames of "fanatical extravagances," Christians were then able to live out their religious freedom more fully.[57]

One aspect of Neander's interesting analysis of the Cordoban martyrs that does not show up in any other Christian church history I am aware of is his consideration of the religiously mixed marriages of many of the martyrs. Neander indicates that most of the martyrs came from mixed Christian-Muslim families. According to Eulogius, writes Neander, these faithful Christians often used their Muslim family ties to gain access to the Muslim courts to make their public denouncement of Muhammad. The judge assumed the accused were coming forward to take *shahada* and convert to Islam, only to be confronted with the public blasphemy against the Prophet.[58] In other words, for Eulogius, the Christians strategically took advantage of the good names of their families to go before Muslim courts. Neander makes no assessment on the veracity of Eulogius's claims. Nevertheless, he opens the door to recognition of the reality of interfaith marriages in the Islamic empires, which are often neglected in other historical studies.[59]

As with his analysis of the Cordoba martyrs, which derided a Christian polemic against Islam, Neander narrates two examples of nonpolemical Christian evangelism among Muslims with respect to the lives of Francis of Assisi (1181–1226) and Raymond Lull (1232–1316). These two stories are embedded in a larger section on the medieval period that includes missions to the "Heathen" in Eastern Europe, Scandinavia, and Russia; to the Tartars and Mongols in Asia; to the "Mohammedans"; and, finally, to the Jews. Like Mosheim before him, Neander places Muhammad and the Arabs in a larger narrative of the many peoples who were to be missionized and converted. Islam is not the sole antithesis to Christendom. Francis and Raymond are only two among many Christian missionaries that Neander extols as faithful witnesses for his readers.

Neander does not provide a full biography of Francis. Instead, he focuses this short section on the famous meeting of Francis with Sultan Kamil, the Mamluk sultan of Egypt, as derived from the "eyewitness" account of Jacob de Vitry, bishop of Acre, at the battle of Damietta in 1219.[60] It is Vitry who narrates the earliest record of Francis's preaching to the sultan, and the famous response by the sultan: "Pray for me, that God may enlighten me, and enable me to hold firmly to that religion which is most pleasing to him."[61]

Using the Latin biography of Raymond Lull, Neander relates Lull's desire to write an apology of Christianity to Muslims by providing logical and sound arguments, which he had hoped would entice Muslims to consider converting. Lull traveled to North Africa three times over the course of his life to present an apology for the Christian faith to Muslim scholars who would listen to him, before he was ultimately martyred for his own public denunciation of Islam in Bugia, North Africa (in what is now Algeria) in 1315. In contrast to his introduction of Francis, Neander includes a thorough analysis not only of Lull's life but also of his views on dialogue as a method of evangelism with Muslims. Throughout his record, Neander makes a distinction between the "fanatic" Muslim crowds and some of the more thoughtful Muslim religious scholars who were willing to hear out Lull's arguments. Neander also notes how Lull spent his life trying to convince the pope that his method of interaction with Muslims was more faithful than the previous attempts at Crusade. Lull also wanted to develop a cohort of "spiritual knights" rather than contribute to the ongoing bloodshed and carnage of the Holy War to which the papacy was committed. Thus, Lull proposed creating schools of Oriental languages among European colleges to train Christian missionaries who could read the Qur'an and speak the language of the "Saracens."[62] Interestingly, other than Samuel Zwemer, who wrote a biography of Lull, Neander is the only Western Protestant scholar to use Lull to encourage future young American missionaries.[63]

Finally, an important distinctive characteristic throughout Neander's history is his use of the word "Saracen." Previously the word had come to be used in a general way to refer to Muslims. The Latin medieval literature conflated Arabs with Muslims, or at least there was little effort expended to understand such distinctions.[64] By the early modern period, the term was also used synonymously with "Turk." Neander, however, uses the word specifically as an ethnic category. He refers to pre-Islamic and Islamic Arabs as "Saracens." The "Saracens" were the Arabs who followed Muhammad and created an empire. They were not representative, however, of the whole of "Mohammedan" faith as the antithesis of Christianity. The term as a reference to Muslims was dropped from the American nomenclature by the nineteenth century, but whether Neander's history had a part in this is unclear. Nevertheless, Neander's widely used history in seminaries and his portrayal of Islam marked a distinct turning point for American theological education. He provided a more sympathetic understanding of Muhammad's role in history, nuanced and complicated relations between Muslims and Christians, and models of interaction that belie antagonism.

The Impact of Philip Schaff (1819–1893)

The prevalence of the church histories of Mosheim, Geiseler, and Neander point to the important contributions that German historical scholarship made to American Protestant education during the nineteenth century. These histories were all at various times required reading in American seminaries and thus affected the way that American seminary students and then clergy were introduced to Islam. For example, Roswell Hitchcock, the Washburn professor of church history at Union seminary from 1855 and the president from 1880 until his death in 1887, relied upon Neander in his courses on church history. Hitchcock had an important influence on what students were taught for over thirty years. There was, however, an even more influential voice in the historical interpretations of Islam at American seminaries: the scholarship of Philip Schaff.

Philip Schaff, the Edward Robinson professor of biblical theology from 1875 to 1887 and the Washburn professor of church history from 1887 to 1893 at Union seminary, was one of the most influential Protestant scholars and certainly the most decorated American church historian of his day. He had a distinguished career as an influential teacher, but he was also widely known for the important research projects that he organized, directed, and published. Schaff was responsible for chairing the North American committee for the Revised Version of the Bible from 1867 to 1877. He was a founding member of the Society of Biblical Literature and Exegesis (1880) and the American Society of Church History (1888), both of which are still very active and thriving societies with their own highly regarded academic journals. In addition, Schaff was the general editor of several major reference works used by most seminaries throughout the United States: the thirteen-volume *Schaff-Herzog Encyclopedia of Religious Knowledge* that was finally completed posthumously in 1914, the fourteen-volume English translations of the patristic writings known as the *Nicene and Post-Nicene Fathers of the Christian Church* from 1886 to 1890; and the twelve volumes of the *History of the Christian Church* from 1838 to 1893, which Adolf Von Harnack called "the most notable monument of universal historical learning produced by the School of Neander."[65] These projects provided Schaff the opportunity to interact with a wide variety of scholars in Europe and the United States, increasing his network of colleagues and his reputation. In addition to his scholarship and influence as a teacher of fifty years in German and American seminaries, one of his biographers highlights the person behind the scholarship: "Philip Schaff had sparkling eyes, a grand sense of humor, a big heart, and love enough for the world. He was a visionary, a prophet, a man of hope, a Christian scholar. Perhaps that is really all that should be said for now of one who was, after all, a truly great man."[66]

Philip Schaff was born in Chur, Switzerland, in 1819. He was educated among German-speaking pietists during the early days of the unified Lutheran-Reformed Church. He combined his pietism with a healthy historical skepticism and honest scholarly effort. He was not a biblical literalist by any stretch but held the scriptures in high regard as the criterion of truth. Schaff had studied under Ferdinand Baur at Tubingen, under August Tholuck at Halle, and under Isaak Dorner and

Augustus Neander at Berlin. Schaff might have succeeded Neander in Berlin had he not received a call from the growing German-Reformed community in the United States asking him to come and teach at the newly formed seminary at Mercersburg, Pennsylvania. The immigrant German communities in the United States were in desperate need of German-speaking pastors. The twenty-four-year-old Schaff was considered a prime candidate to properly train German American students.

Schaff joined John Williamson Nevin as the two professors of the Mercersburg seminary. Together, they developed what came to be known as "Mercersburg Theology," an inclusive vision of the church. In his inaugural address, he outlined his understanding of the history of the church since Pentecost as a history of ecumenism and eventual reunification. Schaff's view of the church was influenced by Hegel, whose ideas would be a common thread throughout his whole public career. For example, Schaff's final lecture—which was read for him at the first Parliament of the World Religions in Chicago in 1893, because he was too feeble to attend—was titled "The Reunion of Christendom."[67] Schaff's views ran against the predominant current of the German Reformed Church, however, and he was ultimately tried for heresy by the German Reformed Church in America, but eventually exonerated, because of his claim that the Roman Catholic Church was a legitimate branch of the church. Such a view was unthinkable at that time and is still held as such by some Protestant evangelicals.

The German American communities had long been at odds with the larger English-speaking Protestant churches, such as the Anglicans and Presbyterians. Of course, Anglo Americans also had deep-rooted prejudice against Germans, who they believed showed little interest in assimilating.[68] German American theology and practice had been tied directly to the German language. However, Schaff, like his compatriot, Samuel Schmucker, president of Gettysburg seminary, encouraged German integration into the larger English-speaking culture.

Schaff taught at the Reformed seminary in Mercersburg from 1843 to 1863, until the Civil War disrupted life in central Pennsylvania. As Mercersburg was located only a few miles from the Maryland border, incursions by southern cavalry into Pennsylvania, especially during the Gettysburg campaign, negatively impacted daily life and forced the seminary to close. Mercersburg was not alone, of course. Gettysburg seminary's campus was the center of that epic battle, and its building became a hospital for months. The ongoing struggles of the war prompted students throughout the country to either leave seminary education and go home or sign up to serve in the army (of either side).

Ultimately, the war provided Schaff an opportunity to become more involved in the larger life of American Protestantism, rather than just the German Reformed Church in a little corner of Pennsylvania. When the seminary closed, he left to pursue his interests elsewhere. He eventually moved to New York City, where he served as the secretary of the New York Sabbath Committee until he received a call from Union seminary in 1870. It was at Union where Schaff became most well known, domestically and internationally. He worked at Union until 1893, when he retired after fifty years as a theological educator, having taught thousands of seminary students who would go on to become pastors and leaders in their communities.[69]

Schaff's teaching about Islam was limited at first to a few brief comments on the "Ishmaelite" religion during his lectures on biblical history to first-year students.[70] Islam was peripheral to Christianity, linked only through references to the Arabs and Ishmael in the Hebrew Bible. Thus, for him Islam grew out of the Jewish tradition. "It may be called a bastard Judaism," he wrote, "as the Arabs are Ishmaelites, or children of the bastard son of Abraham."[71] It was not until a family tragedy shook his life in the summer of 1876 that he was provided with an occasion to take a sabbatical from teaching, and travel to the Near East. In July 1876, the Schaffs' twenty-year-old daughter, Meta, died of typhoid. Her death profoundly shook her parents. To help them deal with their grief, Philip managed to take a five-month sabbatical from teaching after the fall semester. He, his wife, Mary, and their remaining daughter traveled to Europe and then on to "the Bible Lands."[72] There he encountered Muslims and began to read up on Islam and the Qur'an as portrayed by Western studies. It was along this Protestant pilgrimage to the Near East that Schaff was "transferred as by magic to the age of the apostles, the prophets, and the patriarchs."[73] The trip was not only a necessary cathartic diversion from his pain but a chance to make connections to the land, the monuments he encountered, and the biblical narrative. He found new insights for his teaching—and his faith. The result was a published travelogue, *Through Bible Lands*, which is a lively reflection on his experiences and an exposition of the history of the biblical sites, utilizing many of the latest studies on the geography and land of the Near East. He regularly refers to Edward Robinson's *Biblical Researches in Palestine, Mount Sinai, and Arabia Petraea* (1841) and William Thomson's *Land and the Book* (1858). Robinson was a legend at Union, having preceded Schaff and was one of the most prolific American biblical scholars of the nineteenth century. He was most famous for his travels to Jerusalem and the "discovery" of "Robinson's Arch" on the Temple Mount.[74]

As Schaff traveled throughout the Near East, he was hosted by missionary colleagues of the American Mission in Egypt and in Syria. He toured their mission schools and was impressed with their work. While he was in Egypt, the Presbyterian missionaries Gulian Lansing and John Hogg managed to gain Schaff access into al-Azhar University to experience a lecture and the pedagogy of classical Islamic education. Amazed by the sheer size and scope of the university and its ability to draw Muslim students from around the world, Schaff became convinced that it was this Islamic education that would keep Islam "a force in Africa and Asia."[75] He then visited the newly founded Cairo University, created by Khedive Ismail in the style of a modern European university. He was not impressed. Schaff was skeptical that such a Western-style system of education would win the hearts and minds of Muslims. "Time will show whether the new civilization is able to conquer the old fanaticism," he wrote.[76]

In Beirut he was hosted by colleagues of the Syrian Protestant College, including Cornelius Van Dyck and its president, Daniel Bliss. There had already been a strong connection between Union seminary and the American Mission in Syria. The missionaries Henry Jessup and James Dennis were graduates of Union, and Van Dyck and Bliss taught at the seminary when they were on furlough or traveling in the United States. So, it was only natural that Schaff would rely on seminary connections during his travels and strengthen the ties for the future.

After his return home, Schaff concluded that, if possible, all seminarians should make such a journey to the "Bible Lands." Such a trip would make more of a positive impact on their preaching than any seminary lectures on the history of those lands or dry exegesis of biblical passages. It was during his pilgrimage, however, that he also came into direct contact with Muslims and Islamic cultures. Schaff regularly refers to the "fanatic Mohammedans" and the "oppressive Turk" throughout the book, especially during his visit to Damascus, where he recalls the 1860 massacre of the local Christian population by "white-turbaned and long-bearded" fanatic Muslims.[77] His travels highlighted for him the importance of British oversight of Ottoman territories to secure a "civilized" rule and protect the American missionaries to regenerate true monotheism. "And while we are filled with mingled feelings of pity and indignation at the melancholy condition of the native population and religion under the corrupt despotism of the Turks, we are inspired with the hope of a new Jerusalem that is gradually springing up by the pious and benevolent efforts of foreigners, who labor for the revival of Bible Christianity in this Bible land."[78] In the end, "The lands of the Bible are a vast mission-field, which must be conquered with spiritual weapons for Christ and Christian civilization by the Western nations, in discharge of a debt of gratitude for the blessings received from them."[79]

In *Through Bible Lands*, Schaff inserted two chapters in his section on Egypt describing "The Mohammedan Religion" and "Christianity in Egypt." His chapter on Christianity provides a quick reference to the Coptic Orthodox Church but focuses primarily on the work of the American (Presbyterian) Mission. The chapter on Islam focuses on the basic beliefs and practices of Islam. For example, he provides details about Muslim prayer practices and the ecstatic prayers of Sufi dancers he witnessed in Scutari and Cairo. However, what is most important for our purposes is his description and interpretation of the life of Muhammad and the Qur'an that he developed both during his visit and afterward upon further research and reflection.

After his travels to the "Bible Lands" Schaff compared Muhammad to Brigham Young. This was not an uncommon comparison as Protestant detractors of Mormonism had already created a well-worn path between these two post-Christian religious traditions.[80] On the one hand, Schaff lauds Muhammad for being temperate and living humbly with his wives. On the other hand, he rebukes him for polygamy. Schaff also accepts Neander's opinion that as Muhammad became more successful in his prophetic mission, he gave in to the seduction

MOSQUE OF OMAR

Figure 3.3. Dome of the Rock from *Through Bible Lands* by Philip Schaff (1878), p. 255. Courtesy of HathiTrust.

of power, and that he "grew more sensual and cruel as he advanced in life."[81] In the end, for Schaff, Muhammad was a product of his cultural upbringing and heritage. He was by birth a "savage" son of the desert. He may have had good intentions, but his innate cultural traits would lead a fanatical band of his followers to reduce "the lands of the Bible to a dreary ruin."[82]

Schaff appreciates Muhammad's attempt to preach monotheism and eradicate idolatry among the Arab tribes. He was not an impostor who tricked his way into leadership. Rather, he was the consummate Arab tribal leader. And yet, for Schaff, the Arabs were a fanatical, semibarbarous people. Thus, Muhammad successfully led his people out of polytheism to worship the one God. And yet, for Schaff such a religious movement was of the ancient past, of a premodern era. The Muslim Orient needed the strong hand of British rule and the gentle guidance of American evangelicalism to bring the Arabs into the modern world. One of his own guides through Egypt was Edward Lane's *Customs and Manners of Modern Egyptians*. Lane's popular ethnographic description of early-nineteenth-century Egypt became a blueprint for how Schaff experienced and interpreted the Arab world and Islam. Lane had an Orientalizing effect on Schaff. Channeling Lane, Schaff would later go on to write that the "noble physique [of the Arab] is worthy to be the tent of a noble spirit. Conversion to Christianity would emancipate them from their vices and strengthen their virtues by associating them with the higher Christian graces."[83] This perspective was consistent with his views of Native Americans, Africans, and even enslaved African Americans. Schaff held the view that slavery was an evil and a punishment from God for the sin of Noah and the "curse of Ham." It had fallen on Africans. The solution for Schaff, however, was not the abolition of slavery but its use to civilize Africans. For Schaff, the institution of slavery could be used to civilize Africans slowly and steadily, while supporting the American economy. In a sermon he preached on slavery in the Bible that was later published in 1861, Schaff stated emphatically, "The sooner we take the vexing and perplexing question out of the turmoil of federal politics, and leave it with the several slave States, in the hands of Christian philanthropy, and of an all-wise Providence, the better for the peace of the whole country."[84]

In the same manner, Muslims were not to be feared as eternal antag-
onists against the faith but to be evangelized and civilized. For Schaff,
Islam is a product of its Near Eastern upbringing, if even a lesser product than Judaism. Schaff writes that the Bible and the Qur'an

> are thoroughly oriental in style and imagery, and born under similar
> conditions of soil, climate, and habits of life. Both contain the moral and
> religious code of the nations which own them; the Koran, like the Old
> Testament, is also a civil code, for in Mohammedan countries the civil and
> ecclesiastical governments are one. . . . The Bible is the book of the world,
> and is constantly travelling to the ends of the earth, carrying spiritual food
> to all classes of the People; the Koran stays at home, and is insipid to all
> who have once fully tasted the true Word of the living God. Even the po-
> etry of the Koran never rises to the grandeur and sublimity of Job or Isa-
> iah, the lyric beauty of the Psalms, the sweetness and loveliness of the Song
> of Solomon, the sententious wisdom of the Proverbs and Ecclesiastes.[85]

On the one hand, the Qur'an is to be admired for its beauty and form.
On the other hand, it is limited in its vision. Following Edward Gibbon's
lead, Schaff accepts the critique that the Qur'an gives in to Oriental sen-
sibilities and sensualities. This Orientalized view of Islam was consistent
with his overall view of history. Schaff's view of the history of the world,
and the history of the church in particular, was quite Hegelian in nature;
he saw these histories as a process of moving forward and being checked
by forces that posed challenges (spiritually, philosophically, culturally, or
politically). He believed that American Protestantism, working through
its missionaries, whom he met on his travels, would correct and overcome the challenge of an aberrant religion and culture.[86]

After the publication of *Through Bible Lands*, Schaff began to compile
his notes on Islam into lectures he titled "Conflict with Mohammedanism." These lectures served as part of the required church history curriculum at Union and were recopied by bright-eyed seminary students
from 1878 until his retirement in 1892. He also published his lectures as
a chapter on Islam in volume 4 of *The History of the Christian Church* for
students to read well into the twentieth century.[87]

The final form of the published lectures includes a general overview
of the current Western literature on Islam, statistics on Muslim commu-

nities around the world, a general history of Islam, an overview of the life of Muhammed and the "Koran," beliefs and practices of Muslims, and Christian theological responses to Islam. Each section includes an up-to-date bibliography.[88] Interestingly, Schaff concludes his chapter on Islam by quoting recent events in Utah in 1877, denoting his attempt to frame Mormonism as an American Islam for his students.

Schaff's general overview of Western literature on Islam provides an extensive list of sources on the Qur'an, the Sira, and Islamic history ranging from Marracci's seventeenth-century Latin translation of the Qur'an up to Henry Jessup's then recent *Modern Missionary Problem*, published in 1879. Schaff also includes the important historical studies by Weil, Muir, Sprenger, and Nöldeke, as well as Western travelers Burkhardt, Burton, and Lane. Schaff also includes the works of the two most prominent nineteenth-century Muslim reformers, Syed Ahmed Khan and Syed Ameer Ali.

Schaff had read the Qur'an in translation, using J. M. Rodwell's most recent 1876 translation, based on Gustav Flügel's 1834 Arabic edition. Rodwell had reorganized the surahs according to what he believed to be the natural and historical order of their revelation, rather than according to the canonical ordering of surahs by length. Thus, Schaff was not reading a traditional text of the Qur'an.

When it comes to the contents of the Qur'an, Schaff follows Rodwell's assessment that Muhammad's understanding of monotheism came from apocryphal Eastern Christian sources and Talmudic Jewish traditions.[89] While such "borrowing" from the oral traditions of Christians and the Jews with whom he came in contact certainly cuts against orthodox Islamic beliefs, Rodwell's perspective was more positive than those of previous Western detractors. "The Korán deserves the highest praise for its conceptions of the Divine nature, in reference to the attributes of Power, Knowledge, and universal Providence and Unity," he writes. "That its belief and trust in the One God of Heaven and Earth is deep and fervent—that it never speaks otherwise than with respect and reverence of the great characters and saints of the Old Testament as well as of the Founder of Christianity, whose miraculous Birth and more than human nature is fully acknowledged . . . has proved that there are elements in it on which mighty nations—though not, perhaps durable— empires can be built up."[90]

Finally, Schaff was also influenced by Rodwell's assessment that Muhammad "started with the over-powering conviction of the unity of God and a horror of idolatry, and wished to rescue his countrymen from this sin of sins and from the terrors of the judgment to come; but gradually he rose above the office of a national reformer to that of the founder of a universal religion, which was to absorb the other religions, and to be propagated by violence. It is difficult to draw the line in such a character between honest zeal and selfish ambition, the fear of God and the love of power and glory."[91] For Schaff, like Neander before him, there was a natural human element in Muhammad's progression from prophetic warner to ambitious political leader. We do not find the same invective against the Prophet's intentions that seep through the medieval sources. Rather, he has a more sympathetic response to the constraints of leading a reform movement among semicivilized Near Eastern polytheists. Lastly, one cannot escape Schaff's Orientalizing and racializing of Muslims.

What makes Schaff's brief foray into Islam so important for our understanding of Islam within Protestant seminaries in North America was his ability to introduce many students to the latest Western Orientalist research on Islam that evaluated the beliefs of Islam beyond the broader histories of Mosheim and Geiseler. He even moved beyond the more nuanced assessment of Muhammad of Neander, by providing important insights from the Qur'an. There is appreciation of Islam and yet a confirmation that Protestant Christianity is the only true answer to humanity's moral and spiritual needs and social progress.

Schaff demonstrates that he was aware of the latest studies on the Qur'an and the life of the Prophet and used them effectively in the classroom, even if he did not spend much time in the study of Islam. The sheer number of students and pastors who listened to his lectures and read his work ensured that his views would dramatically impact American Protestant perspectives on Islam. Only two years after volume 4 of the *History of the Christian Church* was published, even before he completed all twelve volumes of the complete compendium, a second edition was required. A third edition was then published posthumously in 1910 and was continuously reprinted up until 1996, when it became available online through the Christian Classics Ethereal Library. Throughout the twentieth century Schaff's was a standard seminary church history textbook and still remains on library shelves. However, aside from the apocalyptic references to Muhammad from Milo Mahan at General, or the reading of George Bush's biography of Muhammad in antebellum America, seminary students would have been subject to other church history lectures based on Orientalist sources or the compendiums of Mosheim and Geiseler. It was Neander's and Schaff's Orientalized cultural and religious perspectives that would become the most common portrait of Islam and Muhammad for most students after the Civil War and well into the twentieth century.

While students were introduced to Islam through their studies in church history, biblical studies was always the primary field of study for seminary students. The Bible was the primary focus for the Protestant faith. Islam was only introduced peripherally through some of the apocalyptic books like Daniel and Revelation. However, Arabic and the Qur'an became an important vehicle for engaging Hebrew throughout the nineteenth century. As we will see in the next chapter, the earliest seminary professor, Moses Stuart, published his own Arabic grammar, and at the end of the century John G. Lansing had students reading portions of the Qur'an to better learn how to interpret Hebrew.

4

Arabic as a Biblical Language and the Study of the Qur'an

In 1831, a young Edward Robinson, the extraordinary professor of sacred literature at Andover seminary, reflected in an article in the *Biblical Repository* on the state of the field of biblical studies, and more specifically on the role of Near Eastern linguistics in the study of the Old Testament:

> With reference to Biblical Criticism and Ecclesiastical Histories, we know that the sacred scriptures, particularly those of the Old Testament, abound in modes of expression, and allusions to customs, in many cases imperfectly understood in Europe, but still prevailing in the East. That light confessedly *derived from the Arabic* and other sister dialects of the Hebrew, has been thrown on the text of Scripture, by the rabbinical and other commentators, few will deny; yet *volumes of Arabic Grammar, Rhetoric and the more ancient productions of the Arabian poets* which approach most nearly in style and sentiments to some parts of the Hebrew Bible, still lie in MS. in our libraries, either entirely neglected, or at best accessible to few. . . . Perhaps no people possess more extensive stores of History, Biography, and Polite Literature, than the Arabs and the Persians. The accounts which their historical and biographical works contain of their own and the surrounding countries, are necessarily the principal sources from which information can be obtained relative to the history of those regions, and of the extraordinary persons to whom they have given birth.[1]

The indefatigable Robinson was one of the original students of Moses Stuart, the first seminary professor of Hebrew in the United States. Robinson would become a professor in his own right, first at Andover, then the first professor of sacred languages at Union seminary from 1838 to 1863. While Robinson did not go on to pursue research in Arabic literature as a key to understanding the Bible, he did recognize the importance of Arabic, not only as an "Oriental" language but as a cognate biblical language.[2]

Robinson's own student at Andover, Joseph Packard, who would become the professor and dean at the Episcopal Theological Seminary in Virginia, expounded on this topic several years later: "As Hebrew has been so long a dead language we are peculiarly fortunate in thus having the testimony of a cognate and living dialect, so fertile and copious, of which we can attain a more complete knowledge than we ever can of the Hebrew."[3] Packard expounds on what was a common nineteenth-century view of Arabic as a Semitic language. First, he notes that Hebrew and Arabic are of the same Semitic family, built upon triconsonantal roots with various cognate words and similar verb tenses. Second, Packard sees linguistic and cultural similarities built into the biblical record. For example, he highlights that Joseph's brothers could communicate with the Ishmaelite traders when they sold him into slavery in Genesis 37:27–28 because they had similar languages. Finally, Packard asserts that the spoken Arabic of the biblical and pre-Islamic days is most definitively captured within the pages of the Qur'an. Thus, for Packard, Arabic is a key to the philological study (that is, relating to its linguistic origins, development, and relationship to other Semitic languages) of the Hebrew text of the Bible and warrants its place as a "venerable object of curiosity."[4]

This chapter delves into the ways in which Arabic, and eventually Qur'anic Arabic, was utilized as part of biblical exegetical training in many seminaries in the nineteenth century. Building on the studies of European scholars during the movement of *ad fontes*, American biblical scholars viewed Arabic as one of the most important cognate languages of biblical Hebrew, if not *the* most important. Because there were Arabic texts much older than any then extant Hebrew codices, and certainly due to a great deal of anti-Jewish sentiment, the Qur'an was viewed as a more trustworthy source for biblical Hebrew than Jewish sources, including the Talmud.

The Study of "Oriental" Languages in Early Modern Europe

To examine why American seminaries included Arabic as part of their Protestant Christian education in nineteenth-century America, we need to detour back to the early modern period in Europe. It was during this time that an interest in Eastern texts and the Arabic language grew out of the intersection of disparate political, commercial, scholarly, and religious interests. As a result of these European interests, Orientalist knowledge production of Eastern Arabic literature was transported to North America.

From the fifteenth to the seventeenth century, Portuguese, Dutch, Italian, and English merchants were looking for new Eastern markets. These traders were the first of the Europeans to begin exploring Eastern lands and were tasked by their sovereigns not only to open up new markets but also to learn about and from the Ottomans, who controlled access to the East. The British Levant and East India Companies, the Dutch East India Company, and Portuguese explorers were all competing with one another to extend control over new Eastern markets. A byproduct of this international imperial cold war, however, was the "discovery" of languages. These traders were exposed to a whole new world of Eastern languages, or, as they were normally called then, "Oriental" languages. As these traders and travelers began to learn these languages, they began to bring back a wide variety of Eastern texts to be studied by interested parties back home. For example, Edward Pococke (1604–1691) served as the chaplain to the English Levant Company in Aleppo, Syria, which was a major trading center. During his time in Syria, he learned Arabic and collected Arabic manuscripts. When he returned to England, he became the first chair of Arabic studies at Oxford in 1636. It was his translation of the twelfth-century Syriac historian Bar Hebraeus that opened up the history of Islam to non-Arabic-reading scholars. The study of Arabic by the likes of Pococke led to the examination of original Islamic texts. However, Arabic as a cognate language to Hebrew was of primary interest to many, including the Dutch scholar Thomas Erpenius (d. 1624), who was absorbed in the linguistic connection between Arabic and Hebrew.[5]

Imperial trading and colonization provided opportunities for Christian scholars to expand their knowledge of Eastern languages. The Reformation and then the Renaissance created a desire in scholars to return to ancient texts and sources to rediscover the wisdom of the ancient Greeks. While there were Latin translations of original Greek sources through Arabic intermediaries, Europeans quickly discovered that there were also a vast number of original Arabic writings on astronomy, math, and geography by Arabic scholars from the medieval period. This movement of *ad fontes*, "back to the sources," also focused on the Bible, particularly the sources of the Old Testament. Since the fourth century, the Western church had accepted the Latin Vulgate as the official scripture of the church. However, it was widely known that Jerome had learned Hebrew from local rabbis in the Holy Lands to assist him in translating the Bible. For many centuries, the church had accepted the Vulgate as an authorized version of the Bible and thus there was no need for further study of its original sources. By the sixteenth century this view began to change. There was a renewed interest in understanding the Hebrew Bible both as a source of faith and doctrine and as an ancient and Eastern book.[6]

Jewish texts had long been on the Vatican's forbidden reading list since the medieval period. Engaging in the study of Hebrew was a dangerous game. The Hebraist Johannes Reuchlin (1455–1522) embroiled himself in a controversy over the use of Hebrew texts. Reuchlin argued that Hebrew and other Eastern languages were important keys to understanding the Bible. He wrote, "The language of the Hebrews is simple, pure, uncorrupted, holy, brief and consistent. It is the language in which God spoke with man, and men with angels face to face rather than through an interpreter."[7] By the time Martin Luther made a translation of the Hebrew Bible into German in 1534, the study of Hebrew had gained acceptance in universities of Europe. For Luther, as for others, Hebrew was the language God used in the Garden of Eden. It was even considered the language of all humanity until the sin of the people of Shinar and the destruction of the Tower of Babel (Genesis 11:1–9); there, at the tower of Babel, God introduced the many different human languages, including Arabic.[8] As Hebrew became a prominent focus of study for humanists and Protestant scholars, this also led to their interest in the study of Arabic, not as a language of Islam but as a biblical Semitic language.

For the Latin Catholic Church, Arabic was never seen as the sole purview of Islam. As early as the Crusades, Latin Christians came into contact with Eastern Arabic-speaking Christians. By the eighteenth century, many of the indigenous Arabic-speaking Christian communities of the Near East had significant relations with various Catholic missionary orders (such as the Lazarists, the Capuchins, and the Dominicans). In fact, the Congregation of the Propagation of the Faith's primary raison d'être was to bring the Eastern Orthodox communities back into communion with Rome. Founded in 1622, the society succeeded in creating break-away communities from among all the Arabic-, Armenian-, and Greek-speaking Orthodox churches. These became known as the Eastern Rite Catholic Churches. The Latin missionary orders and the Eastern Catholics created a channel for the flow of Arab Christian knowledge production, including Arabic translations of the Bible and bilingual liturgy manuals, as well as Arabic theological treatises, which became part of the Catholic worldview. This is demonstrated through the rich collection of Arabic Christian works in the Vatican's library.[9]

One particular community of Arabic-speaking Christians who became important coreligionists with Rome were the Maronites of Mount Lebanon.[10] In 1584, the Maronite College was established in Rome. Its purpose was to bring Maronite clergy to Rome to solidify the "unification" and to begin translating Latin texts into Arabic, and Arabic texts into Latin. Maronites such as Jibra'il al-Suhyni and Yunna al-Hashruni translated Arabic texts and helped with the research and publication of the polyglot Bibles.[11]

The Maronite College was not the first Catholic initiative to translate Arabic texts, however. The Toledan collection of Islamic sources, including the Qur'an, had been translated back in the middle of the twelfth century. Robert of Ketton's 1142 translation of the Qur'an into Latin became the standard Qur'anic text throughout all of Europe from the twelfth to the seventeenth century, when there was a flurry of translation activity. Ludovico Marracci's *Alcorani textus universus* was completed in 1698 and supplanted Robert's translation.[12] Prior to that, in 1647, the French diplomat to the Ottoman Empire, Alexander Du Ryer, had made a French translation, *L'Alcoran de Mahomet*. Du Ryer's French Qur'an was then translated into English by an anonymous author in 1649.[13] This was the standard English version of the Qur'an available until George Sale's 1734 translation made directly from Arabic, which would remain the most popular English edition until the late nineteenth century, when a variety of English translations became available.[14] By the nineteenth century, Beirut became the center for an Arab Christian arms race between the Maronites, the newly forming Protestant community, and the Jesuits. Each set up a publishing house to print new Arabic Bibles, devotional material, and theological treatises (aimed primarily against one another).[15]

Arabic as a Key to Biblical Hebrew

Medieval Spanish and French rabbis had previously made important connections between Arabic and Hebrew, and even used Arabic to help them in their own interpretations of scripture.[16] Aware of these medieval connections, Robert Wakefield (d. 1537), the first Regius professor of Hebrew at Oxford, began to examine the connection between the two languages. Wakefield gave a lecture at Cambridge in 1524 entitled "De laudibus et tulitate trium linguarum," examining the relationship among Hebrew, Chaldean, and Arabic. He argued that there were important benefits in reading Arabic medieval texts, especially for those interested in science and philosophy. Wakefield was primarily interested in philological connections, that Arabic as a Semitic language had developed from ancient Hebrew and was just as essential as Chaldean (as noted earlier, the common name for Aramaic) as a biblical tool.[17] Wakefield argued that without a knowledge of Arabic, "the holy Scripture and the Hebrew language cannot be fully appreciated or properly understood."[18]

Wakefield's argument rested on two primary supports. First, as previously noted, Arabic is a triconsonantal language and functions similarly to Hebrew. Thus, Hebrew, Chaldean, and Arabic complement one another. Because medieval Arabic scholars spilt so much ink examining Arabic grammar, there were tools within the vast array of Arabic literature to help interpret those Hebrew words that were vague or unclear. Wakefield's explicit argument about the relationship of Semitic languages would become the accepted view among Protestant Old Testament scholars until the early twentieth century.

The other support for the study of Arabic was a commonly held anti-Judaism perspective in early modern Europe. As was seen with Reuchlin's controversy over Jewish texts in sixteenth-century Germany, there was an accepted belief that the rabbinical literature was inherently corrupted and openly anti-Christian. Martin Luther particularly distrusted rabbinical writings.[19] This suspicion of the rabbis focused on the work of the Masorites, who had standardized the vowel pointing of the Hebrew Bible from the fifth to the seventh century. There was a common view that the Masorites had corrupted the original reading of the Hebrew text through their insistence on inserting the *nakkud*, or vowel points. Thus, one of the only Jewish texts believed to have any validity as an authentic key to interpreting the Hebrew Bible was the Arabic translation of the Torah by Sadiaa Gaon (d. 942). Sadiaa, or Saʿid bin Yusuf al-Fayyumi, was the widely heralded head of the Jewish academy in Surra, Iraq, during the Abbasid Empire. Sadiaa lived and breathed in the Arabic culture of the Abbasids. It was here that Jewish, Christian, and Muslim scholars created a broadly shared Arabic-Islamic dominant culture, thanks in part to the availability of ancient Greek texts in Arabic. Sadiaa's translation of the Torah, which he called his *Tafsir*, became the basis for later Western Christian interpretation of the Hebrew Bible.

After Wakefield, the most influential early modern European scholar to influence the field of the study of Hebrew was Thomas Erpenius. Appointed the professor of Arabic and Oriental languages at Leiden University in 1613, Erpenius had been a student of Josephus Scaliger (1540–1609), who published the *Thesaurus linguae arabicae*. Scaliger was the first scholar to begin reading the Qur'an for philological purposes rather than to refute it.[20] Erpenius gleaned from Scaliger that Arabic was an important linguistic tool for understanding Hebrew. In 1620, Erpenius published his own *Rudementa linguae arabicae*, where he elaborated on the affinities between Arabic and Hebrew. Like Wakefield, he argued that medieval Muslim grammarians provided opportunities for further erudition of Hebrew words and phrases.

In his first year at Leiden, Erpenius gave a lecture to encourage his students to study Arabic.[21] Erpenius began his lecture by providing a fairly accurate picture of the history of Islam, correcting some of the fanciful Latin medieval rumors and stories of Muhammad. Nonetheless, Erpenius still held to the traditional Western Christian view labeling Muhammad as "the pseudo-prophet—the most dangerous enemy of the divinity and the cross of Christ."[22] He then proceeded to praise the Arabic language, the role of learning among the Arabs, and their books in medieval libraries, which could now be found throughout Europe. With these Arabic sources available, students might delve into the medieval works not only to learn about Islam so as to refute it but also to learn about medicine, math, geometry, geography, Roman law, philosophy, and the great poetry of the Arabs. Most importantly, Erpenius asserted, Arabic provided keys to understanding Hebrew. "Hebrew is the mother of Arabic and the first of all languages." Thus, Arabic should be learned before one learns Hebrew, "since it is easier and more regular" with simple grammatical rules and no exceptions.[23] Erpenius went on to lay out what would remain the accepted philological rationale for the study of Arabic by Christian clergy and scholars for centuries to come.

> Hebrew—of which some knowledge should be as desirable to us as an exact understanding of the faith and mysteries of our salvation—is susceptible of so much illumination from Arabic, both with regard to expression and to figures of speech and meaning, origin, and etymology of words, as to deserve a book in itself. My *Commentarius in linguam Arabicum* with its six hundred examples will confirm this. It will also provide certain rules useful and necessary for a solid grasp of Hebrew expressions that I have brought out of the inmost recesses of the Arabic language. . . . I do not mean by this that Hebrew words are derived from Arabic, but that the meanings and origins of the more obscure words in the Hebrew language, of which only defective and scanty evidences remain in the Old Testament, may be illustrated and explained by the same words that still exist in the Arabic language, which is preserved entire and has very many roots and word patterns in common with Hebrew.[24]

Erpenius asserted that to teach students Arabic one should begin with grammar and then read together a bilingual version of the Psalms in Arabic and Latin, then the story of Joseph from the Qur'an, and then other Arabic historical texts.[25] Here, Erpenius not only provided a curriculum for Arabic language learning but set in motion the reading of the Qur'an as a tool for understanding the Hebrew Bible, an approach that, as we will see, would later become a blueprint for several American Protestant seminaries.

The London Polyglot Bible

It was one thing to encourage students to study Arabic, but it was something else entirely to provide them the tools to do so. While Erpenius's arguments were persuasive, students would have to wait another generation before such tools were readily available. It was not until after the publication of the polyglot Bibles that an Arabic translation of the Bible was made available to a wide variety of readers.

As early as the third century, the Egyptian church father Origen recognized that the Bible could be better understood by comparing the
various texts of its original languages. His Hexapla, which is no longer
extant, provided a pre-Masoretic Hebrew text in parallel columns with
various Greek translations. In the fourth century, Jerome also compared
various versions of the Hebrew text with the Septuagint as the basis for
his Latin Vulgate. Thus, there was precedent from the early church fathers for the use of various translations to better understand the Hebrew.
With such a wide assortment of Latin, Hebrew, and Arabic texts in the
libraries of Spain, Cardinal Francisco Jiménez de Cisneros (1436–1517)
had in mind to follow in Origen's footsteps by laying various translations
side by side for readers to examine: Hebrew on the left, the Latin Vulgate
in the middle, and the Septuagint on the right. He added an Aramaic
Targum and a free Latin translation of the Targum at the bottom of each
page for the Pentateuch portions only. What has come to be known as
the 1521 Complutensian Polyglot Bible took fifteen years to complete and
included a team of Christians and Jewish *conversos* (or converts, as they
were then labeled) to complete the six-volume edition of the Old Testament. Incidentally, the Bible was dedicated to the previous sovereigns
Ferdinand and Isabella, who provided the necessary legal sanction for
the study and use of Hebrew.

This important tool for biblical study contributed to an international
textual arms race.[26] The Complutensian Bible was followed by other versions, including the Antwerp Polyglot in 1572 and the Paris Polyglot in
1645. Each of these added additional Eastern biblical languages in the
separate columns, such as the Samaritan version of the Torah and various Syriac versions of the New Testament.[27] In 1657 an Arabic version
of the Hebrew Bible was added as a column to the London Polyglot.[28]

The archbishop of Canterbury, William Laud (1573–1645), who
founded the Laudian Chair of Arabic Studies at Oxford and donated
his own collection of manuscripts to the Bodleian Library, supported a
new Protestant polyglot translation project to be headed by Brian Walton (1600–1661), then bishop of Chester. Even though the project had
official Anglican support from the highest levels, there would continue
to be ongoing controversy over the inclusion of the Hebrew Masoretic
text.[29] As previously mentioned, it was generally accepted that the vowel
points in the Masoretic text were a late invention of the rabbis. Due

to anti-Jewish views, some even argued that the rabbis had placed the vowel points to corrupt the Hebrew text out of "hatred to the Christians."[30] Walton argued, however, that while the vowel points did come late to the text through the Masorites, the rabbis were only following a received tradition of vocalization and recitation that came directly from the Apostles on the day of Pentecost and that this tradition had been accepted by both Origen and Jerome. Walton recognized that Syriac and Arabic, as Semitic languages, were also originally unpointed. Unlike the Complutensian and Antwerp polyglots, Walton included Arabic, as well as Ethiopic and Persian translations. For the Arabic translation of the Pentateuch, Walton used the popular tenth-century version of Sadiaa Gaon, mentioned above. It is still not clear which Arabic New Testament manuscripts he used; there were several translations in contemporary use by the Eastern churches, particularly that of Jibra'il al-Suhyuni, whose edition was used in the Paris Bible.[31] Significantly, as part of this project Walton recognized how important the Qur'an was as a key to understanding the unpointed pre-Masoretic text of the Hebrew Bible.[32] American seminary biblical scholars, like Robinson and others after him, came to the same conclusion.

The Study of Semitic Languages in North America

With this background of European biblical translations in mind, we now return to North America. The study of Semitic languages in North America is woven together from at least two strands. The first strand was a theological one. There was a strong belief among seventeenth-century New England colonists that God had made a covenant with them. References to America as the New Israel of the Old Testament in New England Puritan literature is ubiquitous.[33] This led to a desire to better understand the Old Testament as a blueprint for North American society. For example, Cotton Mather (1663–1728), the most renowned early colonial Puritan theologian, believed in the importance of reading the Hebrew to fully interpret and understand God's will for the new nation. Mather saw the Hebrew Bible as the foundation for American Protestant civilization. The earliest American colleges founded by Protestant Calvinists—Harvard, Yale, and Dartmouth—required Hebrew to be studied along with Greek and Latin.[34] Stephen Sewall, the Hancock professor of Hebrew and other Oriental languages at Harvard from 1765 to 1785, and Ezra Stiles, a former student of Sewall and later the president of Yale from 1778 to 1795, instilled in their students a belief in the importance of Hebrew and Semitic language study.[35] In fact, Stiles encouraged the valedictorians of Yale to give their graduation speeches in biblical Hebrew, as he claimed to have done when he graduated with top honors!

The second interwoven strand of interest in Semitic languages was due to commerce. American mercantile enterprises facilitated the dissemination of Eastern texts that were transported from places like Aleppo and Constantinople across the Atlantic and landed on shelves in private libraries.[36] New England ports had extensive mercantile connections not only with Europe but also with the Ottoman Empire, especially after the establishment of a "most favored nation" treaty that was signed in 1830. Well-to-do or well-connected clergy were able to acquire Eastern books and manuscripts for their own edification and amusement.

Jeffrey Einboden, in *The Islamic Lineage of American Literary Culture*, highlights the role that Arabic played for several early American clergy. He examines Ezra Stiles's daily devotional life, and his interest not only in Hebrew but in Arabic as well, once translating the Psalms into Arabic in his diary.[37] Einboden also analyzes the role that Arabic played in the life of William Bentley (1759–1819), another student of Sewall at Harvard and a popular Unitarian minister, who was considered "the most learned man in America" of his day.[38] Bentley was pastor of Second Congregational Church in East Salem, Massachusetts, one of the notable ports for American trade. In his diaries, Bentley records his requests to local merchants to procure Oriental books and manuscripts for him, including Arabic texts. Arabic phraseology, including the references to the *shahada*, run throughout his diaries. Einboden demonstrates that Stiles and Bentley, among others, learned Arabic not only out of intellectual curiosity but also as part of their devotional life in reading, translating, and understanding the Hebrew Bible.

Bentley is perhaps an extreme example of this interest in Arabic. Nevertheless, the availability of Eastern texts and goods not only provided an avenue for a few well-educated clergy to become exposed to Arabic and other Eastern languages, but by the middle of the eighteenth century, trade also resulted in a shift in American attitudes towards the

Ottomans. As the United States emerged from the War of 1812 and the Barbary War of 1815 as a new transatlantic nation and growing economic power, there was a newfound self-assurance. With a growing international trade network, a new treaty with the Ottoman Empire, and a navy to protect their ships, Americans no longer felt threatened by piracy. Ottoman material culture, its clothing styles, architecture, and literature, were romanticized. By the 1830s the Ottomans were no longer the purveyors of barbarism and piracy but now the wardens of a romantic Orient. As Timothy Marr has stated, there was a change from "oppositional repulsion and more toward the celebration of romantic liberty" of the East.[39] The growing availability of Eastern and Arabic books and texts supported not only the intellectual curiosities or the devotional studies of East Coast clergy but new opportunities to study Arabic and other Eastern languages in order to better understand scripture in general. Those students who "read theology" with these ministers were instilled with a belief in the importance of reading cognate Oriental languages to better understand the Hebrew Bible. This revived a stagnating field of studies in the Hebrew Bible.

As important as Hebrew was for some New England divines, it was never particularly attractive to young students at Harvard and Yale. It never gained the prominence of Greek and Latin. Students relentlessly complained about their required Hebrew recitations and rarely showed up for class. In fact, students complained enough that eventually they were able to waive the requirement if they produced a note from their parents requesting this.[40] By 1785 Hebrew was dropped from the Harvard curriculum and left up to interested divinity students to pursue on their own initiative. The lack of excitement for Hebrew among students can probably be explained with a few reasons. First, the general piety of Americans had changed dramatically since the days of Mather. The effects of French Enlightenment thinking and the disruption of the American War of Independence had noticeably changed American religious interests. While covenantal theology was still an important part of American religious perspectives, positivism, the belief that what is true can be scientifically verified, challenged traditionally held views of Providence. Overall, fewer students were interested in reading divinity. But there may also have been other practical reasons why Hebrew dropped from general interest: the difficulty of the language, the lack of available resources to learn from, or even poor instruction. Unlike Latin and Greek, which could be taught by reading a variety of different kinds of texts, the Hebrew Bible was the only acceptable text available to read. Other Hebrew texts, such as the Talmud, would have been considered corrupted by Jewish thinking and would have been off limits. The lack of books or other helpful linguistic resources from Europe was undoubtedly affected by the American Revolution, which disrupted the importing of books from Europe and derailed education in general during the 1770s and 1780s.

Interest in the Hebrew language waned in the American colleges at the end of the eighteenth century but was revived in the first third of the nineteenth century as seminaries were established. These new seminaries required Hebrew and Greek, and eventually offered other cognate languages as part of the curriculum. The seminaries invested not only in teachers and students but in the research and publication of their own textbooks. For example, Moses Stuart (1780–1852) was appointed the professor of sacred literature at Andover seminary in 1810 and served in that capacity until 1847. As the first professor of Hebrew at an American seminary, Moses Stuart was responsible for reenergizing the Christian philological study of Hebrew and other Semitic languages in North America.[41] However, when he was appointed to his position, he confessed that he could barely read Hebrew even with a lexicon! As he took up the task of learning the language to teach it to his students, he decried the lack of available quality resources, including grammars and even Hebrew Bibles. So, Stuart traveled to Germany for assistance and guidance. There he attended the lectures of William Gesenius (1786–1842), professor of Hebrew at Göttingen and then at Halle. Gesenius's interest in Hebrew was philological. In 1813, Gesenius published *Hebraische Grammatik* and *Hebräisches und Chaldäisches Handwörterbuch über das Alte Testament* two years later. These two language resources would revolutionize biblical language study in Europe and North America. Stuart mastered German enough to be able to use Gesenius's grammar and lexicon and to develop his own lectures on Hebrew based on Gesenius's work, and then ultimately to publish his own Hebrew grammar in 1821.[42]

Two of Stuart's most notable students, Josiah W. Gibbs and Edward Robinson, would go on to become exceptional scholars in their own right. Gibbs became the professor of sacred languages at Yale and Robinson the professor of sacred literature at Union seminary. Stuart en-

A

HEBREW AND ENGLISH LEXICON

OF THE

OLD TESTAMENT

WITH AN APPENDIX CONTAINING THE BIBLICAL ARAMAIC

BASED ON THE LEXICON OF

WILLIAM GESENIUS

AS TRANSLATED BY

EDWARD ROBINSON

LATE PROFESSOR IN THE UNION THEOLOGICAL SEMINARY, NEW YORK

*Edited with constant reference to the Thesaurus of Gesenius as completed by E. Rödiger, and
with authorized use of the latest German editions of Gesenius's
Handwörterbuch über das Alte Testament*

BY

FRANCIS BROWN, D.D., D.Litt.

DAVENPORT PROFESSOR OF HEBREW AND THE COGNATE LANGUAGES IN THE UNION THEOLOGICAL SEMINARY

WITH THE CO-OPERATION OF

S. R. DRIVER, D.D., Litt.D.   AND   CHARLES A. BRIGGS, D.D., D.Litt.

REGIUS PROFESSOR OF HEBREW, AND CANON OF   EDWARD ROBINSON PROFESSOR OF BIBLICAL THEOLOGY
CHRIST CHURCH, OXFORD   IN THE UNION THEOLOGICAL SEMINARY

CLARENDON PRESS: OXFORD

Figure 4.1. Title page to the Brown-Driver-Briggs 1906 edition of *A Hebrew and English Lexicon of the Old Testament*. Courtesy of HathiTrust.

couraged Gibbs to translate Gesenius's grammar, which he eventually did in 1824 as *A Hebrew and English Lexicon, including the Biblical Chaldee*. In 1836, Robinson translated Gesenius's Latin *Lexicon Manuale Hebraicum et Chaldaicum* into English. This would become an important tool for the transmission of German linguistic scholarship on the Bible to North America. It also had a great impact on the understanding of the relationship between Hebrew and other Semitic languages, including Arabic. Robinson would continue to edit and add corrections to the lexicon throughout his career, publishing updated editions. It was his final 1854 edition that ultimately would become the basis of the famous Brown-Driver-Briggs (BDB) *A Hebrew and English Lexicon of the Old Testament*, first published in 1906 and as of the writing of this book still available in its 2015 edition.

Thus, we see a direct connection between Gesenius's philological study of Hebrew, Moses Stuart's early scholarship, and Edward Robinson, who cemented the work of Gesenius into American biblical scholarship into the twenty-first century. Of particular importance is Gesenius's views on the original unpointed Hebrew text and its linguistic relationship with the other Semitic languages, particularly Arabic.

The Philological Study of Hebrew

When Moses Stuart began to learn and teach Hebrew at Andover seminary in 1810 it was commonly accepted that the oldest and most pristine form of the Hebrew language did not have vowel points. And, as already noted, it was also generally accepted at this time that the Masoretic text of the medieval rabbis was a corruption of the unpointed original Hebrew.[43] In fact, the first Hebrew grammar printed in the United States that did not include vowel points was that of John Smith, professor of English, Latin, Greek, Hebrew, and Chaldee at Dartmouth. Smith's grammar was first written in 1773 when he was a student at Dartmouth.[44] Because there were not adequate Hebrew fonts available for printing until the beginning of the nineteenth century, the book was extremely expensive to publish. Students could not afford the book, and library access to it was limited. Thus, it had a very constrained impact on the study of Hebrew. This underscores one of Stuart's complaints about the lack of available good language resources in the young republic.

In a short essay on the debate about using the vowel points and the Masoretic text, Smith concludes that "whether we read with or without vowel-points, the sense and meaning of the language must entirely depend upon the written characters, destitute of points and accents, as they still remain in the most ancient and authentic manuscripts."[45] Stuart initially used Joseph Smith's unpointed grammar to teach but eventually began using the Masoretic text to assist his students in learning the language. He believed that while the unpointed text represented the earliest and most ancient of texts, the vowel points assisted his students in learning the language.[46] His decision was very controversial.

Prior to Stuart, the primary focus of study of the Hebrew Bible among American clergy related to its theological import. American divines read the Old Testament as the Word of God, as part of the message of salvation history that found its culmination in the life of Jesus of Nazareth in the New Testament. As Stuart introduced Hebrew Bible reading at Andover, students began to spend more time focusing on the textual intricacies of the Hebrew language, not only attending to its theological sense but seeking to analyze the text to distill important insights. The work of Gibbs and Robinson accelerated this tendency in Protestant scholarship. This textual approach suddenly exposed American scholars to the field of philology and a new world of Near Eastern languages. Frances Brown highlighted in the introduction to the BDB that,

> Semitic studies have been pursued on all hands with energy and success. The language and text of the Old Testament have been subjected to a minute and searching inquiry before unknown. The languages cognate with Hebrew have claimed the attention of specialists in nearly all civilized countries. Wide fields of research have been opened, the very existence of which was a surprise, and have invited explorers. Arabic, ancient and modern, Ethiopic, with its allied dialects, Aramaic, in its various literatures and localities, have all yielded new treasures; while the discovery and decipherment of inscriptions from Babylonia and Assyria, Phoenicia, Northern Africa, Southern Arabia, and other old abodes of Semitic peoples, have contributed to a far more comprehensive and accurate knowledge of the Hebrew vocabulary in its sources and its usage than was possible forty or fifty years ago.[47]

Thus, while Hebrew was still the central language of Old Testament study, there were few opportunities to compare Hebrew literature with other biblical manuscripts or documents, unlike in New Testament study where a variety of versions, canonical and noncanonical, abounded. The oldest Hebrew texts of the Bible available could only be traced back to the medieval period. The Aleppo Codex, generally viewed up until the twentieth century as one of the oldest Hebrew texts of the Torah, has been dated to the tenth century. The Leningrad Codex, which is the oldest complete Hebrew Bible in codex form, has been dated to the early eleventh century. The availability of Arabic, Syriac, and Ethiopic resources whose origins were hundreds of years older contributed to the ongoing study of this limited biblical Hebrew lexicon. This changed, however, when the Dead Sea Scrolls were uncovered in 1947. Sections of these scrolls included full texts of the Hebrew Bible dated to the Second Temple period. These scrolls could now be compared with other finds, such as the Cairo Genizah documents found in 1896, which included various portions of the Hebrew Bible. These discoveries allowed scholars to begin using various Hebrew versions to expand their knowledge of the language. However, this was not the case throughout the nineteenth century. As the Brown-Driver-Briggs lexicon demonstrates, the other Oriental languages were pivotal for interpreting many of the hapax legomenon, or sparsely used Hebrew words or phrases.

In nineteenth-century American Hebrew Bible study, Arabic became a tool, as it had for Wakefield in England in the sixteenth century. Even Moses Stuart, who never learned to read Arabic, stated, "In Arabic, there exists a great variety of MSS. and books, historical, scientific, and literary. The means of illustrating this living language, are very ample and satisfactory."[48] In fact, Arabic became the prominent cognate Semitic language for the study of biblical Hebrew not only because there was a vast body of medieval material but because it was assumed that this ancient language had not "decayed" over the years, as had Talmudic Hebrew. Qur'anic Arabic had managed to escape the vicissitudes of linguistic transformation or assimilation. As Gesenius himself had previously noted, "Aramæan dialects suffered the earliest and greatest decay, and next to them the Hebrew—Canaanitish. The Arabic longest retained the natural fullness of its forms; remaining undisturbed, among the secluded tribes of the wilderness, in its fully stamped organism."[49] The key to understanding the Hebrew Bible within its ancient Near Eastern context was aggressive study of these cognate languages: Aramaic (or Chaldean, as it was then called) and its later derivative form of Syriac, Arabic, and to some extent Ethiopic.[50] It was this view of Arabic as an important source for understanding biblical Hebrew that led to the prominent use of the Qur'an in advanced-level biblical textual studies.

The Specialization of Biblical Languages

Each of the early American seminaries appointed a professor of sacred languages who was responsible for teaching Hebrew and the "cognate" languages. Professors not only taught biblical theology or exegesis but offered tutorials and electives in many of the Semitic languages to advanced-level students. It was not uncommon that the prized students of the early faculty members were encouraged to go on for further study and were then hired as the next generation of seminary faculty at their alma mater, or they would be hired at another seminary to teach the cognate languages. We have already met Josiah Gibbs and Edward Robinson, two of Moses Stuart's early protégés. They would go on to be prolific biblical scholars at Yale Divinity School and Union seminary, respectively.

The reading of biblical texts became highly advanced and technical, and the seminary curricula reflected this. Whereas originally one professor served to teach the whole Bible and its original languages, by the 1870s two instructors were required to teach the Old and New Testaments. For example, at New Brunswick seminary, the Reverend Alexander McClelland (1794–1864) was appointed as the professor of biblical literature in 1832. He taught all aspects of biblical exegesis and theology. In 1840, his title was changed to that of professor of Oriental languages and literature and evidences of Christianity, which reflected the changing view of the need to study all the Semitic languages to better understand the Bible. By 1898, however, the Reverend John Howard Raven (1870–1949) was appointed as the professor of Old Testament languages and exegesis. His colleague John DeWitt then became the professor of Hellenistic Greek and New Testament exegesis. In addition to courses solely in the Christian Old Testament, McClelland also offered electives in Arabic, Aramaic, and Assyrian (which at the turn of the twentieth

134 | ARABIC AND THE STUDY OF THE QUR'AN

century was becoming one of the more popular languages of the ancient Near East due to archaeological discoveries), while a separate department for the New Testament carried on the study of Greek and early church patristics. The titles of professors reflected the growing specificity of their profession, from simply biblical literature to specific kinds of biblical literature and other Near Eastern languages.

A brief review of the teaching of Hebrew at Princeton also reveals this shift in the field of biblical studies from a focus solely on biblical theology to the more technical and philological aspects of Hebrew and other languages. Archibald Alexander, the first professor of the seminary, taught all aspects of the Bible. His focus, however, was on Old Testament theology. In 1822, Alexander hired his student Charles Hodge, who was named as assistant in Oriental languages and biblical literature. Shortly after his appointment Hodge traveled up to Andover to visit with Moses Stuart and seek his advice on how to prepare for his work. At Stuart's suggestion, Hodge went to Germany for two years to study with Gesenius. Hodge even spent some time in Paris to study Arabic under the premier European Arabic scholar of the day, Silvestre deSacy.[51] However, unlike Stuart, Hodge would remain primarily known as a theologian rather than a biblical scholar. In 1840, he was appointed as the professor of exegetical, didactic, and polemical theology.

The next faculty members appointed to teach the Bible at Princeton were Joseph Addison Alexander in 1838 and then William Henry Green in 1851. Green graduated from the seminary and was immediately hired as an instructor of Hebrew. He then became the chair of Oriental and biblical literature. In 1859 his position changed, and he became the chair of Oriental and Old Testament literature, a position that he held until his death in 1900. Throughout the 1860s and 1870s, Green would teach not only Hebrew but Syriac and Arabic as a part of this view of better understanding the Old Testament in its Near Eastern milieu.[52]

One of Green's prized students, James F. McCurdy (1847–1935), graduated from Princeton in 1873 and was immediately appointed the librarian and instructor of Hebrew. Only four years later he was appointed the instructor in Hebrew and other Oriental languages. While Green focused on Old Testament history and theology, McCurdy taught Semitic philology. In addition to Hebrew, McCurdy also offered special courses in Chaldean, Syriac, Arabic, and even Sanskrit. However, McCurdy left in the spring of 1882 to return to his home in Canada and teach at the University of Toronto.[53] In 1893, Geerhardus Vos (1862–1949) was then appointed the professor of biblical theology. He did offer some courses in Syriac and Arabic, but there were very few students who were interested or who had time to focus on these electives in the curriculum. Like Hodge, Vos would become known for his standing as a theologian rather than as a textual scholar. He would go on to represent a conservative Reformed theology that contributed to the modernist-fundamentalist debate and the schism at Princeton, leading to the creation of Westminster Seminary in 1929. Thus, we see that while Princeton Old Testament scholars were swept along with the tide of philological study, some faculty maintained a staunch focus on the theology of scripture.

This wider trend in the specialization of biblical and cognate languages can also be seen through a review of the curriculum at General seminary in New York. General was unique among the seminaries in that, because students had to pass exams to be considered for ordination in the Episcopal Church, the bishops of the church had a direct hand in approving the curriculum, whereas at the other seminaries the faculty had the primary role in determining the curriculum. Because of this, readings in patristics and Anglican ecclesiology took up a significant amount of space in the General's curriculum.[54] Any curricular revision was complicated and took a long time to complete. The process had to pass muster with both the faculty and the bishops of the denomination. For example, in the 1850s, no one was happy with the curriculum—faculty, bishops, or students. The curriculum was stale and overcrowded with older reading requirements. However, as with most other schools, whenever there was a discussion about the need for a curricular change, most of the faculty argued that their fields and methods were instrumental to the training of clergy. No one wanted to give up what they saw as vital to theological education. The result was that a new curriculum was finally instituted in 1867 that required seven departments of specialized learning: (1) Hebrew and Greek languages, (2) biblical learning and the interpretation of scripture, (3) systematic divinity and dogmatic theology, (4) ecclesiastical history, (5) ecclesiastical polity and law, (6) evidences of revealed religion, and (7) pastoral theology.[55]

In 1893, the same thing happened again. This time students complained directly to the board, declaring that the methods of instruction were "behind the times." Another curriculum was instituted, but instead of reimagining the fields of study, the faculty added three additional areas: Oriental languages, ecclesiastical music, and moral theology and Christian philosophy.[56] To allow for those gifted students who wanted to go on for specialized study, a fourth year of "postgraduate" study was allowed. In the case of Oriental languages, however, courses were offered but not required. Rather, "instructions in these languages [were] given when desired" by adjuncts and former missionaries when they were available on home assignment.[57] Presumably, this was the case because there were no faculty with expertise in the cognate languages, and no faculty member received such a title as part of their portfolio. By 1903, the Oriental languages were only offered to postgraduate seminarians who would attend classes at Columbia College. This was the same option at Union seminary, where after a long and distinguished period of offering various Semitic languages in its biblical studies department, in 1895 Arabic courses at Union were offered through New York University or at Columbia College by the newly appointed Orientalist scholar R. J. H. Gottheil.[58]

Qur'an as Chrestomathy

The use of Arabic as a key to interpreting the Hebrew Bible reached new heights in the 1880s and 1890s in seminaries when several Old Testament professors began including passages from the Qur'an in their chrestomathies, that is, collections of passages for students to translate as part of their language exercises. Charles Briggs (1841–1913), the professor of Hebrew and cognate languages at Union from 1874 to 1890 and then the Edward Robinson chair of biblical theology until his death in 1913, offered elective courses in Syriac and Arabic, alternating years with Hebrew and Aramaic.[59] Briggs would teach Syriac in the fall term and Arabic in the spring. The Arabic reading included portions of Saadia Gaon's Arabic Pentateuch and then sections from the Qur'an. In 1892, he had nineteen students in Arabic class and nine in Syriac. This represented 12 percent and 5 percent of the total student body, respectively, not an insignificant number of students.

For Briggs, the cognate Semitic languages were critical to understanding the Old Testament in relation to the wider ancient world. Like many before him, Briggs believed the Masoretic text was a later development of the ancient biblical Hebrew and included rabbinic interpolations. He believed, however, that the Arabic of the Qur'anic text was a purer form of the Semitic roots than the later rabbinic literature. He wrote that the Qur'an "has kept the Arabic so fixed to its classical style that it has taken a thousand years for the vulgar Arabic to reach the stage of linguistic development presented in the earliest Hebrew of the Bible."[60] Thus, using a Qur'anic text without vowel points or other diacritical marks (*tashkeel*) was an important way to learn how Semitic language functioned. It should be remembered that prior to the discovery of the Dead Sea Scrolls in 1947, the earliest extant Hebrew texts available were from the ninth and tenth centuries. Thus, it was believed that the Arabic text of the Qur'an predated the Hebrew texts by several hundred years.

In 1884, John G. Lansing (1851–1906) was installed as the Gardner Sage professor of Old Testament languages and exegesis at New Brunswick seminary. Lansing was the son of the Presbyterian missionary Gulian Lansing, and was born in Egypt. He spent his early childhood there, speaking Egyptian Arabic as well as English. He was sent back to the United States at age ten to live with family. After graduating from Union College in Schenectady, New York, in 1875, he married Mary Counsaul. The two returned to Egypt, not as missionaries but for him to study at the Protestant seminary for one year. Lansing then returned to the United States and was admitted directly into the senior class of New Brunswick seminary because of his previous knowledge of the biblical languages and his studies at the Egyptian seminary. He graduated in 1877. Lansing was immediately ordained into the Presbyterian Church of North America, where he served two congregations in upstate New York until he was elected to the professorship at the New Brunswick seminary in 1884. Throughout his professional career Lansing suffered from what the doctors called "cerebral disintegration," which may have been chronic depression, although it is not clear. He was required to take several leaves of absence and retired early in 1898 when he moved to Colorado to be with his only surviving daughter, who took care of him until his death.[61]

Prior to Lansing's arrival at the New Brunswick seminary there was only one Bible professor. Lansing was hired as the first professor specifically assigned to the Old Testament. His work adds to our understanding of how Arabic was viewed by many Old Testament scholars at this time. In his inaugural lecture as professor, Lansing provides eight arguments stressing the importance of the study of Arabic to understanding the Old Testament.

First, Lansing notes that Arabic is an old language. In fact, there was a minority perspective among some German scholars that Arabic was actually older than Hebrew, although this went against a long-standing Christian belief that Hebrew was the original language of the Garden of Eden.[62] To support this, Lansing provides many examples of Arabic roots underlying names and places in the Old Testament. For example, he asserts that Kiriath-Arba in Genesis 23:2, which was the original name of the village that became Hebron, is an Arab place and that the "ath" or "at" is an Arabic construction. On the basis of this and other examples, he argues that the Canaanites were native Arabs who spoke Arabic. Thus, Arabic helped not only by illustrating Hebrew but by providing a "comprehensive knowledge and interpretation of Hebrew" in its ancient Near East context.[63] Second, Lansing asserts that as a triconsonantal language Arabic possesses many commonalities with Hebrew that can assist in understanding how the Semitic language functions. Third, Arabic is a logical language with strict grammatical rules that can help explain more obscure Hebrew words or the hapax legomenon, those words that only occur once in the Bible. Fourth, Arabic has remained relatively pure throughout the years and has been codified by the text of the Qur'an, which has kept the language static. Fifth, the richness of the Arabic lexicon can assist in understanding Hebrew words and provide further nuances. Sixth, Hebrew forms and conjugations can be reconstructed from many detailed examples in Arabic literature. Seventh, the literary corpus is so vast that it allows for a variety of comparisons and understandings of the Hebrew. Finally, Arabic is still a living language that continues to draw on the richness of its literary past.[64]

Lansing passionately laid out his Arabic sympathies: "We have literary productions composed and written two and three centuries before the time of Mohammad, i.e., between 400 and 300 AD. These productions show a literary vigor and polish unsurpassed; exhibit a language already perfect in its form and application; and by a variety of inflections, a regularity of syntax, and a harmony of prosody, give simple proof of the high degree of culture the Arabic had already attained. Such a state

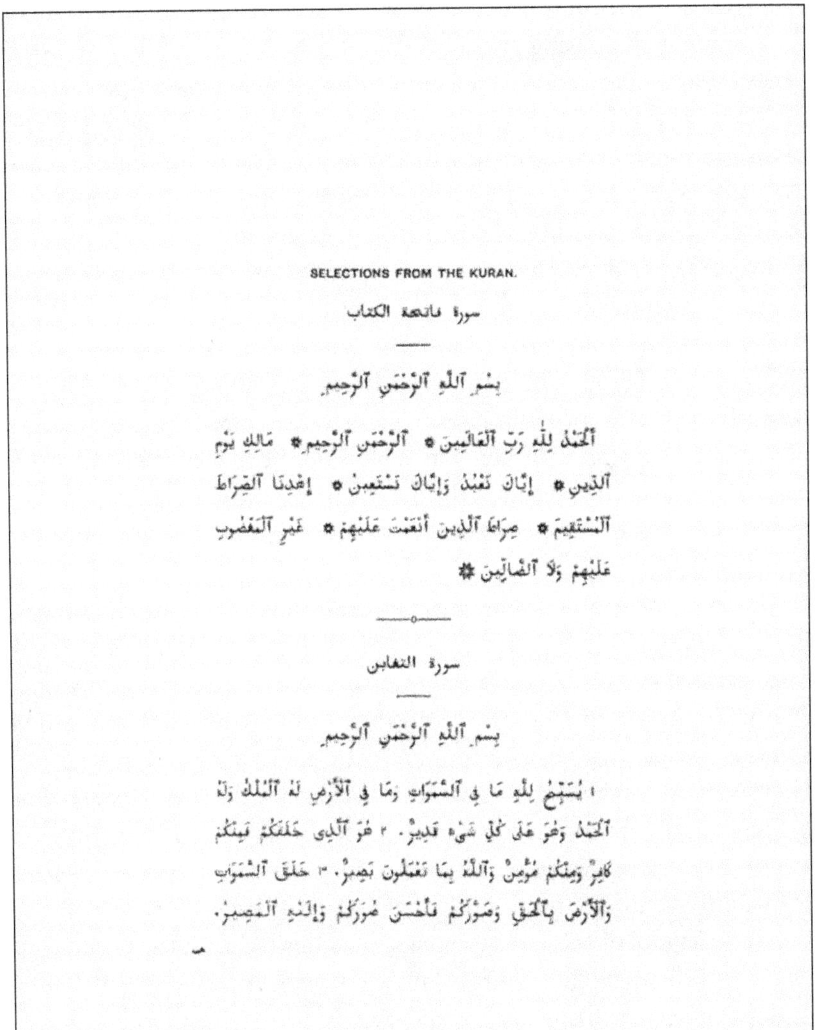

سورة فاتحة الكتاب

بِسْمِ ٱللّٰهِ ٱلرَّحْمٰنِ ٱلرَّحِيمِ

ٱلْحَمْدُ لِلّٰهِ رَبِّ ٱلْعَالَمِينَ ۞ ٱلرَّحْمٰنِ ٱلرَّحِيمِ ۞ مَالِكِ يَوْمِ
ٱلدِّينِ ۞ إِيَّاكَ نَعْبُدُ وَإِيَّاكَ نَسْتَعِينُ ۞ إِهْدِنَا ٱلصِّرَاطَ
ٱلْمُسْتَقِيمَ ۞ صِرَاطَ ٱلَّذِينَ أَنْعَمْتَ عَلَيْهِمْ ۞ غَيْرِ ٱلْمَغْضُوبِ
عَلَيْهِمْ وَلَا ٱلضَّالِّينَ ۞

---o---

سورة التغابن

بِسْمِ ٱللّٰهِ ٱلرَّحْمٰنِ ٱلرَّحِيمِ

١ يُسَبِّحُ لِلّٰهِ مَا فِي ٱلسَّمٰوَاتِ وَمَا فِي ٱلْأَرْضِ لَهُ ٱلْمُلْكُ وَلَهُ
ٱلْحَمْدُ وَهُوَ عَلَى كُلِّ شَيْءٍ قَدِيرٌ ۰ ٢ هُوَ ٱلَّذِي خَلَقَكُمْ فَمِنْكُمْ
كَافِرٌ وَمِنْكُمْ مُؤْمِنٌ وَٱللّٰهُ بِمَا تَعْمَلُونَ بَصِيرٌ ۰ ٣ خَلَقَ ٱلسَّمٰوَاتِ
وَٱلْأَرْضَ بِٱلْحَقِّ وَصَوَّرَكُمْ فَأَحْسَنَ صُوَرَكُمْ وَإِلَيْهِ ٱلْمَصِيرُ ۰

ـ

Figure 4.2. J. G. Lansing's Arabic chrestomathy, including Surahs 1 and 64 from *A Manual of Arabic*, 2nd ed., 1891. Courtesy of HathiTrust.

of linguistic perfection necessarily presupposes a long anterior state of development."[65] Lansing goes on to point out that the pre-Islamic Arab poets Imru al-Qays and Lubaid demonstrate the linguistic "perfection" of Arabic that finds its final fixed form in the Qur'an. Thus, at the end of his grammar, Lansing includes a chrestomathy, or selections of readings, from Genesis 1, 2, and 3 with pointed and unpointed portions from Saadia Gaon's translation. He then provides selections from surahs 1, 64, and 93 of the Qur'an. His Arabic text is based on Fleugel's 1858 Arabic edition, which was in his personal library.

For Lansing, Arabic is the key to understanding the language of the Hebrew Bible. "From where the waves break on the shores of the Hadramaut, from where the palm rises in gracefulness amid the fragrant airs of Yemen, from where the soft winds blow on the hills of the Nejd, from beneath the stars that gleam so brilliantly in the firmament of Hejaz, we gather richest gems of speech wherewith to enrich our knowledge of the Word of God."[66]

This view of Arabic found another prominent advocate in Duncan Black Macdonald (1863–1943), professor of Semitic languages at Hartford seminary from 1892 to 1932. Macdonald was a Scottish Presbyterian who graduated from the University of Glasgow. He had learned Hebrew, Syriac, Arabic, and Ethiopic both in Glasgow and in Berlin.[67] He was hired by the board of Hartford seminary to teach Hebrew, but quickly began offering electives in advanced Arabic by 1894 and offered a course on Islam that used Islamic primary sources the following year. He would eventually teach both at the Hartford seminary and in the Kennedy School of Missions (which was associated with the seminary), where he provided other courses in Islam to assist missionaries to better understand Islam "from the inside," that is, as Muslims would understand Islam.[68] He was the first prominent internationally known Arabist and Islamicist in North America. He was known internationally for his highly acclaimed *Development of Muslim Theology* and for providing several entries for the first edition of the *Encyclopedia of Islam*.[69] In addition, he is known for having a significant collection of editions of *The Arabian Nights*, currently housed at Hartford International University's archives. Macdonald viewed these stories and tales as a way to appreciate the Qur'anic worldview. They were also an avenue into understanding the stories and cultures of the Hebrew Bible.

For over a century German and then American biblical scholarship focused on the historical critical method as a tool to interpret ancient texts. With the recent developments in archaeology at the turn of the twentieth century, scholars were literally uncovering the texts and artifacts of the ancient Near East. The prevailing view was to see the Hebrew Bible within the larger cultural framework that was being uncovered in places like Nineveh and Tel el-Amarna. Macdonald, however, viewed the Bible as part of a larger cultural frame of reference that was reflected in Arabic literature. Duncan Black Macdonald opined, "That the Semites were, and are, a story telling people is commonplace. *The Arabian Nights*, whatever its ultimate origins, is a demonstration of that fact for the Arabic-speaking peoples and the Old Testament for the Hebrews. But all primitive peoples, at all times, have told stories; the records of folklore are full of such stories. Yet no one will doubt that both the Arabic and the Hebrew literatures are rich in stories which have a difference, a peculiar appeal, because they are of a peculiar humanity. Their stories go home to us all in a way quite different from the common, bare folklore tale."[70]

Thus, by reading Arabic literature—including the Qur'an—the student of the Bible not only learns more about the meaning of the Hebrew words or phrases but engages with a larger Semitic literary and cultural world. Macdonald's lectures on the Old Testament are replete with comparisons between the Hebrew Bible and Arabic literature and folklore, with references to *The Arabian Nights*, pre-Islamic poets, the Islamic Stories of the Prophets, or the Qur'an. Arabic stories, poetry, and prose would help the student understand the nuances of the Hebrew language. In his lectures on the Old Testament, Macdonald also introduces students to the ancient Arabic culture of storytelling and poetry. The story of Job and David's odes are compared with the poetry of Imru al-Qays. The wisdom literature and the lyrical poetry of Miriam, Job, and the Psalms find their kindred spirits with the pre-Islamic poets and the soothsayers noted in the Qur'an. The ecstatic experiences of Elijah and Elisha find their equivalent with Muslim Sufis. The preaching of judgment and guidance of the classical prophets like Micah finds its comparison in Muhammad.[71] All of these Arabic and Muslim examples could be found in ongoing Islamic literature and cultures. Thus, Macdonald drew a straight line from the Hebrew Bible to the Qur'an.[72] In this regard, Macdonald was either out of step or ahead of his time within the field of biblical studies, which continued to focus on textual and form criticism until the 1970s, when narrative and literary forms of interpretation finally began to take hold.

For Macdonald, the distinctiveness of the Old Testament was not its form but its message. The "genius of the Hebrew Bible," he wrote, was its answer to the questions of the "eternal human spirit."[73] The religious experiences of the Hebrews and the pre-Islamic Arabs grew from the same soil, and their roots were intertwined in a common human experience.[74] Yet, from that soil the Jewish and Islamic traditions developed two distinctive views of God. For the Hebrews, the God of the patriarchs struggles with a particular people. In their literature, God walks, sees, and hears, is angry and repents. God has a covenantal relationship with his people. For the Arabs, God in the Qur'an is completely other and transcendent and can only be described by his attributes. What distinguished these two religious experiences, asserts Macdonald, was their depiction of the personality of the one God, the Hebrews providing a more anthropomorphic reflection and the Arabs a totally transcendent Other. It should be highlighted that for Macdonald, the Qur'an was a product of this human religious experience. Like other Orientalists, Macdonald believed the Qur'an to be a human compilation, albeit an Arabic literary masterpiece, composed by the Prophet. The Qur'an was to be read along with the Psalms, Proverbs, and other poetic and prophetic literature of the Hebrew Bible to fully appreciate and understand the world and worship God. The Hebrew Bible and the Qur'an represent a fugue of the Semitic desire to express truths of the human experience before God.[75]

What can be said of this Protestant use of Arabic and the Qur'an as part of nineteenth-century biblical studies in seminary education? Of course, one can raise objections to the assumptions made by both Lansing and Macdonald that there was a uniform literary and religious culture throughout the ancient Near East that was shared by all kinds of people, for which Arabic can provide access. Such assertions gloss over the vicissitudes of history and even run roughshod over the development of language and the diversity of medieval Muslim linguistic interpretations of Arabic. While Macdonald does recognize that the descriptions of God in the Qur'an differ from the personality of God in the Hebrew Bible, he argues that "in essence, in arrangement of ideas, in spirit, in form even, it is impossible to make a distinction between" the Hebraic and Arab Islamic worldview. His view reflects the Orientalist perspective of "the unchanging East."[76] Nevertheless, within nineteenth-century Protestant seminary education there were important reasons to engage with Arabic Islamic texts. First, there was widespread acceptance that Hebrew was part of a larger family of Semitic languages, and that those languages were an aid to understanding the nuances of the Hebrew language, whose lexicon was limited to the Masoretic text of the Hebrew Bible. The hundreds of medieval commentaries on the Qur'an, with their exploration of the minutiae of Arabic grammar and syntax, provided a great reservoir of literature to analyze philologically. However, these commentaries were only available to a select few Protestant scholars who were adept at handling these Arabic sources. Even though the teaching of Arabic in seminaries ended in the twentieth century, it still is present through the Arabic references in the BDB, which is still an important reference tool for those seminarians still required to learn Hebrew.[77]

Second, Arabic was not seen as exclusive to Islam. Rather, Arabic was the cultural expression of all the people of the medieval Near East: Jews, Christians, Muslims, and even Arab polytheists. Saadia Gaon's translation of the Torah into Arabic and its inclusion in the polyglot Bible signified that Arabic was inherently a biblical language. By the 1870s there were several new Arabic translations of the Bible that had been published by various missionary agencies for use primarily among Eastern Arabic-speaking Christian communities. The Society of Propagation of Christian Knowledge (SPCK) of the Anglican Church sponsored a Bible translation project by Faris al-Shidyaq that was completed in 1851. The American Mission in Syria finished its translation of the complete Bible in 1865 under the auspices of Eli Smith, Butrus Bustani, and Cornelius Van Dyke (for whom the translation continues to be known). In response to this "biblical Cold War," the Jesuits responded with their own Arabic translation based on the Latin Vulgate. While these translations were undertaken for use among the Arabic-speaking religious communities of the Near East, a wide variety of European and American biblical scholars took part in the editorial and review process, and in the case of the Van Dyke translation, it was published in New York

City while Van Dyke was visiting at Union seminary. Thus, Arabic was not alien to, but rather a constitutive part of, a world Christianity being made more available to seminary biblical scholars who commented on and read proofs of the newly translated Arabic Bibles.[78]

It is interesting to note, however, that for professors like Briggs, Lansing, and Macdonald, who were conversant with the medieval Islamic tradition, the medieval Arabic Christian theological tradition was not utilized or even highlighted as a continuation of this Arabic religious tradition. The Arabic Bible and the Qur'an became the focus of an Arabic expression of Semitic monotheism, but there was no interest in or evaluation of the deep Arabic Christian theological tradition that explores the language and understanding of the Bible and God in response to the development of Islamic orthodoxy.[79] Perhaps this was due to a Protestant bias against Eastern Catholic or Orthodox traditions. If Briggs, Lansing, and Macdonald had explored the important Arabic Christian expressions of language and theology, one wonders how their research and writing would have added to their views of Arabic not only as a culturally Semitic and Jewish expression of God but specifically as a Christian expression of God. How would this have changed their general perspective that Islam grew out of a specifically Jewish milieu?[80]

A third reason why Arabic was taught in seminaries was pure, unadulterated naive curiosity. It is important to remember that for most American scholars during this period, their exposure to Arabic would have been purely textual as part of an overall Orientalist worldview. The American colonial antipathy toward the Barbary Pirates noted earlier faded by the 1830s. Hostility leveled at the Ottoman Empire in response to the atrocities against Armenians and Assyrian Christians was yet to be expressed. Even then, when American missionaries in the Ottoman Empire began to speak out about genocide against the Armenians and Assyrians in the 1890s and during the years from 1915 to 1923, the events were interpreted through the lens of Turkish despotism.[81] It was the Turks who would be branded as evil, not Arabs, the Arabic language, Arabic culture, or to some extent even Islam. It was, rather, "Oriental" despotism. In other words, from the 1830s until the end of the nineteenth century, the Near East itself was not a threat to American Christian identity but was still a place of wonder and mystery. Americans had been streaming to the Holy Lands in large numbers for pilgrimages, adventure, and curiosity, and many wrote about their exotic experiences.[82] Moreover, the Chicago World's Fair and the 1893 Parliament of the World Religions brought to the American heartland an image of the Near East and Islam that was strange but exciting. From the 1830s till the 1890s, the followers of Muhammad were not considered an existential threat, an idea that would later develop within Protestant evangelical thought in the 1970s and 1980s. On the contrary, there was much to learn from what was believed to have been Muhammad's careful crafting of ancient Arabic wisdom literature.

By the 1890s, the philological study of biblical and cognate biblical languages had reached a level that rivaled the study in Germany. American textual scholars could hold their own, and Americans contributed significantly to scholarship that revised the King James version of the Bible. However, within the next twenty years, during the rise in interest in mission societies to evangelize among Muslims, the study and use of the Arabic language disappeared in American seminary curricula. What happened? There were at least three primary reasons that involved curricular changes in seminaries and universities.

First, in the mid-1880s seminaries began to introduce into their curricula more areas of study beyond the Bible, theology, and history. There had been a growing call for more practical components to education, like preaching, hymnody, and administration. In addition, there were newfound scientific areas of study to assist pastoral care—such as psychology, sociology, and comparative religions. The addition of further topics of study within a three-year curriculum could only mean that some other courses needed to be shortened in length and depth to make room. Students were also allowed to select certain courses as specialized electives rather than as a required part of the curriculum. This was part of a broader movement in American higher education to provide new pedagogies for teaching and learning, such as the seminar format and advanced elective courses. Cognate biblical languages fell into the elective category.

The second reason Arabic disappeared from seminary curricula was that the study of cognate biblical languages became part of a broader field of ancient Near East studies. As the philological study of the biblical and other Semitic languages developed, there was an increasing specialization in these languages. Charles Briggs and Francis Brown at Union began to insist that students arrive in their classes already prepared to read Hebrew. This required the creation of independent language classes, normally staffed by recent graduates. As senior faculty delved into the intricacies of the biblical texts and engaged in textual criticism, they had less time to provide overall instruction in the cognate languages that had been brought into view through the polyglot Bible period.

Third, there was a shift in focus in biblical studies from the philology of ancient biblical texts to other material forms of antiquity. The pure scriptural philological interest in the Near East languages opened up to an interest in specific ancient Near East cultures—Assyria, Phoenicia, and Egypt. By the turn of the twentieth century, Near Eastern archaeology or Egyptology, became a prominent and exciting way through which ancient Near Eastern texts were approached and interpreted, that is, within the broader material culture left behind. The study of Near Eastern languages and civilizations became prevalent in universities and was eventually dropped from seminary curricula altogether.

New and larger universities, such as the University of Chicago, Johns Hopkins, and New York University, were successful in securing private and government funding to explore and dig up the ancient Near East to compete with European universities. As American universities established themselves and became successful institutions, they were able to draw on private and public funds to support their educational endeavors and projects. Seminaries, still run by individual denominations, could not keep up with a financial arms race of higher education. Government funding for these types of projects only expanded over time. For example, well into the twentieth century, at the end of World War II, the US government realized that the Middle East was a necessary strategic region to counter Russian foreign policy and became an important front of the Cold War. Government funds were secured to provide Middle East studies centers for national strategic purposes at major universities like Harvard, Princeton, and the University of Michigan.[83] Islamic studies programs began to emerge from these centers, while seminaries abdicated their interest in Arabic and Islam.

It was during the 1890s that universities reorganized themselves and came into their own. The historic boarding college that had focused on reading classics developed into a complex institution with different departments and "schools." Higher education in America was becoming more professionalized. This affected seminaries in many ways. Bachelor's programs became more structured, which meant that postbaccalaureate programs had to step up their expectations of education. In addition, as universities developed their own graduate programs, they began to draw on the pool of available seminary students, especially those who were interested in the ancient Near East. For example, Columbia College organized its Faculty of Arts and began offering courses in a structured curriculum. Due to the proximity of Union to Columbia, it began to draw advanced-level seminary students directly into its courses, such as Gottheil's Arabic and Islamic studies classes, leaving the seminary classes to focus on biblical exegesis and theology.[84]

This was not to be the case at Hartford, however. Arabic continued to be offered not only as part of the study of biblical languages but also for the purpose of Christian mission to the Muslim world. In the final chapter we will turn to those graduates of the seminaries who went out as missionaries and engaged not only with texts but with real people. However, the advanced study and comparison of ancient Near Eastern religious texts also led to comparison of the religious beliefs and practices of adherents. The next chapter explores how the study of various languages led to the study of various religions, ancient and contemporary. Islam came to be categorized in a variety of ways, but always in its relationship to Judaism and Christianity.

5

The Study of Islam as a "Comparative Religion"

The study of ancient Near Eastern languages was not the only specialized field that led to the intersection of Christianity with the study of
Islam in seminaries. By the late seventeenth century, European scholars
became interested in ancient cultures and religions. Ultimately, however,
the study of ancient religions expanded into the area of the phenomena
of religion as a human experience. This chapter explores the development and shift in interest from ancient religions to living religions, their
commonalities and differences. As part of the Enlightenment project to
observe and categorize, Islam was compared with both Western Protestant Christianity and other Eastern religions. Islam came to be viewed
as an "Oriental" religion that was somehow deficient but at least shared
more in common with Christianity than other more "primitive" or
"ethnic" religions. Islam's relationship with Protestant Christianity was
contested, at times an important part in the development of human civilization and at others, evidence of a backward East.

As we have seen, a number of the English Orientalist works on Islam
were available to American colonial and early republican clergy in their
private libraries. Many of these books were later donated or purchased
by seminary libraries. Two common works that show up in these private and seminary libraries were copies of Alexander Ross's *Pansebeia*
(1657) and William Turner's *History of All Religions in the World* (1695).
These books became popular throughout the eighteenth century, especially as the Enlightenment shifted focus away from the idea of religion as a miraculous revelation to positivism, which sought rational
human explanations for the development of religion. As Ziad elMarsafy
notes, in seventeenth-century England there was a veritable "paradigm
shift" regarding the view of other religions as colonial and imperial expansion brought scholars into further contact with other cultures and
religions.[1] The discovery of religious texts in the Near East led biblical scholars into a new world. In Germany, the History of Religions

School—*Religionsgeschichteschule*—begun by Julius Wellhausen through his thesis of the Documentary Hypothesis of the Pentateuch, prompted its adherents to see the Bible in the context of a broader ancient Near Eastern culture. Ancient Near Eastern texts were read in parallel with biblical stories to determine the origins and forms of the Bible. German scholars of the nineteenth century developed a variety of historical-critical methods to do this with great acumen. In reading up on the latest German biblical scholarship, American professors and students also became interested in the philological study not only of the traditional biblical languages of Hebrew, Aramaic, Syriac, Arabic, Greek, and Latin but of ancient Near Eastern cultures.

In reading Akkadian and Egyptian texts alongside the Bible, for example, scholars began to construct images of the ancient Near Eastern religions. In addition to written texts, one of the means utilized to discover ancient Near Eastern cultures was the newly developed and exciting field of archaeology. Archaeology provided academics with tools to compare ancient material culture, that is, buildings and relics. Eventually, the History of Religions School, which had done so much to try to uncover the world "behind the texts," would give way to the term "science of religions"—*Religionswissenschaft*, that is, an objective study of religion. While the terms "History of Religions School" and "science of religions" were often used interchangeably, by the twentieth century they came to recognize different fields, the latter focusing more on the phenomenology or even the sociology of religions, while the History of Religions School continued to focus, in this case, on text critical approaches to the Bible. As Clare K. Rothschild has noted, these definitions are "slippery," with many "variations."[2] American seminary professors used the tools of the History of Religions School while never jettisoning their underlying belief that in the end the text told a theological story.

The nineteenth-century scholars of the science of religions began to compare the Abrahamic religions with what European and American scholars considered the more "primitive, prehistoric, or rudimentary religions."[3] This shift in comparing different religious traditions with Christianity was not only a product of Orientalism per se, that is, a Western attempt to describe, organize, and ultimately control swathes of the world it conceptualized as "the East," as Edward Said has defined the term Orientalism, but it was also part of the nineteenth-century attempt to scientifically classify and understand the natural world. As Eric J. Sharpe has noted, Darwin's *Origin of the Species*, first published in 1859, began to provide a "Darwinian canopy" that covered over all fields of observation, including the study of religions, past and present.[4]

In 1905, Louis Henry Jordan (1855–1923), a Canadian Presbyterian minister, published *Comparative Religion, Its Genesis and Growth*, which was the result of years of traveling and researching in Europe and around the world.[5] Jordan advanced the idea that comparative religions was a new and distinct field of theology. He wrote, "Comparative Religion is that Science which compares the origin, structure, and characteristics of the various Religions of the world, with the view of determining their genuine agreements and differences, the measure of relation in which they stand one to another, and their relative superiority or inferiority when regarded as types."[6]

Jordan would go on to describe the contours of the fields that had taken root in American and European universities that would later come to be known as religious studies. He notes the determination in his writing to justify the work of "placing the numerous Religions of the world, side by side, in order that, deliberately comparing and contrasting them, it may frame a reliable estimate of their respective claims . . . without haste and without prejudice."[7] As a Christian minister, Jordan explicitly states that Christian mission still has a role to play in the engagement of other religions, but so too does the role of a scientific analysis of other religions based on their own merits. As Jordan was writing at the height of the "Great Missionary Age," it might be suggested that he was swimming upstream against the predominant sentiment of Protestant thought of the day. However, while he may have been one of the more systematic recorders of early religious studies in its infancy, he was not the only one interested in such a comparative approach. In fact, there had been a significant interest in comparative studies nearly thirty years before. The interest in studying other religious traditions for purposes other than evangelization did have its roots in the History of Religions School among biblical scholars. The original research on ancient religious texts expanded further from those texts to the contemporary beliefs and practices of living adherents of other religions. This shift was embraced by many professors in American theological seminaries for a variety of different reasons. Certainly, those interested in Christian missions saw the new field as a tool for better methods of evangelizing other cultures. However, some saw this method as a way to better understand the roots of Christianity, in the case of comparing Jewish and Islamic traditions. Others saw the method as a way to better understand human psychology—what makes humans tick religiously. Nevertheless, as the discipline of comparative religions developed and became more sophisticated, many of its American adherents maintained a position that American Protestant Christianity had demonstrated itself to be the pinnacle of human spiritual achievement. In this vein, Islam was viewed in multiple ways, as both part of the Near Eastern monotheistic prophetic tradition but also as a heterodox form of Christianity. Most comparative religions scholars believed that Islam was an important part of the human religious story, but fell short.

Jordan was not the originator of the field of comparative studies, but rather was the ambassador of it. The person credited for developing the Western field of comparative religion was the German scholar, Max Müller (1823–1900).[8] In a series of lectures delivered in 1870, appropriately entitled "Introduction to the Science of Religion," Müller set in motion the field of comparative religions, or as it ultimately developed into, the study of "World Religions."[9] This chapter examines the origin and development of the budding field of comparative religions, specifically as it dealt with the conceptualization of Islam. This new field was grafted onto the curricula of the seminaries from the 1870s through the early part of the twentieth century. Comparative studies took root in North America in the seminary system first and later became established in the universities as what we now call religious studies. Comparative religious studies provided seminarians many opportunities to learn about other religions, especially Islam.

Max Müller and Comparative Religions

The German-born Max Müller taught for most of his career at Oxford, as the professor of comparative philology. Trained in Sanskrit, he is most well known for his translation of the Upanishads and other Indic texts. It was from his deep engagement with Sanskrit texts that he began to ponder the broader relationship not only of languages but of the religions themselves. He began to ask why humans in all cultures developed a spiritual or religious response to life and wondered what might be held in common.

In 1856, Müller published *Comparative Mythology: Lectures on the Science of Language*, and in 1873, his *Introduction to the Science of Religion* was ultimately what drew attention to his work in the field of comparative religions. However, Müller's most popular and widely read publication was his fifty-volume anthology, *The Sacred Books of the East*, which he edited from 1879 to 1910. This project included a variety of international collaborators who translated many of the known religious texts of what have become known as the world religions. The Qur'an, which was included in volumes 6 and 9, was translated and edited in 1880 by E. H. Palmer, professor of Arabic at Cambridge. This new Qur'anic translation became readily available in the early twentieth century as the whole series was published together as a standard reference collection in seminary libraries.

When Müller began exploring the relationship between religions, he started by creating a threefold designation for classifying the associated languages: Semitic, Aryan, and Turanian (the latter was his term for all East Asian languages). Judaism, Christianity, and Islam were grouped together as the Semitic religions, while Brahmanism (what is now generally called Hinduism), Zoroastrianism, and Buddhism were classed as Aryan. Müller's use of these terms—especially "Aryan"—which was originally intended to classify languages, has come to carry racial dimensions. In fact, he has been charged with inventing the "Aryan race." His term later became synonymous with antisemitism in the twentieth century.[10] The final categorization was the Turanian group of religions, such as Confucianism and Taoism. While this nomenclature never took hold, the classification of "Eastern religions" did.

Müller's categorization of the Semitic languages was broadly accepted by American biblical scholars. Biblical scholars had already made use of the comparison of Near Eastern languages to produce the various polyglot Bibles. Church history scholars also began to use Müller's linguistic categories. It was only a matter of time, then, before comparisons between the religious beliefs and practices and then the theology of the religions were studied in seminary classes.

While the arrangement of religions fit into the larger scientific worldview of the "Darwinian canopy," Müller did not see these "world religions" as part of an evolution of human spirituality, of an ever-evolving actualization of human achievement from the earliest or more "primitive" religions—what were often designated as "ethnic religions"—to Protestant Christianity as the moral pinnacle of human religious belief. On the contrary, his examination of these different spiritual systems led him to believe that there were important constitutive elements in all religions. "Yet more and more the image of man, in whatever clime we meet him, rises before us, noble and pure from the very beginning. . . . As far as we can trace back the footsteps of man, even on the lowest strata of history, we see that the divine gift of a sound and sober intellect belonged to him from the very first; and the idea of a humanity emerging slowly from the depths of an animal brutality can never again be maintained again in our century."[11]

Müller was arguing not simply against Darwin's "origin of the species" but against social Darwinism or, more accurately, a "religious Darwinism." In his 1870 lectures on comparative theology Müller argued at length that in comparing religions one should be careful not to be drawn into one's own preconceived notions about "borrowing"—that is, one religion serving as the basis for others. He provides several examples of how some scholars erroneously argued that Semitic forms of religion actually had their roots in Brahmic traditions from India.[12] Müller was cautious about, if not simply flat out against such interpretations of religious Darwinism. This would not be the case across the pond, however. It became quite popular among American biblical scholars, including Henry Preserved Smith at Union, among others, who argued that as Christianity borrowed from its ancient Jewish sources, so too Islam borrowed from Judaism and Eastern Christian forms.

It was not until later in his career, the last decade of the nineteenth century, that Müller wrote about Islam. This was after a visit he made to Turkey, during the Hamidian reforms, where he had discussions with several Muslim scholars, whom he does not name. In his article, Müller reviews the six pillars of belief of Islam and argues that there is much in common with orthodox Christianity. In fact, he writes that if Christians were to understand Jesus' title as "Son of God" metaphorically, there would be general agreement with Muslims that Jesus was the "Word of God," as this is a Qur'anic term and understanding (see 4:171, for example). He also argues that the doctrine of the Trinity is a later historical development of Christian theology and that Muhammad's critique of this doctrine was a valid response to heretical Christian sects in or around Arabia in the seventh century, a common perspective of the Qur'an that is still held.[13]

Müller is also critical of Western Christians who concentrate on the view of Muhammad as a "sensualist," with their myopic critique of his polygamous lifestyle. Rather, Müller asserts that if his actions were understood within their historical framework of seventh-century Arabia, where women outnumbered men, especially after the death of warriors in battle, his polygamous activities should be seen as a way to provide protection for women. He underlines this suggestion by noting that the Prophet only had one wife, Khadijah, for twenty-five years. It was only after her death that he began to marry various women to support and protect them as the circumstances arose. Finally, Müller states that Western Christians should focus more on the prophetic narrative of Muhammad's life, that of a lowly shepherd boy who gained followers for his vision of the oneness of God and the judgment against idolatry, rather than concentrating on old and tired medieval tropes of his personality.

After Müller we do see a shift, or at least a different emphasis, among American Protestants scholars in their critiques and classification of Islam. Interestingly, while Americans used Müller's terminology, they came down on the opposite side of the fence as Müller. Among American Protestant scholars of religion, the focus of Islam shifts from its traditional role as an anti-Christian or heretical Christian sect to that of an Arab tribal religion of the Near East. As noted by Tomoko Masuzawa, as a Semitic religion Islam became "viewed as narrow, rigid, and stunted, and its essential attributes were said to be defined by the national, racial, and ethnic character of the Arabs, the most bellicose and adversarial of the Semites."[14] Thus, contrary to Müller's argument against an evolution of religions, American Protestants wholeheartedly accepted the evolution of Christianity as the universal message that would transcend the tribal religions of the Israelites and the Arabs. White Protestant Christianity would become the apex of a religious Darwinism.

Early American Comparative Religion

Müller was not the first scholar to address the phenomenon of religious plurality, but he did create widespread interest in the field on both sides of the Atlantic. American curiosity about the topic of comparative religions in the colonial period was purely a hobby of those with enough leisure time to pursue such matters. Jeffrey Einboden has shown how wealthy aristocrats of the colonial period were able to pursue their linguistic and cultural interests in other religions. The Boston Unitarian pastor William Bentley, for example, was able to hire captains and agents to procure Eastern texts and artifacts from abroad.[15] Slowly but surely these American Orientalists acquired more information about the wider world and its peoples, their cultures, and their religions. They came to be considered the North American experts on the Orient, and the new American government relied on them to provide information and even translate Arabic and Ottoman Turkish letters.[16] By the nineteenth century, however, another group of New England intellectuals was curious about the "newly discovered" world of religions, including the world of Islam. Two in particular are worth noting, Hannah Adams as the first prominently recognized American woman intellectual and James Freeman Clarke as the father of the American field of comparative religions.

Hannah Adams (1755–1831) was an incredibly popular author primarily due to the novelty of her status as a woman from outside the class of male landed aristocracy. She was more than likely the first professionally published American woman author.[17] Among other books, Adams published in 1784 what was ultimately to become titled *A Dictionary of All Religions and Religious Denominations, Jewish, Heathen, Mahometan, and Christian, Ancient and Modern*. It was so popular that by 1817 there had already been three editions. The dictionary provided a handy reference for any reader interested in the broad scope of world religions during this period of Darwinian classification. Whereas the previous century's taxonomy focused on the traditional fourfold "Jew, Christian, Mohammedan, and Pagan" of Hugo Grotius, Adams's dictionary opened the door for a wide assortment of religious traditions from antiquity up to the present.

While Adams was not strongly attached to her Unitarian beliefs, the central belief of the Oneness of God in Islam did naturally interest her.

Sandwiched between "Magdalenettes" and "Manicheans," the lengthy entry on "Mahometans" in her dictionary includes a short biography of Muhammad's life, drawn primarily from Humphrey Prideaux's critique of the Prophet. The majority of the entry, however, includes an explanation of the pillars of Islamic beliefs and practices, a description of the distinctions between Sunnis and Shi'a, and a short description of Islamic theology, all drawn primarily from George Sale's "Preliminary Discourse" in his translation of the Qur'an. In several instances, Adams makes comparisons between Islam and Christianity by equating the Qur'an to the Bible and the caliph to St. Peter.[18]

Adams's entry on "Mahometans" is not a remarkable addition to what other Americans might have known about Islam from other sources, but Adams' popularity helped lead more readers into further fascination with Islam as an "exotic" religion. The format of short entries and a collection of interesting topics was appealing to a growing American reading public. Despite her being a female author without aristocratic connections or education, her dictionary was able to find its way into many libraries. This was an important milestone that went against the patriarchy of the day. The dictionary also served as a convenient reference work for the growing seminary libraries of the time. After all, what student would not prefer to garner information quickly using a handbook or dictionary, rather than reading through the other larger and more antiquated English works on Islam that were available?

Another example of how other comparative views of religions were making their way into the private reading spaces of Americans was Samuel M. Schmucker's *History of All Religions: Containing a Statement of the Origin, Development, Doctrines, Forms of Worship, and Government of All the Religious Denominations in the World*, published in 1859. Schmucker was not from the same social and cultural tradition as Adams' New England Unitarianism but was reared in mid-Atlantic Lutheranism. The son of Gettysburg seminary president Samuel S. Schmucker, Samuel Mosheim Schmucker attended Gettysburg seminary in 1843 and was ordained by the West Pennsylvania Synod in 1844. He served as a pastor in Lewistown, Pennsylvania, until 1845, and then at St. Michael's in Germantown, Pennsylvania, until 1849. He retired from the ministry and went on to study law and write history.[19] *History of All Religions* provides further insight into the information on religions that was being circulated to the broader reading public. By 1883, the book had gone through six different editions and found its way into the seminary libraries.

This work is encyclopedic in nature, providing entries on major religious traditions as well as Christian denominations. Schmucker's ten-page entry on "Mahommedans" relies primarily on Sale's "Preliminary Discourses." Like Adams's entry, Schmucker's provides an overview of Muhammad's life and the basic beliefs and practices of Muslims, as well as an introduction to various sects within Islam. In addition to including references to the four major Sunni legal schools (Shafi'i, Hanafi, Maliki, and Hanbali), Schmucker also describes the Sunni theological disputes among the "Montazalites, Hashbemians, Nohamians, Jabehians." Schmucker is referring here to the variety of medieval theological schools known as Mua'atlzili that developed in the ninth century. His anglicization of the names of these views is misleading, and the various complicated and nuanced debates about God's supreme knowledge and human free will were issues of which he most certainly was not aware.[20] Schmucker does rehash some of the widely noted Christian accusations of Muhammad, such as that he was an impostor, "pretended to receive revelations," and had to "compel mankind to embrace" Islam.[21] Like Adams, Schmucker does not directly engage with Muslim sources, but only European Orientalist ones. What is significant about Schmucker's entry, however, is that the life of Muhammad is no longer the sole focus of interest or even the center of moral disparagement that we find in earlier references; rather, there is further interest in the beliefs and practices of Muslims and their theological diversity.

While Adams's and Schmucker's dictionaries provided easily accessible information on Islam for Americans and became available as reference works in the seminary libraries, it was another prominent New England Unitarian who would grapple with the same questions over comparative religions as did Max Müller, and whose work would dramatically affect what seminarians were taught about Islam from their professors. Writing at the same time as Müller, James Freeman Clarke (1810–1888) provided Americans with their first opportunity to read and explore the concepts and implications of the "science of religion." In 1868, three years before he published his own *Introduction to the Science of Religion*, Clarke serialized "Ten Great Religions: An Essay in Comparative Theology" in the *Atlantic Monthly*. Shortly after the completion of the series, it was published as *Ten Great Religions: An Essay in Comparative Theology* in 1871.

Covering the major religions of the world, Clarke classifies them as the "catholic religions" as opposed to the "ethnic religions." The "catholic religions" transcend continents and peoples while the "ethnic religions" appeal only to an indigenous community and culture from which the religion grew. Buddhism, Christianity, and Islam are considered "catholic religions" because they have adherents all around the globe, located and embodied in different cultures. However, Confucianism, Hinduism, and African traditional religions have been confined to particular ethnicities or "races" of peoples, as Clarke labeled them.

Clarke argues that among the great "catholic religions" (what Müller also calls the "great religions"), Christianity is the most advanced. He states that while all religions possess "some truths . . . Christianity possesses all; and that, while they are stationary, Christianity is progressive."[22] On the one hand, Clarke attempts to provide a fair and appreciative evaluation of these religious traditions, showing both the good and bad in all. On the other hand, he argues that while the religions have some good and truth, they are all a "preparation for Christianity."[23] Clarke's comparison of religious traditions concludes with what would become the traditional American Protestant understanding of comparative religions. Contrary to Müller, he wrote that "each religion of the world is a step in the progress of humanity" that finds its end in a higher religion, which is Protestant Christianity as the pinnacle of human spiritual achievement.[24]

It should be noted that the underlying theory behind Clarke's view of comparative religions was a nineteenth-century racial theory, what he called "the science of ethnology." It is worth quoting this in full, noting the derogatory language that became acceptable terminology of the day. He writes, "That mankind is so divided into races of men it would seem hardly possible to deny. It is proved by physiology, by psychology, by glossology [philology], and by civil history. Physiology shows us anatomical differences between races. There are as marked and real differences between the skull of a Hindoo and that of a Chinaman as between the skulls of an Englishman and a negro. . . . Now we find that each race, beside its special moral qualities, seems also to have special religious qualities, which cause it to tend toward some one kind of religion."[25]

Clarke's view of comparative religion was racist in nature, eschewing what Müller was arguing in England. Clarke's view became the underlying framework among most American Protestant views of comparative religion at the time, and certainly the predominant view held at the first Parliament of the World Religions in 1893, that American Protestantism was not only spiritually superior but was part of a superior culture and civilization.

Clarke tackles Islam in chapter 12 of *The Great Religions*, the last before he concludes with Christianity, even though Christianity predated the development of Islam. He proffers that of all the religions of the world, Islam is the most interesting and curious from the Christian perspective. It is the only religion to come after Christianity and create its own new civilization "in the broad daylight of history."[26] In reviewing the history and beliefs of Islam, Clarke availed himself of the latest Western biographies of Muhammad, including Sprenger, Weil, and Muir. He also used Renan, de Perceval, Carlyle, and Goethe's evaluations of Muhammad's life. Clarke does provide a brief, patronizing nod to the writings of the Indian Muslim scholar Syed Ahmad Khan, who wrote rebuttals to Western studies on Islam. Clarke retorts that "something, however, is always gained by hearing what the believers in a system have to say in its behalf, and these essays of the Mohammedan scholar [Khan] may help us in this way."[27] This being said, he never examines Syed's views and simply piles on the Western scholarly critical tradition. While Clarke appreciates Muhammad's intention to preach monotheism to the Arabs, he excoriates the Prophet for perpetuating a God of the Qur'an who is an Oriental despot.

Accepting the traditional biography of Muhammad's life, Clarke shows sympathy for Muhammad's sincerity as a religious leader. He writes, "Now, it is impossible to read the detailed accounts of this part of the life of Mohammed and have any doubt of his profound sincerity. His earliest converts were his bosom-friends and the people of his household, who were intimately acquainted with his private life. Nor does a man easily begin an ambitious course of deception at the age of forty; having lived till that time as a quiet, peaceful, and unobtrusive citizen, what was he to gain by this career?"[28] Whereas he had been a successful merchant in Mecca, his later years were spent preaching the unity of God in the face of Meccan opposition and persecution. Clarke compares

Muhammad's steadfastness to Martin Luther's stance against the pope. However, when describing Muhammad's *hijra*, his movement from Mecca to Medina to become the head of the state there, Clarke posits, "What sadder tragedy is there than to see a great soul thus conquered by success?"[29] In taking up his role as the leader of the community in Medina, Muhammad now takes on the mantle of power, which he uses for his own benefit, writes Clarke. He then compares Muhammad's decision to that of the temptation of Jesus by Satan, who offered Jesus the kingdoms of the world if only he would bow down and worship him. It is in this moment that Clarke suggests that Muhammad's character changes and he gives in to worldly power and violence. In the end of his assessment of Muhammad, Clarke writes, "He was a great man, one of the greatest ever sent upon earth. He was a man of the deepest convictions, and for many years of the purest purposes, and was only drawn down at last by using low means for a good end."[30]

After the hijra and his ascension as a political ruler, Clarke offers that Muhammad was overcome by "worldly purposes and temporal triumphs."[31] As the political leader in Medina, Muhammad then led a new state that expanded throughout the peninsula through violent means, and after his death, his companions continued the expansive policies to create a new empire. Thus, for Clarke, in establishing a state, Muhammad relinquished his role as a spiritual renewer and gave in to mundane power.

Continuing further, Clarke reviews the condition of Islam in various Muslim-majority nations around the world during the eighteenth and nineteenth centuries. He notes that whereas the original effect of Islam in seventh-century Arabia was to instill a moral monotheism as a necessary protest against the barbaric polytheism of the Arabs, Muhammad's emphasis on the "will of God" and submission to God's power led to political domination and social decay.

> The merits and demerits, the good and evil, of Mohammedanism are to be found in this, its central idea concerning God. It has taught submission, obedience, patience; but it has fostered a wilful [sic] individualism. It has made social life lower. Its governments are not governments. Its virtues are stoical. It makes life barren and empty. It encourages a savage pride and cruelty. It makes men tyrants or slaves, women puppets, reli-

gion the submission to an infinite despotism. Time is that it came to an end. Its work is done. It is a hard, cold, cruel, empty faith, which should give way to the purer forms of a higher civilization. No doubt, Mohammedanism was needed when it came, and has done good service in its time. But its time is almost passed.[32]

Clarke's perspective was not unique. We have already seen how Archibald Alexander, in his *Brief Outline of the Evidences of the Christian Religion*, had made the same argument that Protestant Christianity leads to prosperity and Islam leads nations to decay.[33] Underlying Clarke's interpretation was his overall assumption that the inherent progress of human spirituality would ultimately lead a nation to adopt Christianity, Unitarianism specifically. Contrary to Müller, Clarke believed that Christianity fulfilled the necessary moral and spiritual needs of humanity in the modern world. Given that the United States was living through its own industrial revolution and expansion westward toward and into the Pacific, Clarke's views represent a confident America. Gone were the days when the government had no answer to the repeated piracy attacks on its ships and the enslavement of its sailors. After four years of a civil war and entry into a robust Reconstruction, as a New Englander, Clarke was feeling confident in the United States' role as a world culture, ready to examine others from paternalistic heights.

Courses on the "Great" and "Ethnic" Religions

While many would not associate themselves with Clarke's Unitarian views, his embrace of religious Darwinism was widely accepted within Protestant seminaries. That humans were religious beings set apart in a hierarchy of the ordered world was an accepted American Christian principle. Islam, then, was generally viewed as an expression of human religiosity in a step along the path toward a more morally and spiritually pure society that was ultimately achieved by Protestant Christianity. It is important to recognize that both Müller and Clarke evaluated the "great" or "ethnic" religions and weighed them on the basis of what they perceived as their spiritual, theological, and ethical perspectives. The complex relationship among state power, social contexts, and economics was overlooked.

James C. Moffat (1811–1888), professor of church history at Princeton, responded to the growing interest in comparative religions through his lectures that were ultimately published in 1873 as *A Comparative History of Religions*.[34] Between 1873 and 1889, the book went through fifteen editions. Volume 1 begins with the phenomenology of religion, of "man as a religious being," and then provides a survey of the ancient religions of the Persians, Indians, Egyptians, and Assyrians. Moffat lauds the role of previous Orientalist studies of these religions' ancient texts as keys to unlocking the common principles of the different religions. Volume 2 of *A Comparative History* explores various spiritual themes shared by the ancient religions. For Moffat, humans are created as spiritual beings, with freedom and will. "True" human beings actualize these spiritual aspects of human existence not only individually but socially. "True religion" liberates humanity from its "abject submission to natural forces and bald necessity, as well as from moral corruption" by providing ethical guidance for society.[35] Thus, for Moffat, the movement of history is not only a progression from one civilization to another, building upon the cultural or scientific advancements of previous societies, but a progression of spiritual and moral projects. Western Christianity, he posits, is the evidence of human progress and achievement, of overcoming "barbarism" with "civilization."[36] Moffat concludes that the Gospel responds not only to individual spiritual human needs but also to social and temporal ones. However, Moffat warns that the "true civilized human" can be derailed by falling back into moral degeneracy, or sin, by following his baser or more "savage" or "primitive" ways.

Ironically, Moffat argues that while civilization progresses through the purer forms of religion, humanity is merely returning to reclaim the true human spirituality that was given by God at the Garden of Eden. True religion was present from the beginning, but as humans have moments of regression, there has been the need to return to the original form of "true religion" through the messages of the prophets like Abraham, Moses, Jesus, and even Muhammad.[37] These reform movements come to correct the backsliding toward polytheism: Abraham comes to correct the religion of Noah's generation, Moses to correct the polytheism of Egypt, Jesus to correct Pharisaism, Muhammad to correct the polytheism of Darius of Persia, and even the Buddha came to correct the polytheistic excesses of the Brahmins.[38] All true religion actually points back to one monotheistic origin, argues Moffat. In this way, Moffat is unknowingly expressing the classic Islamic doctrine of the *fitra* of humanity. For Moffat, Islam represents the best elements of true religion by insisting on worship of the one God. He does not, however, draw on any direct Islamic sources for his ideas, nor does he delve into the biography of Muhammad. Rather, he sees Islam as fitting into the larger movement of history as a positive force, but culturally limited to the Arab culture from which it arose.

Francis L. Patton (1843–1932) was called to Princeton as the Stuart professor of the relations of philosophy and science to Christian religion in 1881. The chair was created in response to the debates about religion and science. There was a growing concern among Presbyterian clergy and professors to find a Christian voice to respond to growing public views about science as a critic or antagonist to revealed religion in light of Darwinian ideas. However, it would be almost another twenty-five years before Patton, other Princeton faculty, and its graduates contributed to "The Fundamentals" in 1928—pamphlets that set forth the traditional Protestant views commonly known as fundamentalist Christianity.[39] Nevertheless, in the fall of 1882, Patton began giving lectures on "The Relations of Philosophy of Science to Religion" and "Theism." Lecture notes written by Patton's student and future doyen of Presbyterian missions, Robert Speer, record Patton as stating that "Mohammedanism [has] much in common with Judaism."[40] According to Speer's notes, we see the continuation in the view that the monotheistic religions in general were an important expression of true religion, even if he did not provide an assessment of the beliefs and practices of adherents.

By the 1890s, Müller's and Clarke's concepts of comparative religions were fully employed in seminary curricula in one way or another. In 1893, John Preston Searle, the professor of didactic and polemic theology at New Brunswick seminary, was offering courses in comparative religions. Philander Kinney Cady, professor of the evidences of revealed religion at General seminary, offered a specialized course in "The Great Ethnic Religions, and the Primitive Religions."[41] George William Knox was hired by Union in 1898 as the professor of philosophy and history of religion as part of a new philosophy and history of religion department in New Brunswick. He began teaching a "Survey of the Ethnic Faiths" to "provide a rapid sketch of the history and teachings of Primitive Religions, Hinduism, Buddhism, Confucianism, and Islam."[42]

Public Lectures on Comparative Religions

An introduction to different religions—"great" or "ethnic"—was not only left to specific class lectures; it also gained a larger audience through public lectures that were later published. Throughout the last quarter of the nineteenth century, numerous lectureships were established by donors for the purpose of addressing any number of important religious issues and theological topics that were on the minds of those financially supporting seminaries. Prominent scholars or pastors were invited by the faculty, the president, or the board and normally asked to provide six to ten public lectures on a timely topic. This tradition began in Britain, where prominent lectures were endowed through a trust and associated with a major university, such as the Baird and Cunningham and Gifford lectures in Scotland, and the prestigious Hibbert Lectures in England (for which Max Müller was the inaugural lecturer in 1878). The American seminaries were quick to follow suit and establish their own lectures to cement their role as institutions of intellectual repute. Two public lectureships were established at Union seminary, the Ely and Morse lectures. Princeton established the Stone Lectures, and in Chicago, the Haskell Foundation provided funds through which John Henry Barrow, a graduate of Union and the organizer of the Parliament of the World Religions, gave the inaugural lectures at the University of Chicago.

The Ely Lectures

Founded by Z. Stiles Ely in memory of the Reverend Elias P. Ely of New York, the Ely Lectures at Union seminary were intended to support "the evidences of Christianity" in the modern world. The Ely Lectures were established "to serve the proposition that Christianity is a religion from God, or that it is the perfect and final form of religion for man."[43] According to the stipulations of the endowment, the faculty and board of the seminary were free to select the lecturer and the topic as they saw fit. The topic of the first lecture demonstrates the interest in and importance of the study of comparative religions during this period. The Reverend Frank Ellinwood (1826–1908), a graduate of Princeton seminary and the corresponding secretary of the Board of Foreign Missions of the Presbyterian Church (US), delivered the 1891 Ely Lectures on the topic of "The Conflict of Christianity with the Great Non-Christian Religions of the World."[44] Ellinwood argued in his presentation that the reality of non-Christian religions is no longer a matter of "academic interest," that other religions "are no longer far off. . . . There is no longer any excuse for ignorance of the rich treasures of Oriental Literature. They are at our doors."[45]

Ellinwood served as the pastor of Presbyterian congregations in New Jersey and New York, but his longest tenure was as the secretary of the Board of Foreign Missions of the Presbyterian Church (US) from 1871 to 1906. He, along with Robert Speer, would be the primary engineer behind the creation of large-scale Presbyterian missionary work around the world. It was under his direction that the Presbyterian Church began missions in China and Korea, in particular.[46] For Union, he delivered a series of ten lectures under the title "The Oriental Religions and Christianity." The final presentation was entitled "The Divine Supremacy of the Christian Faith," in which he culminated his argument that only Christianity provides salvation for humans and refuted the comparative religious approach.

> The religions of men, like their social customs and political institutions, are placed in contact and comparison. The enemies of the Christian faith here, in Western lands, naturally make the most of any possible alliances with other systems supposed to antagonize Christianity; while a multitude of others, having no particular interest in any religion, and rather priding themselves upon a broad charity which is but a courteous name for indifference, are demanding with a superior air that fair play shall be shown to all religions alike. The Church is therefore called upon to defend her unique position and the promulgation of her message to mankind.[47]

Here, Ellinwood takes aim at the liberal wing of the church, especially Union's faculty.

Ellinwood's sixth presentation is titled "Mohammedanism Past and Present." His purpose is to refute any positive role of Islam in history.

Ellinwood relies on several Western sources, including Palmer's translation of the Qur'an in the Sacred Books of the East series, edited by Müller. He also relies heavily on William Muir and the Presbyterian missionary Elwood M. Wherry's *Comprehensive Commentary on the Qur'ān*, published between 1882 and 1886. Both Muir and Wherry presented Muhammad as an impostor and Islam as a false religion. The basis of Ellinwood's argument in this presentation is that the Hadith collections that provide the basis of Muhammad's life show a clear connection with the ancient polytheistic practices of the Kaaba. Ellinwood claimed that Muhammad learned of an early type of monotheism from the Jewish tribes in the Arabian Peninsula and from his wife's cousin, Waraqa, who was a Christian. However, these Jewish and Christian believers had fallen away from their true religions and been overcome by local traditions and various forms of idolatry themselves—such as the belief in the Trinity as Father, Son, and Mary, which he believes is reflected in surah 5:116.

Ellinwood argues that while Muhammad truly believed himself to be a religious reformer, once he fled to Medina to carry on his mission, he then was transformed into a political leader and "conqueror." Ellinwood argues that the personality and character of a true man of God, or a true prophet, become better and purer, whereas Muhammad was the opposite. His actions and activities demonstrate a "moral trend downward," and he became a "remorseless tyrant."[48] Focusing on Muhammad's relationship with women, Ellinwood remarks that Muhammad went from being in a devoted marriage with Khadijah to having multiple wives, and then sanctioning the slavery of women captives.

Similarly, Ellinwood opines that the civilization of Islam has deteriorated over the course of history. He does not deny that there were great Islamic civilizations in Spain, Baghdad, and India but claims that these all deteriorated due to the weight of their own immorality. "The world will never forget that by the burning of the great library of Alexandria the rich legacy which the old world had bequeathed to the new was destroyed."[49] As an abolitionist, Ellinwood also notes that it cannot be argued that Islam spread throughout Africa by traders and marabouts, but rather that it spread through conquest and the slave trade. Referencing William Blyden's *Christianity, Islam, and the Negro Race* (1887), he states that Arab Muslims "have been, chiefly responsible for the horrors of that trade, and . . . even when Americans bought slaves for their plantations, Moslem raiders in the interior instigated the tribal quarrels which supplied the markets on the coast . . . [and] at the present time both the supply and the demand depend on Mohammedan influence."[50]

Ellinwood then turns to refute another positive view of Islam, that of the Anglican canon Isaac Taylor, whose *Leaves from an Egyptian Notebook* (1888) argued that Islam was more successful than Christianity in "civilizing" Africa and more successful in promoting abstinence from alcohol than any Methodist missionary organization. The evidence of the truth of Christianity, concludes Ellinwood, is that it unlocks the higher natures of humanity: "humility, purity of heart, forgiveness of injuries, sacrifice of self, to man's moral nature."[51] These virtues are exemplified through the life of Jesus, but they have no place in Islam or the life of Muhammad, says Ellinwood. Therefore, Christian mission in Africa is necessary to exemplify the best of Christ and sow the seeds that will someday be reaped by the conversion of Muslims to Christianity.

Ellinwood's lectures given in 1892 were well received by those supporting not only Presbyterian mission but Christian missionary efforts in general. His views of Islam were not unique and reflected many of the pejorative Western Christian perspectives on Muhammad and his life. However, this was not the only perspective of Islam that was provided through the Ely Lectures. In 1897, Henry Preserved Smith would be invited to lecture, and his view of Islam was radically different from Ellinwood's.

At Union seminary, Henry Preserved Smith (1864–1925) was hired as the Davenport professor of Hebrew and cognate languages. He came to Union after a long and controversial career as a scholar. He had been previously brought up before the Cincinnati Presbyterian Presbytery and found guilty of heresy while he was a faculty member at Lane Seminary, where he had taught from 1872 to 1892. Like many other American Protestant scholars, Smith had traveled to Germany to study in Berlin and researched the latest methods in biblical exegesis.[52] It was in Berlin that he learned about higher biblical criticism and relished in the concepts of the History of Religions School. Smith brought this learning back with him to Lane Presbyterian Seminary in 1872 and began teaching these critical methods to his students. As a result, he was caught up in the debates of biblical inspiration and inerrancy. His views became quite controversial, eventually leading to the charges of heresy by the local presbytery (consisting of local Presbyterian pastors). Found guilty, he was defrocked and required to resign from his faculty position. Moving east, he spent the next fifteen years teaching as an adjunct at Andover seminary and Amherst College. Finally, in 1907 he was hired by Union seminary to serve as the librarian and professor of Hebrew until his retirement in 1925.

Union seminary had also experienced a heresy trial within the Presbyterian Church in the same year as Smith's trial, that of Charles Briggs, the eminent Old Testament scholar. Whereas Smith found little support from the board of Lane, Union's seminary board was insistent that the school be a place of freedom of inquiry and wholeheartedly supported Briggs. Briggs's heresy trial was a debate not only about the infallibility of scripture but about control of what was taught in the seminary. Union saw itself as a progressive institution and because of the Briggs trial established itself as a freestanding institution, free from ecclesiastical control of any presbytery or denomination. Thus, Union was only too glad to attract another "heretic" as a symbol of its progressive Protestant Christianity.[53]

As a biblical linguist, Smith was interested in philology. He was a devotee of Müller's perspective on the relationships of languages. He imbibed Müller's ideas as they related to Judaism, Christianity, and Islam, and he applied these views to his understanding of the historical development and interaction of the Abrahamic scriptures. In fact, Smith's interest in Islam derived from his study of higher criticism of ancient Near East texts, which he learned to appreciate in Germany. But it was the debate about biblical inerrancy and inspiration that led him to first examine and juxtapose Jewish and Islamic views of scripture from his own Protestant Christian understanding.

Led by the likes of Charles Hodge and then Benjamin Warfield at Princeton seminary, Presbyterian presbyteries began to ask their seminary professors for proof of their orthodox Calvinist views. Like Briggs, Smith was a target of the more conservative wing of the Presbyterian Church, which had a high view of the revelation of scripture and believed in the concept of verbal inspiration of the Bible. He was asked to provide an accounting of his beliefs, which he would later publish. In his apology, Smith demonstrates his erudition of classic higher criticism, along with knowledge of European Orientalist studies of Jewish and Islamic texts. From Smith's perspective, the Protestant principle of "justification by faith" is the first article of Christianity. This doctrine asserted a theological perspective of relationships between humanity and God. It was not the Bible and its inerrancy in all matters theological, historical, or factual that proved the truth of Christianity. Quoting Luther, Smith wrote that "it is clear that Luther would claim no further infallibility for the Bible than this, and, indeed, he expressly declares as much in his judgment of the Canon. He proposes this rule: What proclaims Christ is Scripture."[54] For Smith, the truth of the Bible was its message, not its historicity.

In responding to charges of heresy, Smith argues that those demanding biblical inerrancy, such as Charles Hodge or Benjamin Warfield, were themselves ascribing to an Islamic and rabbinical Jewish view of scriptural inspiration. In his own defense on the distinction between inspiration and inerrancy Smith begins with the Qur'an. He opens his argument by recalling the Islamic view of the revelation of the Qur'an to Muhammad, its recitation to his companions, its transmission to scribes, and finally the compilation of the *mushaf* (or written text) as the authoritative and unaltered speech of God. He then notes how the rabbis developed a view of the oral Torah given to Moses to supplement the written Torah and its transmission to the faithful through the rabbis. In essence, Smith argues that the Christian proponents of the inerrancy of scripture are following an Islamic and rabbinical Jewish view that believes in the oral transmission of revelation to Muhammad and Moses. "The point I make is: This is the kind of Bible we should like to have God give us, and when we construct for our selves a theory of revelation we do it along these lines."[55] In other words, those who adhere to the verbal inspiration of the Bible adhere to an Islamic perspective of the Qur'an. But his point is that the Bible is not so constructed nor was it intended to be. To hold such a position, says Smith, is problematic.

If we assume with the Muslim that the sacred text is in every word the declaration of God himself, or with the Christian theologian [i.e., Hodge and Warfield] that every word of the Bible was inerrantly inspired, it is quite conceivable that the meaning is not exhausted by what appears to be the natural sense of the words, but that the divine author has concealed under the text things that can be discovered only by the chosen few who possess key to the treasure. The trouble comes when we compare the various interpretations which result from the application of the theory and find that they disagree. This we find to be true in Christian exegesis, and we must expect a similar result in the exposition of the Quran.[56]

In other words, for Smith, such a high view of the verbal plenary inspiration of scripture in the Islamic sense is merely created to support one's own concept of inerrancy, and thus one's own interpretation of the text. Such a view is not supported by historical facts or textual transmission, he asserts.[57] Rather, higher criticism allows believers to examine the texts in their historical and cultural contexts to better apply the Protestant theological truths rather than the interpreters asserting the text itself as the truth.

After his expulsion from Lane seminary, Smith spent what must have been a difficult fifteen-year desultory sojourn in New England without an official appointment. During that time, he was invited to Union seminary in 1897 to give a series of presentations on "The Bible and Islam" as part of the endowed Ely Lectures. Here Smith found a welcome reception.

The ten lectures given by Smith would later be published and would also serve as the basis of his History of Religions course.[58] We see Müller's fingerprints throughout *The Bible and Islam* and Smith's lectures on world religions. In his opening introduction to the course, Smith reiterates Müller's perspective that there is a commonality in all religions based on the "internal experience of man." Even when religions may exhibit unique claims or have distinctive marks, they are all grounded in the human experience, that is—the "phenomenon" of religion.[59] Like Clarke, Smith sees the monotheistic Abrahamic traditions as providing a corrective and reform for the earlier, more "primitive" religions.

Smith describes Islam as flowing out of Judaism and Christianity as a natural example of religious borrowing. "There is a sense in that the great historical religions have started out with a single leading thought; but they have not been able to make progress without taking up some features from their predecessors," he wrote. This "syncretism" is a reality that the religions must accept primarily because cultures and civilizations do the same thing—they borrow and build off ideas and concepts.

"Beneath the contrasts and rivalries of national and theological thought may be found deep resemblances in ideas, words and customs."[60] Thus for Smith, just as Christianity built off Judaism, so too did Islam build off both Judaism and Christianity.

While we do not have Smith's manuscript notes for his lecture on Islam, we do have an outline. The outline highlights dates for the life of Muhammad, the importance of the Qur'an, Hadith, rituals and prayers, the six pillars of belief, marriage, holy war, slavery, magic, amulets, saints, and dervishes.[61] While the lecture outline does not provide any sources, Smith more than likely relied on Thomas Hughes's *Dictionary of Islam* (1885) for his background information, as this was his primary source for the publication of his earlier *The Bible and Islam*.[62]

The Bible and Islam served as the basis of Smith's constructive views of Islam throughout his life. Even though he believed that the Islamic views of the revelation of the Qur'an were misconstrued, Smith repudiated the Christian stereotypes of Muhammad as a charlatan—or worse. He acknowledges that, like King David, who was capable of morally culpable actions, Muhammad, too, was a product of his own time and culture. And yet, Muhammad possessed a genuine religious persona, intellect, and skills to provide religious guidance to the Arabs. Because there were no Arabic scriptures, writes Smith, Muhammad used well-known biblical stories that were recited to him orally from Arabic Jews and Christians to "furnish a framework" that could be recited and later written down in the Qur'an.[63] It was in this Jewish-Christian milieu that he further developed his monotheistic ideas "adapted to Arabic conditions."[64]

Smith's assessment focused on many of the theological similarities with Christianity, such as monotheistic worship, ethical renewal, and the day of judgment. Smith's views were quite progressive for the time. Yet, by claiming that Muhammad was the author and creator of the Qur'an who borrowed from the Abrahamic traditions, he expressed views that would still be seen as patronizing or offensive to Muslims. However, using Müller's and Clarke's categories, as well as his own training in philology, Smith subjected Islam to the same rigorous examination as he carried out for the Old and New Testaments. He concluded that "if thoughtful men of all confessions are to come to a common understanding of the man and his book it must be by a really historical method. The man [Muhammad] must be understood as a member of Arabic society of the seventh century of our era, and the book must be interpreted in the sense in which it was taken by the men who first heard it. The exegesis we are criticizing errs, like so much Christian exegesis, both by defect and by excess."[65]

Ultimately, for Smith, it is the message and meaning of the religions that carry theological truth, not their historicity. Like Clarke, Smith believed that if Islam was to be faulted for anything, it, like Judaism, lacked a universal appeal. It was focused on one ethnic community and language group, whereas the message of Christianity could be translated into other cultures and languages. In this regard, Smith seems unaware of or uninterested in the global presence of Islam, on which Samuel Zwemer would later focus. Ellinwood, who represented a mission approach, and Smith, who represented a "history of religions" approach, epitomize opposing views about comparative religions in general and about Islam among Protestant clergy and seminary professors at the end of the nineteenth century.

Stone Lectures

In the same year that Ellinwood gave the Ely Lectures, Samuel H. Kellogg (1839–1899), a graduate of Princeton seminary, professor of the Presbyterian seminary at Allegheny in Pittsburgh, and a missionary of the Farrukhabad Mission in North India, provided the Stone Lectures at Princeton seminary. The Stone Lectures were founded in 1871 by Levi Payson Stone, a Presbyterian businessman and trustee of the seminary. Stone became a "born again" Christian after reading Dr. Charles Hodge's *Way of Life*. Stone was so grateful to the seminary for its mission and ministry to the Presbyterian Church that he wanted to give back. So, he endowed a lectureship that had no restrictions other than that it should not "contravene the system of doctrine taught in the standards of the Presbyterian Church."[66]

Samuel Kellogg was a well-respected "missionary-scholar." He graduated first in his class at Princeton in 1864 and went straight out to serve as a missionary in the Farrukhabad Mission in northern India. He wrote a Hindi grammar, for which he received a prize from the International Congress of Orientalists. After the sudden death of his wife, Antoinette, in 1876, he returned to the United States and served as a pastor in Pittsburgh and Toronto. While in Pittsburgh he was asked to teach at the Presbyterian seminary at Allegheny. In 1892, he was asked to come back to India by the Farrukhabad Mission to work on a new Hindi translation of the Old Testament. It was on his way to India that he stopped at Princeton to give these lectures, which were later published in 1899 as *A Handbook of Comparative Religions*.[67] The title of the eight lectures on the phenomenology of religion was "The Genesis and Growth of Religion." "Religion essentially consists in man's apprehension of his relation to an invisible Power or powers, able to influence his destiny, to which he is necessarily subject, together with the feelings, desires, and actions, which this apprehension calls forth."[68]

Following in Müller's footsteps, Kellogg develops a view of religion from his experience among the religions of India, primarily what are now known as Hinduism and Buddhism. He believed that all humans are created with a spiritual desire for religious life but ultimately, all humans fall away from the worship of the true God. According to Kellogg, all religions have an innate sense of the "invisible Power" but usually fall into error and need to be corrected. In this way, he turns Müller's concept of the positive role religion plays among all peoples into a negative—humans feel "apprehension" about an ultimate power. It seems he has taken his cue from Luther's *anfechtung*, his anxiety and feelings of despair about God and an afterlife. In the end, Kellogg believes that the human spiritual need can only be rectified through belief in Christ.

Lecture 8 focuses on "Shemitic Monotheism" and provides the crux of his argument about Christianity as the ultimate end and goal of all religion. For Kellogg, Christianity provides the answers to all human religious experiences. He argues that the Israelites had monotheism revealed to them, but they, too, fell away "from monotheism into nature-worship of various forms, ancestor-worship, polytheism, fetishism, and idolatry," and prophets had to bring them back to true worship.[69] The Old Testament, then, is a classic example of the true human religious experience. This perspective of prophetic religion also aligns with the Islamic perspective, of what Sydney Griffith calls Islamic "Prophetology"[70]—that is, that prophets are sent by God to bring people back to the true worship of God. Kellogg argues that Muhammad was one of these prophets who brought monotheism back to the idolatrous Arabs. However, according to Kellogg, Muhammad ultimately did give in to the idolatrous whims of the Arabs by allowing the black stone in the Kaaba to remain as a centerpiece of their focus of prayer.[71] Nevertheless, Islam as a "Shemitic" religion is closer to Christianity in its view of the human experience and concept of revelation and salvation, unlike the Turanian religions of East Asia that lead humans away from God toward "various forms, ancestor worship, polytheism, fetishism, and idolatry," says Kellogg.[72] Even so, Islam falls short of true religion, in his view.

The 1899 publication of his lectures, *A Handbook of Comparative Religion*, which he completed after he returned to India, expands his views and further develops his negative perspectives on Islam. Here he is even much more critical of Islam. For example, he writes that in Islam the Qur'an calls believers to return and submit to God. However, he expounds on the descriptions of the judgment day as found in the Qur'an and the Islamic traditions that focus on the terror of the judgment day, the graphic torments of hell, and the "sensual desires" of heaven.[73] Rather, the New Testament reveals "a new heaven and a new earth," where the resurrection of the believers provides hope. It is in Christianity, concludes Kellogg, that "sin" can only be rectified through Jesus, rather than willful submission. Submission does not necessarily lead to any type of moral regeneration. In fact, because humanity has always exhibited the tendency to fall back into idolatry and polytheism, even the Old Testament prophets or Muhammad himself could not keep the Israelites or the Arabs from spiritual ruin. In this way, Judaism and Islam, as "Shemitic religions," are similar. They are a step toward belief in God but are in the end incapable of saving humanity. While the Christian understanding of God is one of love and forgiveness, Kellogg writes, the Qur'anic portrayal of God is like an Oriental despot capable of "horrible caprice" and "arbitrary almightiness" who falls short in his understanding of mercy and compassion but demands loyalty and obedience.[74] Only Christianity can relieve human "apprehension" and draw all people back to the one true God, concludes Kellogg.

The American Lectures on the History of Religions

At the same time that the Ely and Stone lectures were given, in 1891 a group of fifteen seminary and university administrators and scholars gathered at the Historical Society of Philadelphia, and at Union seminary the following year, to organize what was to become the American Lectures on the History of Religions. The organizing committee was made up of representatives from the University of Pennsylvania, Columbia, New York University, Harvard, the newly formed Johns Hopkins and Cornell universities, and Union seminary. Union President Frances Brown and Professor Charles Briggs were on the initial committee. The committee wanted to create an annual lecture of the same quality and level as that of the well-known Hibbert Lectures in England. The focus was to provide a "course of lectures on some religion, or phase of religion, from an historical point of view, or on a subject germane to the study of religions." An important caveat in the charter was that "polemical subjects, as well as polemics in the treatment of subjects, shall be positively excluded."[75] The association reflected the growing trend toward a nonsectarian, or secular, study of religion that did not make assumptions or normative claims about Christianity, which was the expectation at the denominational seminaries. However, the interest in an objective, or more specifically non-Protestant-centered, field of study of religion would not really take hold until the 1960s when religious studies departments began to take root in colleges and universities. Many of the early scholars who were invited to lecture on comparative religions around the country were Protestant seminary faculty. Thus, religion departments and the study of religion at universities and especially private liberal arts church colleges continued to reflect a dominant "cultural embeddedness" of Protestant Christianity.[76] The American Lectures would eventually rotate among the host institutions until it found a home at Columbia University in 1936 and then within the American Academy of Religion in 1994.[77]

The American Lectures began in 1892, a year after the organizational meetings, with the topic of "The History and Literature of Buddhism." The lecturer was Rhys Davids of the University of London. Davids was an internationally well-respected scholar who had contributed translations of Buddhist texts for Müller's *Sacred Books of the East*. However,

Davids had also worked with the Society for the Promotion of Christian Knowledge, an Anglican organization that seeks to provide resources on Christianity for the broader public. This points to the reality that a supposed fire wall between Christian theological perspectives and objective religious studies was never very clear. Even in places where seminaries became separate institutions from their universities, such as at Princeton and New Brunswick, faculty of the colleges were often made up of seminary faculty who taught in both schools. Where Christian ministers had often made up the core of college and university religion departments from their inception until the 1980s, their role became suspect by a new generation of scholars of religious studies reared in the "science of religion" methodology.[78]

The Morse Foundation Lectures

The Reverend John Henry Barrows (1847–1902) was already a household name in the field of comparative religions when he was asked to provide the Morse Foundation Lectures at Union seminary in 1898. Barrows had been the chairman of the General Committee on Religious Congresses for the Columbian Exhibition in Chicago, better known as the Chicago World's Fair. The first World Parliament of Religions, which took place at the exhibition in 1893, was his brainchild. While the parliament has become synonymous with interfaith dialogue and was designed "to cultivate harmony among the world's religious and spiritual communities," its beginnings were steeped in Protestant theological paternalism.[79]

Barrows grew up the son of a professor at Olivet College, Michigan. He and his brother were two of the six students to graduate from the college in 1867. Barrows studied the classics and became well known for his knowledge of Greek and Latin. In fact, Barrows allegedly gave the opening address at his graduation in Latin.[80] Both brothers had a conversion experience at a revival meeting while at Olivet and both then attended the divinity school at Yale. John Henry was extremely active in the prayer meetings and revivals of New Haven organized by Henry Ward Beecher. However, due to health challenges, he reluctantly abandoned his studies and returned home. Not to be dissuaded from the ministry, he moved to Kansas, where he served as a "home missionary" on the frontier. In 1872, John Henry was called by the Presbyterian Church in Springfield,

Illinois, as their pastor, even though he had not yet completed his theological studies nor been ordained. By 1874, he decided to continue his studies, left Springfield, and enrolled at Andover seminary. However, during his studies he was again offered another position as the pastor of Eliot Congregational Church in Lawrence, Massachusetts. He accepted this position and was then ordained by the presbytery, still not yet having completed his formal theological studies. He served there until 1880, when he was called to the Maverick Congregational Church in East Boston. Barrows had been there barely a year when he was called to be the pastor of the prominent First Presbyterian Church in Chicago, which he then served for eight years. The Chicago years proved to be the most important and productive years of his career. Barrows was constantly on the move with a wanderlust and excitable evangelical spirit that kept him involved in all kinds of social causes, from abolitionism to the temperance movement. Even though he was never able to obtain an official academic degree, he was widely recognized for his keen intellect. He was a popular preacher and speaker, often being invited to speak during summers at the Christian Chautauqua camp in upstate New York.

It was during his tenure in Chicago that he was invited to serve on one of the committees planning the Columbian Exhibition, or the Chicago World's Fair. The purpose of the Columbian Exhibition was to celebrate the endless possibilities of human achievements of a new world. Barrows was interested in showcasing religion as an essential part of the advancement of human civilization. Chairing his committee on the Religious Congress, he developed "the plan of holding a parliament of religions at which the representatives of the great historic faiths shall sit together in frank and friendly conference over the great things of our common spiritual and moral life."[81] As a charismatic and engaging figure, Barrows solicited positive support for the parliament from those with whom he spoke. He managed to secure the participation of the Catholic archbishops in the United States and made arrangements to have Buddhist, Hindu, and Muslim "representatives" at the meetings, including Alexander Webb, the prominent American Muslim convert. Barrows was indefatigable in his efforts to organize and implement the parliament. The year before the parliament he wrote hundreds of letters inviting and encouraging participation. It is likely that the parliament would not have come to fruition without his unrelenting energy. In fact, the Japanese Buddhist contingent almost left Chicago upon arrival due to a cultural misunderstanding. They were only convinced to stay when Barrows made a personal apology and appeal.[82]

In communicating his plans about the parliament, he wrote that the gathering would show "in the most impressive way, what and how many important truths the various Religions hold and teach in common . . . [and] promote and deepen the spirit of human brotherhood among religious men of diverse faiths, through friendly conference and mutual good understanding, while not seeking to foster the temper of indifferentism, and not striving to achieve any formal and outward unity."[83] `His patriarchal language aside, Barrows championed the view that "proper" religion brings out the best of humanity. He believed that, given the chance, believers of like minds but of different religions could agree on peaceful means and methods of advancing civilization. It is worth quoting him at length here.

> I have no doubt that this phenomenal meeting will make apparent the fact that there is a certain unity in religion, that is, that men not only have common desires and needs, but also have perceived more or less clearly, certain common truths. And as the Apostle Paul, with his unfailing tact and courtesy, was careful to find common ground for himself and his Greek auditors in Athens, before he preached to them Jesus and the resurrection, so the wise Christian missionary is discovering that he must not ignore any fragment of truth which the heathen mind cherishes, for, thus ignoring it, he makes an impassable barrier against conviction in the non-Christian mind. I believe that the Parliament will do much to promote the spirit of human brotherhood among those of diverse faiths, by diminishing ill-will, by softening rancor, and giving me the privilege of getting their impressions of others at first hand.[84]

While Barrows may have been the most prominent public interreligious persona in America, he was not a theological pluralist. He did not see the world religions as different and complete ways toward salvation. In his stout belief that rational believers would be able to work together to bring about peace and prosperity, he also was just as certain that serious religious practitioners would come to understand the full truth about God in Christ; it was only a matter of being polite and hospitable enough until they would see the logical truth. Barrows' naïve intentions about the role the conference would play rested upon a purely idealistic intellectual perspective. It never occurred to him that the power structures of the day, colonization, imperialism, international politics, and even American racism had an impact on interreligious engagement. Yet, the turn of the century was the height of the colonial age, in which even the United States would participate during the Roosevelt administration through its occupation of Cuba and the Philippines. Barrows, for all of his idealistic tendencies and best intentions, was steeped in male patriarchy and Western paternalism.

Regardless of how Barrows or other Protestant thinkers evaluated the opportunities of the parliament, the field of comparative religions was now flourishing in the seminaries and other newly formed graduate programs at universities, such as the University of Chicago, New York University, and Columbia, as well as at the venerable colleges of Harvard and Yale. The concept of "great" and "ethnic" religions was prominent and part of the scholarly theological discourse of the day. In his final reflections on the parliament, Barrows wrote,

> [The Parliament] has shown that mankind is drifting toward religion and not away from it; it has widened the bounds of human fraternity; it is giving a strong impetus to the study of comparative religion; it is fortifying timid souls in regard to the right and wisdom of liberty in thought and expression; it is clarifying many minds in regard to the nature of the non-Christian faiths; it is deepening the general Christian interest in non-Christian nations; and it will bring before millions in Oriental lands the more truthful and beautiful aspects of Christianity. The impression that it is making on the unbelieving and secular world is salutary, for it gives the first opportunity for men to see religion in its entirety and to apprehend its greatness. The Columbian Exposition which accentuated the material glories of modern civilization needed the Parliament of Religions to bring back to the human mind the greater world of the Spirit.[85]

This euphoric feeling about the parliament reflected American society at the end of the century. The "Gilded Age" was a time of good fortune and economic prosperity in America and would lead to a brief American experiment in colonization, with expansion into the Pacific and the Philippines, and the Caribbean and Cuba. Scientific innovations and American expansionism created a sense of optimism about human progress and opportunity that would be shattered by "the guns of August" in 1914 and with the genocide of the Assyrians and Armenians by the Turks in 1915. Until then, there was a great sense of social, economic, and religious idealism. This American cultural perspective is reflected in a mural completed by Edwin Bashfield in 1898. Bashfield's mural, *The Evolution of Civilizations*, adorns the inside of the dome of the south pavilion of the Library of Congress. In the painting, Civilization, depicted as a female, is surrounded by angelic cherubs in an inner blue circle and in an outer circle of winged figures representing the great civilizations of the past, including Egypt, Greece, and Rome. Following these are the representations of the modern nations of Italy, Germany, Spain, England, and America. Finally, Judaism and Islam are also included. Islam is represented by a bare-chested man with a turban. The mural intends to portray Islam as an important contribution to the development of Western civilization.

Barrows's success in the planning and execution of the parliament led to several concrete opportunities for his future. First, the parliament made him an instant celebrity and the poster child of comparative religions, even if the Protestant reflection on other religions was naively conceived. After the parliament, Barrows traveled the world and was received by many religious leaders—Christians, Hindus, and Muslims—even the sheikh of Al-Azhar.[86] Second, following the parliament, one of his parishioners at First Presbyterian, Ms. Carol Haskell, gave money to the University of Chicago to establish the Haskell Lectureship for the purpose of exploring comparative religions. Haskell would also found another lectureship at the University of Chicago in Barrows's name: the Barrows Lectures. Upon her suggestion, Barrows was the first invited lecturer in 1894. Third, Barrows was offered a position at the University of Chicago as the professorial lecturer in comparative religions. It was primarily an honorary appointment but one of which he was grateful and proud. Fourth, because of his role in promoting comparative religions, he was invited to Union seminary to give the Morse Foundation Lectures in 1898. The Morse Lectures had been founded in 1865 by Professor Samuel F. B. Morse for the purpose of exploring the relation of Christianity with the sciences. Barrows's lectures, however, focused

Figure 5.1. *The Evolution of Civilizations*, by Edwin Bashfield, Jefferson Building, Library of Congress. Washington, DC, ca. 1898.

on the "world religions." The lectures were published the following year as *The Christian Conquest of Asia: Observations and Studies of Religions in the Orient*. The Morse Lectures were the reflections on his travels to Turkey, Egypt, India, and China in 1896 and 1897.[87]

During his excursion abroad, Barrows and his wife spent several days in "Constantinople," or Istanbul, as the guests of the American missionaries from Robert College. Here, the American missionaries alerted Barrows to the atrocities committed by the Hamidian government against the Armenian and Assyrian communities. He was shocked by these developments. As he reflected on his experience in Istanbul, he had little if anything positive to say about the "wicked and doomed city."[88] He intimates not only that the city is physically erected along the border of East and West, of Europe and Asia, but that it also stands as a metaphor for the conflict between the Cross and the Crescent. His negative views of Islam were shaped and informed by firsthand reports of the massacres of the Christians from the American missionary community that eventually filtered out to US newspapers. It would be this consistent messaging from the American missionaries in Turkey that almost succeeded in instituting an American Mandate over Armenia in 1920.[89]

In his Morse Lecture, Barrows remarks that the original lands of Christianity were now under "the cruel, unrelaxing grasp of Islam."[90] He accords this by referring to Genesis 16:12 and the blessing and curses of Ishmael as the "wild ass of a man."[91] Quoting Edward Gibbon, Barrows reiterates that Muhammad came "with the sword in one hand and the Koran in the other, erected his throne on the ruins of Christianity and Rome."[92] Muhammad "saw it expedient to turn aside from the paths of peace and moderation into those of war, marauding and plunder . . . and [became] a persecuting fanatic."[93] In addition, unlike Müller, who insisted that religion was not a racial category, Barrows followed the well-trodden path of social Darwinism and the racialization of religion. He notes that Christianity predominates in "Caucasian" countries where "the Aryan stock" predominates, whereas Islam prevails in "Mongolian, Malayan, and Negro countries."[94]

The Morse Foundation Lectures of 1898 were a far cry from his earlier hopes about the "common desires and needs" and "common truths" of world religions in 1893.[95] If there was anything positive to say about Islam after his sojourn abroad, it was that the ethics of moderation and the prohibition of alcohol and gambling were laudable. Barrows concludes that to compare a true form of Christianity with a true form of Islam—to compare Jesus with Muhammad—is to demonstrate the superiority of Protestant Christianity. One cannot look to Jesus for the evil and sinful acts of Christian countries, opines Barrows. Quoting Freeman Clarke from *Ten Great Religions*, Barrows notes that Islam "repudiates all change, all advances, all development," whereas Protestant Christianity looks to the future.[96] The best way forward, then, is for American Protestant missionaries who are working and teaching in the Ottoman Empire to lead Muslims to the truth. Thus, a "new crusade is in progress in which the weapons are schools and preachers and printing-presses, arms which, in the end, will be more effective than swords."[97]

Barrows's Morse Lectures reframe Islam. Here, we see another "paradigm shift," a reversion back to the days of the early republic. In a period of seventy years, from the 1830s until the last years of the nineteenth century, Islam came to be viewed not as a spiritual or existential threat, as had been the case in the seventeenth-century North American colonies, but as part of the Near Eastern natural experience of human religiosity. At the turn of the twentieth century, with stories of Turkish atrocities against Christians being conveyed by graduates of American seminaries serving as missionaries in the Near East, the image of a violent and barbaric Muslim would once again return.

The reports of Turkish treatment of the minority Christian communities reversed a previously held interest in Islam as a peculiar Near Eastern religion that somehow grew from Judaism and Christianity. It was the negative reports about the Turks by American missionaries that shifted American views of Islam during the beginning of the twentieth century, returning them to the images of the violence of the Barbary pirates, the "scorpions" of Revelation as portrayed by Johnathan Edwards and Archibald Anderson. Islam may have been considered a monotheistic religion from the cradle of biblical civilization and a source of Eastern Oriental spirituality for some seminary professors for the middle decades of the nineteenth century, but by the conclusion of World War I, some Protestant clergy once again began to describe Islam as a cause of Oriental despotism and violence. Some American missionaries, many of them graduates of the seminaries of the East, primarily Andover, Union, and Princeton, were an important resource through which American seminarians, clergy, and other Protestant Christians were informed about Islam. However, the interpretation of Islam and the portrait of Muhammad by these American missionaries was not uniform. There was a great diversity of opinion about previous and future relationship with Islam. It is to the graduates of the seminaries who went out to serve in the Ottoman Empire, Persia, and India that we now turn.

6

Missions to the "Mohammedan World"

While Muslims had been in the English North American colonies since the first days of the slave trade, their religious identity went largely unnoticed. Occasionally a White American took the time to consider the unique prayer practices or written Arabic script of passages from the Qur'an scribbled on whatever paper a Muslim African was able to acquire.[1] Colonial Americans were more aware of English and European encounters with Turks and their religion.[2] By and large, the first public North American encounter with Muslims was during the Barbary Wars when North African corsairs captured American ships and enslaved their crews and passengers at the end of the eighteenth century. Ransomed Americans wrote about their experiences and even shared views of the religion of the "Moors." As we have seen, Cotton Mather offered up prayers and solicited the donation of funds for the ransom of White enslaved Americans. However, following the conclusion of the Tripolitan Wars, and with the development of advanced naval technology, such as the steamship, Americans began to invade the Near East in increasing numbers. They came not in military retaliation but for commerce, curiosity, adventure, or a sense of spiritual duty. Often they came with a mixture of these motives.[3] While missionaries were not the only Americans to travel abroad, engage with Muslims, and write about their experiences, they were the most noteworthy cohort of Americans to do so. American missionaries had the longest sustained relationship with Muslims and their cultures and went to great lengths to share their reflections on them. They wrote about Islam with increasing passion—some out of frustration over the lack of converts, others out of a desire to warn Americans of the perceived spiritual and moral dangers of Islam, and still others out of sheer interest in and curiosity about Islamic history and civilization. By the second decade of the nineteenth century, Americans no longer had to read old Latin or English Orientalist books on Islam; their own compatriots were sharing experiences about living in Muslim contexts and were writing books based on primary Islamic sources. Most of the American missionaries writing about Islam were educated at American seminaries, and many returned to teach at their alma maters. Long before American universities began establishing study centers to research Islam or Muslim cultures, seminaries were the primary places for the American study of Islam.[4] While Edward E. Salisbury held the first university chair of Arabic at Yale, seminaries had already demonstrated an engagement with Islam from the 1820s through missionary letters, presentations, and student missionary associations. Thus, American missionary views had a significant impact on seminary education as well as for a church-growing Protestant America.

This concluding chapter reviews the role that American missionary fervor played in adding significant primary source material about Islam that came to be taught and learned at these seven seminaries. Surprisingly, however, given the importance of mission work among the earliest seminary students during the second Great Awakening, Christian mission as a field of study was rarely taught and student training for professional service was never regulated. It took nearly the one hundred years covered in this survey before these disciplines could be studied and standards of missionary training could be agreed upon. Thus, this chapter reviews the arc of interest in Christian missions from the genesis of seminary education up to the 1910 Edinburgh World Missionary conference, specifically with an eye toward missionary activity in Muslim-majority lands.

The Lack of a Missions Curriculum

The academic study of Christian mission, or missiology, did not develop in American seminaries until well into the twentieth century. Surprisingly, there were often no specific courses or programs in Christian missions during most of the nineteenth century. This was not the case because the idea of Christian missions was not deemed important. Rather, there had been a general assumption that preaching the Gospel to all ends of the earth, especially among a rapidly expanding European-descent population in North America, was a natural requirement and necessity of the Christian faith. From the origins of formal seminary education, Christian mission—domestic and foreign—was considered part of ministry in general and therefore not established as its own field of study.

A. C. Thompson (1812–1901), who was a student at Hartford seminary in the 1830s, never became a missionary, but he was a central figure in promoting missions when he returned to teach at his alma mater in 1888. Reflecting on the curriculum of Hartford during his years as a student, he affirmed, "Repeated and grateful reference is made to the eminently Biblical training given here, one result of which is a deepening love for the Sacred Scriptures; to the type of Biblical exegesis, which has enabled these brethren to know where and how to find that truth which they are to preach. Among those brethren there is but one voice in regard to the instruction—that the theology taught has stood them well in all their work."[5] It was Bible and theology that were at the heart of all instruction and formation. A solid grounding in these was sufficient to guide ministry wherever it would take the graduate, whether to a congregation in Boston, to the frontiers of Ohio, or to the eastern mountains of Anatolia.

Since the early seminaries had only two or three faculty, professors who taught about Christian missions were often the professors of pastoral theology, didactic theology, or church history.[6] Even when the schools began to grow and become more specialized, priorities were given to hiring a second Bible scholar and then a pastoral theologian. Hiring a professor of mission was not deemed necessary because all professors exuded the call to missions.

Princeton, however, was the exception. It is credited as the first American seminary to hire a professor of missions, Charles Breckenridge as the professor of pastoral theology and missionary instruction, in 1836. The position was short-lived, however. Breckenridge left Princeton after only three years to become the chair of the mission board of the Presbyterian Church, and the faculty position was never refilled. The course and the content of missions were then once again absorbed by other faculty, as they had been previously. In 1850, a course called "Pastoral Theology and Missionary Instruction" was offered, but again it was ultimately dropped from the curriculum in 1856. It was assumed that in studying didactic theology, students would learn all they needed to know about propagating the Gospel, wherever a graduate went. Two examples of this pedagogical experience are available to us in the archives at New Brunswick and Gettysburg seminaries.

Samuel M. Woodbridge (1819–1905) was the longest-serving professor at New Brunswick. He was the professor of pastoral theology, ecclesiastical history, and church government from 1857 to 1865, the professor of ecclesiastical history and church government from 1865 to 1901, and then emeritus professor from 1901 to 1905. This was a total of forty-eight years of instruction. His *Analysis of Systematic Theology*, developed from his lecture notes, published in 1872 and then revised in 1883, was required reading for all students.[7] Like similar works reflecting the theological commitments of the various Protestant denominations, Woodbridge's *Analysis* systematically lays out the Reformed understanding of God's Providence, human depravity, and the offer of God's grace to the repentant sinner.

The New Brunswick archives hold Samuel Zwemer's copy of Woodbridge's textbook. It provides us with interesting insights into his learning as a student. The textbook is littered with marginalia. These include handwritten notes in both English and Arabic as well as pasted passages from the Bible that Zwemer associated with a particular theological argument. Zwemer was not unique in his note taking in this regard; other students often did the same. However, what is unique is Zwemer's attempt to assimilate Woodbridge's Reformed theology into Arabic terms that he would use in his study of Islam with Professor John G. Lansing, and ultimately his work as a missionary in Arabia.[8]

At Gettysburg seminary, among the personal letters and papers of the first president and professor, Samuel S. Schmucker, are lecture notes from his days as a student at Princeton seminary. One set of notes is from Archibald Anderson's "Lectures on Polemic Theology." In these lectures Anderson covers the theological "errors," including "Deism, Paganism, Judaism, Mohammedanism, Humanitarianism, Socinianism . . . Popery . . . Arminianism, Fanaticism," among others. In Schmucker's handwritten notes on this wide-ranging theological encyclopedia of a course, we find the following comments on Islam: "Mohammed was a cruel, sensual man & a robber." The origin of Muhammad's "errors" was what Alexander called "enthusiasm" and "fanaticism." However, Islam was not unique among other human philosophies or created religions. It was one among many errors of humanity.[9]

These lectures by Woodbridge and Anderson reflect the early sentiment that pure seminary pedagogy was to focus on teaching the truth of scripture as understood through denominational theological lenses. A student who learned the truth of the Bible and how to preach and teach this would be able to stand against any wayward "error." It mattered little whether such errors were Enlightened Deists or "Mohammedans."

Visiting Missionaries

While there was no specific curriculum on Christian mission, seminaries were still places of practical activity of mission. The seminaries invited missionaries, many of whom were alumni, back to their alma maters. As we will see, it was often the students themselves who organized these visits and often raised money to support them. Later the lectures were endowed by gifts to the seminaries.[10] These public presentations, which were usually later published, helped to achieve the objectives of student-led missionary societies by providing direct information on missionary life abroad and generating further interest among the students.

The earliest presentation at a seminary about Islam was given by Eli Smith, who served with the American Board of Commissioners of Foreign Missions (ABCFM) in Syria. He came to the United States on a furlough in 1833 and visited Andover and Hartford seminaries. His presentation on Islam was later published as *Missionary Sermons and Addresses*.[11] Smith, who had already traversed much of the Near East by this time, provided an overview of the context and atmosphere of Christian missions among Muslims in the Ottoman Empire. He described the social and political changes to take place in the Ottoman Tanzimat period. These government-imposed reforms from 1839 to 1876 mandated the equality of all subjects before the law, regardless of one's religious identity. The changes were implemented under pressure from several European nations and were opposed by many of the religious leaders and wealthy landowners who believed that these modernizing trends went against the traditional social organization of the empire and their traditional authority.

Smith describes the "despotic" Ottoman Empire and "haughty" Muslims now being "humbled" by the advances of colonial Western nations, like Britain, France, and Russia. This political context was making it possible for missionaries to travel relatively freely as they were working with religious minorities that were being protected by these nations. At this early phase of American missionary activity in the Ottoman Empire, there was a great deal of hope for progress given the political events of the day. However, Smith warned that even as the sultan was engaging in modern political reforms, it was not possible to proselytize among Muslims, as there was too much social prejudice and animosity by Muslims against conversion from Islam. In fact, he provided several examples of the detrimental effects to those missionaries who had tried to publicly proselytize. Nevertheless, Smith maintained that it was an opportune moment for missionaries to work among the indigenous Christians of the empire. It was through them that Muslims would see the true nature of Christianity:

> By turning those churches, which now by their ungodly conduct only prejudice Moslems against Christianity, into truly pious communities, each set as a city upon a hill that cannot be hid; and in the meantime availing ourselves of every suitable opportunity to speak to Moslems themselves of Jesus and him crucified, even this great work may be effected.
>
> Among *the native Christians*, at any rate, in the present crisis of Mohammedanism, has Providence opened a wide field for missionary culture in Turkey. Among them especially are missionaries called for. How urgent is the call, I might show you, had I time, by portraying their wretched spiritual condition.[12]

Smith's views about Islam reflect a common understanding that both Eastern Muslims and Christians were in need of civilizing. However, after years of living in Beirut, his opinions would later become more nuanced. His relationship with Muslim and Christian scholars and acquaintances influenced his views about Islam and Near Eastern cultures, though these revised views did not find their way into later Protestant missionary circles.[13] Nevertheless, this publication served its purpose in promoting missions among its North American constituency.

While Smith's presentations represent a young and energetic missionary early in his career, Cyrus Hamlin's presence at Hartford, fifty-four years later, represents a seasoned missionary looking back on his life "among the Turks." Hamlin worked with the ABCFM from 1837 to 1859, when he left the mission to start Robert College, an English curriculum college open to all subjects of the empire, including Muslims. In 1877, Hamlin was forced to return to the United States against his will, being suddenly replaced as the president of the college. Devastated, he ultimately found employment at his alma mater, Bangor Theological Seminary. He taught there from 1877 to 1880, when he was offered the post of president of Middlebury College, which he held until he resigned in 1885. In 1887, Hamlin was invited to Hartford seminary to fill a short-term vacancy in theology. He stayed only for one year and then retired to a home in Massachusetts.[14] By this time, Hamlin had written *Among the Turks* and *My Life and Times* in 1877 and 1893, respectively. While we do not have a record of Hamlin's lecture notes or documentation of his teaching at Bangor or Hartford, *Among the Turks* was written the year before his appointment at Bangor.[15] Given that he had just returned from Turkey and was in the midst of a major life transition, one cannot but imagine that when he analyzed his previous missionary life at the time, the content of *Among the Turks* became much of the fodder he shared with his students on his missionary educational models.

Hamlin is a unique character among the early American missionaries. He often was at odds with his fellow missionaries, especially regarding mission policies. The ABCFM was adamant that indigenous languages were to be the medium of all activities, with a specific focus on the spiritualizing aspects of preaching the gospel and seeking converts. Hamlin, however, was an entrepreneur. He would come to promote secular education as part of a civilizing mission; he believed in education provided "for all its peoples, without distinction of race, language, color, or faith."[16] It is this irreconcilable difference in missionary methods that led him to leave the mission and found Robert College in 1863. Hamlin believed in the use of English education open to all members of society to promote productive subjects of the empire. This was a radical break from the other missionary associations of the time that sought to reform and revitalize the orthodox communities of the Near East to bring about any hope of converting Muslims.

Much in the same way that John Barrows viewed religions and civilizations, Hamlin believed that Western Protestant culture was the pinnacle of human endeavors. A Protestant Christian education would provide the basis for students to develop morally and religiously. While a Muslim student might not convert to Christianity, such a student would ultimately understand the true value of this "enlightened" education in the modern world. Modeling his views on the experience of missionaries in India, he asserted that English would be used because it was the universal language of international commerce and colonization. More importantly, he argued, it "is the grand store-house of knowledge in literature, science, and religion."[17]

In *Among the Turks*, Hamlin provided an extremely nuanced and complicated view of Islam. He was clear in pointing out that, first, Americans knew very little about Islam, despite there being English translations of the Qur'an readily available. He went on to complain that the information about Islam usually made available to the American public was often from travelers, politicians, or businesspeople, who had spent little time "among the Turks" and had a very shallow experience of Muslim culture. Here, Hamlin asserted that Islam as a religion is a complex entity that relies not only on the Qur'an but also on the Hadith of Muhammad as interpreted by religious scholars throughout the centuries.

Hamlin argued that there are four things that are central to understanding Islam. First is its positive belief in the one God: *theism*. "The worship offered to God is simple and profoundly reverent. It levels all human distinctions, and the highest and lowest bow together, without regard to station, birth, or wealth. There are souls so absorbed in this truth that they retire into it, and take no part in the empty superstitions of the faith."[18] This strong sense in submission to the deity, however, also leads to *fatalism*. Fatalism, he contended, prohibits the natural development of progress. Thus, Western liberal education—not just Christian education for the purpose of conversion—is the cure. Third, centuries of interpretating the Qur'an through the sayings of Muhammad in the Hadith had led to the establishment of empty *ritualism*. This focus on following the rules and laws of the scholars was pharisaical and did not free the mind or the soul.[19] Finally, Hamlin complained about Muhammad's *sensualism*, his permissiveness of polygamy and the promise of a Bacchus-like afterlife. The numerous sayings of Muhammad that focus on the promise of the afterlife, which have been collected and framed by many different religious scholars throughout the ages, have deterred the masses from real religion, he asserted. Ultimately, for Hamlin, Islam is a combination of localized superstitions, complex scholarly traditions about Muhammad, and only then a core message of theism from the

Qur'an. In the end, the general Muslim population of the Ottoman Empire was led astray by complicated interpretations of Islamic laws that are un-Qur'anic, but rather culturally despotic.

Despite all the caveats about Islam and the Turkish government, Hamlin still had hope for progress for Turkey. The Ottoman Empire was slowly reforming itself and would overcome its deficiencies. He noted that religious liberty for the Christians had been steadily increasing and Christian missions had never been more active in printing and distributing Christian literature. Ever the optimist, Hamlin concludes *Among the Turks* with a plea to his American audience to acknowledge and support Western education in the empire.

Years later, reflecting back on his life in his memoir, *My Life and Times*, Hamlin would be more critical of Islam itself, noting that "polygamy, concubinage, slavery, divorce, death penalty—all go together in the social and civil life of Islam."[20] Then again, he was just as critical, if not even more so, of his fellow Eastern Christians. Islam in the Qur'an had always been critical of idolatry, which Muslims "heartily reject, with all the sanctions of reason and conscience. As to worship and dogma [of Eastern Christianity], it saw nothing which it could not despise. It read the four Gospels, and then looked at the Christian church, and saw image, saint, and relic worship, and turned away in disgust."[21] Thus, Hamlin was convinced that the best option for the Near East was a progressive Protestant Christian system of education that could enlighten the mind and spirit. Christian mission must then endeavor toward a civilizing mission. Of course, his views were espoused before the atrocities against the Armenians and Assyrian Christians that became public in 1895, and he would die the year of the genocide of 1915. One wonders what response he would have given to the relationships between Turkish nationalism and Islam then.

Lectures in Christian Missions

These brief presentations by missionaries on furlough visits were eventually formalized as endowed lectures that became required attendance for students. The first was the Hyde Lectureship at Andover, which began in 1867 with Rufus Anderson, chair of the Prudential Committee of the ABCFM, although we have no record of the title or content of his lecture.[22] In 1884, Augustus Charles Thompson established the Lecture on Foreign Missions at Hartford. This was a series of ten to fifteen lectures each year to be offered by an invited lecturer. All students were required to attend and were examined on the content of the lectures. Princeton commenced its Students' Lecturer in Missions program in 1892–1893. Usually, the chosen missionary was an alum. While Princeton sent out many missionaries around the world, only a handful worked in Muslim-majority contexts, primarily the Ottoman Empire and India. The inaugural lecturer of the Princeton program was James S. Dennis (1842–1914), a graduate from 1868, and a missionary of the Presbyterian Church in Beirut. He came to Princeton on a furlough, taught Arabic in the biblical studies department, and provided the inaugural lecture entitled "Foreign Missions after a Century." Dennis worked in Syria his whole career, first under the ABCFM and then under the Presbyterian Mission Board when they assumed ownership of the ABCFM mission stations in Syria in 1870. He lived in Sidon for several years before moving to teach at the Presbyterian seminary in Beirut for the remainder of his missionary career. Upon his retirement in 1896, he was invited back to Princeton to give a second series of lectures as the Students' Lecturer in Missions.

In 1896, Dennis decided not to research documents or textual evidence about missions but wanted to give living testimonials of missionary insights on contemporary social issues. As with the Edinburgh conference that would follow several years later, Dennis sent out questionnaires to three hundred missionaries around the world, soliciting input on all manner of sociological issues they encountered, including individual, family, and tribal "social evils," such as gambling, intemperance, drugs (particularly opium), polygamy, adultery, child marriage, slavery, witchcraft, "uncivilized and cruel customs," "idleness," poverty, and much more. He organized these responses into six lectures that reviewed the missionary data. In the end, he concluded that modern Protestant Christianity could provide answers to all the challenges to human cultures.

The wonder, the magic—the divine wisdom, rather—of Christianity is its power of adjusting itself to all human environments and of Christianizing without destroying them. . . . In this respect it reveals its immense superiority to mere civilization. . . . The highest and noblest achievement of Christianity, however, is its power to lead the individual heart out of and above its environment into spiritual contact with God. The transformed and renewed personality—kindly, unselfish, true-hearted, and pure—is the ultimate solution of social evils and the sure promise of a redeemed society, fashioned at last into the likeness of Christ.[23]

Dennis' initial lectures at Princeton were so popular that he was invited to three other Presbyterian seminaries, Auburn, Lane, and Western (but not Union, interestingly). An expansion of the lectures was published in a massive three-volume work, *Christian Missions and Social Progress: A Sociological Study of Foreign Missions.* This became a standard resource for mission courses throughout the early twentieth century and can be found in all the seminary libraries in this study. However, recognizing that not all students would have the stamina to pore through all three volumes, the Student Volunteer Movement edited Dennis' work down to 171 pages. *Social Evils of the Non-Christian World* provided outlines of the lectures and addressed the specific topics of social ills and "evils" that could be studied by student groups. Because of this publication, Dennis was considered a prominent expert witness of the Protestant missionary age. He would go on to be invited to attend the 1900 Ecumenical Missionary Conference in New York and the 1910 World Missionary Conference in Edinburgh.[24] Thus, he had a profound effect on American Protestant views of mission, world religions, and Islam.

Dennis' premise was a simple one: Christian mission has resulted in social progress wherever it goes. His argument was essentially that preached by Archibald Anderson seventy-five years earlier from the same seminary chapel at Princeton. "That there is a striking apologetic import to the aspect of missions herein presented is evident. It is not merely a vindication of the social value of mission work, but it becomes, in proportion to the reality and significance of the facts put in evidence, a present-day supplement to the cumulative argument of history in defense of Christianity as a supreme force in the social regeneration and elevation of the human race."[25] Responding to the popular trends in the study of comparative religions and the Social Darwinist theories of Herbert Spencer, Dennis argues that "primitive" or "ethnic religions" may have a kernel of transcendent revelation in them, but it cannot be concluded that there is a Hegelian progression of humanity's knowledge, morality, and spirituality. Human beings may have received some revelation of the truth, but in most cases, they have fallen away to follow "half-truths." "Half-truths" are more dangerous for society. Thus, Western Protestant mission provides the opportunity for wayward societies to recover what they have lost or misconstrued. Rather than judging other religions as aspects of God's truth or activity, the only true standard of religion is that which can verifiably lift people from immorality and backwardness.

> The idea . . . that Christianity, including primitive revelation and the Old Testament dispensation, is an involution introduced into the course of human history by the God of Providence for the purpose of promoting individual and social progress, and changing what would otherwise be a downward into an upward evolution, seems to the author to be merely the restatement in modern terms of the unchangeable and ever true doctrine of Redemption. This simply means that in the long struggle of human society toward moral perfection God has contributed a notable—in fact, an indispensable factor in the gift of an ideal religion.[26]

According to Dennis, that gift is Western Protestantism.

While Dennis served his entire missionary career abroad in Syria, Islam is only one part of a larger narrative in *Christian Missions*. Dennis does accept that Islam was originally a reforming movement away from Oriental polytheism toward the worship of the one God. However, he sees it as doomed to fail from the start. What Dennis gives with the left hand, he takes away with the right. He contended that Islam was a true reforming religion but is, in the end, spiritually, morally, and socially irredeemable. He claimed that the cultural environment of the East and Muhammad's leadership and desire for power would not lend themselves to moral or ethical development in a culture that was built upon spiritual and social despotism.[27] He wrote,

> At the close of the era of conquest the real social history of Islam may be said to begin, and it has been marked by a notable absence of progress in political civilization or of moral training and culture in the individual and the family. As regards its relations to the civilized world, it is a gigantic

and demoralizing social incubus, with no power of cooperation, adaptation, and moral adjustment. Its fixed tradition, fatalism, its legislative rigors, its ceremonial exactions, its spirit of despotism, its degradation of woman, its sanction to slavery, and its cruel fanaticism are impassable barriers between Islam and progressive culture. The Koran invariably calls a halt to civilization.[28]

Repeating the same arguments as Archibald Anderson, he averred that Islam brings about "disorder and decay."[29] The difference between the two perspectives, however, is that Dennis had three hundred firsthand missionary perspectives from which he drew. His research was based not on English Orientalist texts but on "objective" missionary experiences. This blistering attack on all things not considered truly Christian sets up a foregone conclusion, where the answers to the problems of humanity are framed by the very people who are proposing the questions. Dennis's three-volume "scientific" sociological analysis of human society was founded upon the descriptions of human societies for which the Protestant missionary population around the world had a front-row seat. They were at the time the ostensible experts of the day on anthropology, sociology, and ethnography.

Unlike Hamlin, who promoted a secular Western education for progress, Dennis argued that enlightened Western education is not sufficient to transform Muslim societies. The answer to human degradation is a true spiritual Western Protestant Christianity that will provide the way only through the true spiritual and moral example of the missionaries. It will only be the individual unbeliever who, faced with the moral and spiritual truth of sin, will repent. Dennis invoked Charles Darwin, who after a visit to a converted community of Maori in New Zealand pronounced, "The lesson of the missionary is the enchanter's wand" that will magically cure all social ills.[30] The third volume of the publication provides evidence of hundreds of Protestant missionaries living and working all over the world who had at their disposal many different avenues to work their magic, through building schools and hospitals, imploring local governments to change laws, and encouraging community leaders to eschew outdated social customs.

A fellow Princeton graduate from 1892 and fellow Presbyterian missionary, William Ambrose Shedd (1865–1918), was also invited to give the Students' Lectures on Missions, in 1902. His six lectures, entitled "The Historical Relation of Islam and the Oriental Churches," were ultimately published as *Islam and the Oriental Churches: Their Relations*.[31] Like Dennis, Shedd also gave these lectures at several other Presbyterian seminaries, including Auburn, McCormick, Chicago, and the Presbyterian Theological Seminary of Kentucky. Growing up as a missionary child in Persia, graduating from Princeton, and now a missionary himself, Shedd was highly valued as a trusted authority for his views on Islam. Thus, he had an important impact on Presbyterian views of Islam.

While Dennis posited a stark difference between Western Protestant ethics and other unreliable Eastern religious cultures, Shedd promoted a positive perspective of Eastern Christianity. In fact, Shedd was quite clear that Western Christians had often been misled in their views of the Eastern churches, especially the Assyrian Church of the East—what was generally known as the "Nestorian Church." Shedd emphatically asserted, "An often and opposite error cannot be expressed more tersely than in the following sentences from the Report of the Ecumenical Missionary Conference in New York: 'When Muhammad arose, Christianity was so dead that it was putrid. Muhammadanism [*sic*] crushed it in its mailed hand as if it had been a Dead Sea apple.'"[32] Rather, he argues, the Assyrian Church of the East was a missionary church with a prolonged and prosperous history. Long associated with the excommunicated patriarch of Constantinople in 431, Nestorius, the more accurately titled Assyrian Church of the East was not able to shed its pejorative association. Shedd was a unique voice in the Western circles who had access to the Assyrian Church and its history and culture. His lectures and subsequent publication were an important contribution not only to missionary thinking about Islam but also to Western scholarship on the Eastern Syriac-speaking churches. His overall perspective was that there was sufficient depth of wisdom and knowledge that Western Christians should support the reform of the ancient Christian church of the East.

Shedd's views of Islam were not unique, however. Much like Professor Preserved Smith at Union, Shedd believed that Muhammad was influenced by Judaism and heretical forms of Christianity. In his first lecture Shedd posited that there are enough musings on the different kinds of Christian heresies in the Qur'an to demonstrate that Muhammad, as the author of the Qur'an, did not have an accurate understanding of Christianity. He only learned of its heretical forms. "Besides this dogmatic contradiction of doctrines that have become identified with historic Christianity, and besides the denial to Jesus of a unique place and authority in religious and spiritual matters, there is in Islam, as we have seen, a misrepresentation and distortion of the facts of the sacred history of Christianity."[33] However, Shedd does not see Muhammad as an impostor or a trickster, as was common in earlier Christian views, but rather as an influential Arab preacher and poet who taught a conglomerated Oriental monotheism.

What is unique about Shedd's approach to the study of Islam was his reliance on Syriac sources. Growing up and living in the heartland of the Assyrian Church in Urumia, Persia, Shedd was able to read Syriac. During his furlough in the United States, he availed himself of two medieval Syriac histories, Bar Hebraeus from the thirteenth century and Bishop Thomas of Marga from the ninth, which he borrowed from the Hartford and Princeton seminary libraries, respectively.[34] Thus, by relying on these medieval Syriac texts throughout his lectures, Shedd highlights the importance of the Assyrian Church's theology and history as the primary Christian influence on Islam and Muslim-Christian relations.

Contrary to promoting Muhammad and Islam as a persecutor of Christians, Shedd notes that in his subjugation of the East, the Prophet did actually provide for the preservation of the Christian communities, allowing them to organize their own affairs freely. In fact, for much of the Arab rule, especially during much of the Abbasid period in Baghdad, Christians "shared in the general fortune of the country, good and bad, perhaps having more than their proportionate share of the wealth, on account of their higher culture . . . in spite of the heavier burdens of taxation that they bore and their lower position before the law."[35] The restrictions on Christians from the Covenant of 'Umar, which required them to wear distinct clothing, for example, were only occasionally enforced and then only in localized instances. There was a general tolerance for religious diversity and relative autonomy for all subjects of the caliph. Shedd reminded his Western audience that Eastern Christians shared the same cultural context as Muslims.

Ultimately, Shedd claimed, it was not Muslim rule that undermined the Assyrian Church of the East but the terror and chaos of the Mongol invasion and rule in the fourteenth century. Nevertheless, he concluded that humanity had progressed in its understanding or expectation of mere tolerance. The world now required religious freedom, something that had been elusive in the Near East. He remarked that medieval and early modern political rule was always arbitrary for Muslims and Christians alike, depending on the ruler and local conditions. At least Christians could turn to Muhammad's practice of tolerance to support their acceptance as second-class citizens, but that was the best they could expect. There was no blueprint for anything more than mere tolerance. In this regard, Shedd concluded that antagonism between Islam and Christianity is inevitable because Islam has required political structures to which Christians must acquiesce. Thus, Islam is still "a problem" for Christians in Asia, Shedd stated flatly. The solution, of course, was the example of a simple Christian faith in its Asian form, free from political and worldly entanglements, that might convince Muslims of the truth of Jesus. Even while breaking with much of the past Christian interpretation of Islamic history through his reading of Syriac Christian sources, Shedd was still a committed evangelist living among Eastern Orthodox Christians, and Turkish, Kurdish, and Arab Muslims. In response to the trends in the seminaries at the turn of the century, quoting the English minister Joseph Parker, Shedd announced, "There are comparative religions, but Christianity is not one of them. The story of Jesus Christ, his character, his love, his death, denied by the Prophet in shallow flattery— the preaching of these shall win men to him. The character of Christ, exemplified in the purity of the home, in the tenderness of the physician, in the righteous life and preaching of the missionary, shall lead men to realize something of holiness and of sin."[36] Shedd believed that Protestant missionaries could provide a living witness to the simplicity of the Christian faith to reinstill in the ancient Assyrian Church its original missionary spirit. This was something he had seen as a boy growing up in the local Assyrian evangelical community and now as the principal leader of the Presbyterian missionary association in Urumia. It is the missionary's job not to establish a Western Christian church but to encourage the indigenous Christians in their true missionary calling. Interestingly, to do this he advocated for the introduction of a Protestant monasticism. Shedd remarked how effective monks had been in the establishment of Eastern Christianity throughout the centuries. Thus, a Protestant monasticism would provide a true image of the faith for both

Assyrians, Armenians, and Syrians and the Kurds, Persians, and Turks. The long tradition of "Bahira the monk" in Islam and the positive connotations of the monks in the Qur'an would even establish credibility among Muslims.

In the end, Shedd was less pessimistic about the opportunities for the Assyrian Church than about the ability of the Turks to change their heavy-handed administration. While Islam was capable of adapting throughout history, the Turks had shown their true colors as despotic rulers, he asserted. Shedd was a realist when it came to protection of the Christian communities in the face of a brutal world war that had reared its head at the beginning of the twentieth century. He believed that the Turkish government was not to be trusted, as he had seen the terrible effects of warfare. Urumia was situated squarely on the border between the Ottoman and Russian empires and exchanged hands throughout the war. Sadly, Shedd would ultimately become one of the war's victims, dying of cholera while helping to evacuate Christians from Urumia in 1918. His life was memorialized by his wife in a bestselling hagiography, *The Measure of a Man: The Life of William Ambrose Shedd, Missionary to Persia*, in 1922.[37]

Another Princeton alumnus invited to give the Student Lectures on Missions and Islam was Elwood Morris Wherry (1843–1927). By the time he arrived at Princeton to give his eight lectures in 1906, he was already well known in Presbyterian circles as a prolific missionary scholar of Islam. Two of his works, *Islam; or, The Religion of the Turk* (1886) and *A Comprehensive Commentary on the Qur'an* (1882–1886), were widely disseminated and promoted among mission agencies, especially after he organized the 1906 Cairo and 1911 Lucknow missionary conferences on Islam with Samuel Zwemer.

Wherry graduated from Princeton in 1867 and immediately went out to serve with the Presbyterian Board of Foreign Missions in India. For thirty-seven years he was involved in publishing Christian evangelical material for the Mission Press or teaching at the seminary in Saharanpur in North India. As was noted above, he worked with Zwemer to put together the publication for the 1906 Cairo conference, helped to host the 1911 Lucknow conference, and published the subsequent proceedings as *Islam and Missions*. Like Zwemer, Wherry saw Islam as in inevitable conflict with Christianity because it was untrue and deceitful. In his *Compre-*

hensive Commentary on the Qur'an, published in four volumes between 1882 and 1886, Wherry regarded the Prophet as ignorant of the true Bible and Christianity and, in the end, as cruel and an impostor. Responding to a recent optimistic biography of Muhammad written by W. Bosworth Smith, Wherry attacked the author for covering over Muhammad's "multitude of sins," moral and spiritual.[38] The commentary was written primarily for missionaries in their direct evangelizing efforts with Muslims. It was widely recognized as a critical tool for missionary work.[39]

Wherry was focused on evangelizing directly among the Muslim community in northern India, something that was not possible in the Muslim-majority Ottoman or Persian empires. Even so, while having much more freedom under British rule to propagate the Gospel openly, he and his missionary colleagues had long learned the negative lessons of public confrontation from the controversy of the former missionary Karl Pfander in his public debate with the Muslim scholar Rahmatullah Kairanawi in 1854. The debate was a disaster for the Christian missionary community. In the Indian public eye, Pfander had lost.[40] In addition, following the bloody Indian Rebellion of 1857–1858, which resulted in India officially being brought under British imperial and colonial rule, the British were wary of any antagonizing efforts by missionaries among the Muslim community. Thus, he warned against direct public debate with Muslims. Rather, the missionary should highlight Islamic errors through reasoned Christian literature.

The eight lectures he gave, which were ultimately published as *Islam and Christianity in India and the Far East*, intended to provide an overall argument of the violent spread of Islam in South and East Asia through both Muslim occupation and subsequent Muslim governments that imposed Islam. Ironically, like Zwemer, Wherry believed that the British Empire in its sovereignty over the East provided opportunities for the fruitful spread of Christianity. In his preface to the publication of the lectures, he wrote, "It remained for Protestant governments to bring to the Moslem world the gospel of religious liberty and to enable the Christian evangelist to present the saving truth of God's Word to his Moslem hearer without let or hindrance."[41]

In his opening lecture, Wherry provided an overview of Islamic history and an introduction to the life of Muhammad, the Qur'an, and Muslim religious practices. He also highlighted the diversity of Muslim communities. Wherry's knowledge of Islam was quite impressive. He demonstrated his knowledge of not only the original sources but even the contemporary effects of the Wahhabi influence in southeast Asia, as well as the reformist positions of Sayyid Ahmad Khan. Wherry also was one of the few missionaries to note the more recent impact of Mirza Gulam Ahmad as a "false Messiah," whose preaching led to the establishment of the Ahmadiyya movement.[42]

Wherry concludes the lectures with a summons to increased missionary work, pointing out two effective methods of evangelization: preaching and the publication of Christian literature, including the Bible, in indigenous languages. He advocated that a preacher should appeal to the fact that Muhammad was a preacher himself. Muhammad preached to the unyielding polytheists in Mecca. Here, the Christian missionary might find some sympathy among Muslims, as long as the missionary called all people to repentance, even the Christians. Wherry seemed to believe that there were enough similarities in the concept of the revelation of God's Word to save one from judgment that Muslims would be able to hear a skilled preacher. The second method of effective evangelization Wherry espoused was the publication of Christian literature. Pamphlets, periodicals, and books provide the missionary with opportunities to provide literature to be read by Muslims in the privacy of their own home, outside of the confines of a public debate. Wherry's final comments were directed toward encouraging young seminarians to follow this missionary path in the Islamic world.

Student Missionary Associations

Despite the remarkable explosion of missionary activity in the early nineteenth century, it was not until the 1890s that the seminaries began appointing faculty specifically to teach Christian missions. Even with the notable exception of Princeton, it was not until after the 1910 Edinburgh World Missionary conference that seminaries began to create full-time chairs in missions or missiology. By that time, students had already been organizing themselves into ecumenical and international networks of associations for over one hundred years! These student-led societies became the backbone of what Kenneth Scott Lattourette called "the great century" of mission.[43]

The Great Awakening in North America at the end of the eighteenth century fostered and generated an evangelical movement among Protestant denominations in North America. This new spirit of revivalism after the American Revolution contributed to and encouraged the founding and initial success of the newly formed seminaries.[44] There was now a willing pool of male students whose hearts had been warmed by the spirit or who had had a conversionary experience and committed themselves to ministry. Many of these students who enrolled in seminary were interested in or enamored with the idea of serving as a missionary, either on the frontier of an expanding United States or overseas.[45] To be a missionary was an appealing career choice. The interest in Christian missions was, then, in many ways commensurate with the establishment of the American seminaries.

Even though there was no mission requirement in the curriculum and no professor of Christian missions or missiology, it was the students who led the way in organizing and advocating for the study of missions. Students organized societies "for the inquiry of missions." Only two years after the creation of Andover seminary, the students formed the Society of Inquiry of Foreign Missions in 1811.[46] At Princeton a society was created in 1814, at New Brunswick in 1820, at Gettysburg in 1826,[47] and at Union in 1837.[48] There are no records that indicate the start of the student missionary society at Hartford or General.[49] However, by the 1880s there was a monthly meeting of the societies at each school. At General, theoretically all members of the student body were included.[50]

The student missionary societies organized themselves in sophisticated fashions. They elected officers, held meetings, raised funds, and began correspondence with other student societies at American seminaries, as well as missionary institutes and colleges in Europe, and missionaries in the field. Within a short time, these voluntary associations also developed an impressive international network of relationships of graduates who had become missionaries.[51] The students gathered monthly to exchange letters with other societies, read papers or books on missions, and put together biographies of former classmates who had died abroad. They also organized several ecumenical meetings and lectureships and published their own tracts on missions. Looking back on his time at New Brunswick, Samuel Zwemer wrote, "The missionary spirit in New Brunswick Seminary . . . was due to several cooperating causes: the Student Volunteer Movement, and Graves Missionary Lectures, the fact most of our professors were missionary minded and the Society of Inquiry which discussed missions at its regular meeting. All these worked together so that even around the dinner table there would be hot discussions on home and foreign missions."[52]

For their part, missionaries regularly wrote letters back to their constituencies who supported the American missionary enterprise, including the students at their alma maters. These letters were often serialized in journals dedicated to missions, to increase interest in and financial support for their work. The ABCFM's newsletter, the *Missionary Herald*, was an important and popular mouthpiece for the work of the American missionaries. The periodicals of the mission boards were sent to the seminary libraries, and the private letters and reports were shared at the student association meetings.[53] The ABCFM and the Presbyterian Church also supported the publication of several books by missionaries, which were purchased for seminary libraries, that provided information on mission to Muslims that piqued the curiosity of evangelical supporters as well as the students.[54]

These networks of correspondence produced a great deal of positive energy that fed into the lifeblood of the student body and led many graduates to apply to mission boards for service. If the seminaries inherently stuck to their denominational loyalties and politics, the students had no qualms about reaching across the confessional aisle for the purpose of Christian missions. The Christian missionary enterprise was the first ecumenical movement, and the ABCFM, which consisted of Baptists, Congregationalists, and Presbyterians, was the largest ecumenical organization throughout the nineteenth century.

As the associations were interested in Christian mission in general, the students only occasionally discussed topics or read papers related to Islam. These were sometimes published and forwarded to the reading public to increase interest in missions. For example, in 1830, the student association at Andover published a tract called *The Condition and Character of Females in Pagan and Mohammedan Countries*, compiled from a variety of missionary letters and travel correspondence. Six thousand copies were initially printed and distributed. However, there was so much interest that an additional twenty thousand were printed! The pamphlet was a simple statement of "facts" related to the "pagan,

Mohammedan or Hindoo culture" and their "degradation" of women and marriage, through polygamy and other "servile" functions. The pamphlet then concludes, "What then must be done? What, to rescue Pagan women from bondage?"[55] This, as Gayatri Chakravorty Spivak has noted, was a call for "white men to save brown women from brown men."[56]

The earliest American missionaries, and graduates of Andover, Princeton, and New Brunswick, went to India to work among the Hindus, as well as to the Sandwich Islands (Hawaii), China, and West Africa. However, some of the members of these societies would go on to be influential missionaries who lived and worked in Muslim-majority contexts, including Eli Smith, Josiah Brewer, and Horatio Southgate (Andover), George Bowen, Elmwood Wherry, Henry Jessup (Union), and James Cantine and Samuel Zwemer (New Brunswick). Other graduates of these seminaries who worked in Muslim-majority contexts were deemed successful by their constituents simply because they chose to work in Muslim lands. These missionaries wrote about Islam to the supporters and spoke when on furloughs. The Turkish, Armenian, Nestorian, and Syrian missions of the ABCFM in the Ottoman Empire, as they were called, proved to be the longest-lasting missionary enterprise for the American seminary graduates from Andover and Princeton, while the Arabian Mission staffed by New Brunswick seminary graduates had a lasting impact on Christian-Muslim relations throughout the twentieth century.[57] The two seminaries that never really established a strong connection to the Muslim world through missions were Gettysburg and General. Horatio Southgate, the first Episcopal missionary to the Ottoman Empire, was originally a graduate of Andover and a Congregationalist before he became an Episcopalian. He was ordained a bishop to engage in mission overseas from 1836 to 1850. His letters and papers are now held in the archives of General seminary. However, he became entangled in theological debates with other missionaries of the ABCFM, and ultimately the controversy led to his return to the United States. In many ways, this was a failed attempt at joining the ecumenical network of missions.[58]

Graduates of Gettysburg would go on to work as missionaries primarily on the frontiers of the expanding US territories. Those who did go abroad went to India and West Africa.[59] American Lutherans would not organize any mission to a Muslim-majority land until 1910, when the Lutheran Orient Mission sent a graduate of Luther Seminary in St. Paul, Minnesota, Ludwig O. Fossum (1879–1920), to evangelize among Muslim Kurds in Urumia.[60] However, the earliest American Lutheran reflection on Islam took place at the Society of Inquiry on Missions at Gettysburg in 1827. One of the founding members of the society and among the first class of students at Gettysburg, Lewis Eichelberger, read a paper entitled "By What Arguments Can We Best Convince the Mohammedans of the Falsity of Their Religion?" The paper was based on the book *A Brief Outline of the Evidences of the Christian Religion* by Archibald Alexander. Samuel Schmucker, the president and only professor of Gettysburg seminary at that time, had been a student of Alexander's at Princeton. Schmucker had heard Alexander's original sermon on this topic in 1823 and purchased a copy of the sermon that was published as a book in 1825. He lent the book to Eichelberger for his presentation before the society.

Eichelberger, as far as we know, had no further knowledge of or interest in serving as a missionary in a Muslim-majority context, as he never wrote about Islam again. In fact, he may not even have read an English translation of the Qur'an, as the quotations from the Qur'an in his paper are taken directly from Alexander's book (based on George Sale's English translation). He also had no other information about Muslim-majority contexts other than what he read through Alexander's book, and possibly from letters from other missionaries serving in Muslim-majority nations. In his paper, Eichelberger argued that Islam rules by violence and despotism. Quoting Alexander directly, Eichelberger recited to his fellow students that "despotism extends its iron scepter over these ill-fated countries, and all the tranquility ever enjoyed, is the dead calm of ignorance and slavery."[61] The presentation was intended to incite fellow students to the missionary life among Muslims. Eichelberger himself would not take up this call, however, becoming a pastor to congregations in Maryland and the Carolinas.

While there was no specific program in Christian missions in the curricula of the seminaries, several professors sponsored or encouraged the student missionary societies, including Archibald Alexander, Samuel Schmucker, A. C. Thompson, Charles Breckenridge, and Leonard Woods. Woods, professor at Andover, documented the early days of the

Society of Inquiry there. He documented the letters to the society from the first American missionaries to the Near East, including Levi Parsons, Pliny Fisk, Jonas King, Isaac Bird, William Goodell, and Daniel Temple.[62] Of particular note among faculty supporters of student missions, however, was John G. Lansing, professor of Old Testament languages and exegesis at New Brunswick. In 1899, he and three students—James Cantine, Philip Phelps, and Samuel Zwemer—gathered to consider founding a mission in an Arabic-speaking country. This meeting led to the creation of the Reformed Arabian Mission.[63] Lansing's important contribution to the use of the Qur'an in teaching Hebrew was discussed earlier. The effect of his teaching Arabic as a cognate biblical language to a generation of seminary students cannot be underestimated. Lansing was the son of missionaries in Egypt. His family history and memories of Egypt created a unique opportunity for students who were interested in missions. His stories and trinkets from Egypt—including papyri and manuscripts—created an "Oriental fervor" among the students envisioning a glamorous and romantic life as a missionary.[64] While Lansing had long desired to return to the Near East as a missionary, health concerns prohibited him. It was, however, his relationships with Cantine and Zwemer that played an essential role in creating the Arabian Mission and setting Zwemer on his path and vocation of "Mission to Islam."

Student Volunteer Movement

Student mission associations were not limited only to the seminaries. The most successful ecumenical student association created was the Student Volunteer Movement (SVM). This student association became not only an avenue for relationship building and information sharing about Christian mission but an effective recruitment agency at colleges and seminaries across the country. As part of a broader idealistic fervor within the late nineteenth century, many middle- and upper-class students were influenced by the growing opportunities of religious revivals through the likes of Dwight Moody and his vision of the Young Men's Christian Association (YMCA) and the Young Women's Christian Association (YWCA). Similarly, the SVM encouraged college and seminary students to take "the mission pledge" and commit their lives not only to Christ but to "home and foreign" missions.[65]

Missionary agencies wanted missionaries who were well prepared and well educated. They desired the "cream of the crop" of their generation of students, encouraging theologically astute and linguistically gifted individuals to enter the ministry as missionaries. The SVM actualized a recruiting system at colleges and seminaries that was predominantly student led.[66] While seminary education may have been helpful for some, it was not a requirement for "the pledge" or for service abroad. This was especially the case for women, who began to volunteer for missionary service in greater numbers.[67] The SVM was an ecumenical and intergender movement that cut against the grain of seminary denominational loyalty and confessionalism common among the seminaries of North America.

In the summer of 1886, nearly fifty students attended the first SVM conference. The conference was the brainchild of Princeton resident and Union alum Robert P. Wilder. By 1912, the SVM claimed that it had a presence in 729 institutions of higher learning and 40,406 students in their association across the United States. By 1914, the SVM claimed that 5,882 volunteers had been sent out by fifty-five different missionary agencies, and almost half were women![68] Princeton itself contributed significantly to this movement. In fact, in addition to Wilder, Frank Ellingwood and Robert Speer both were Presbyterian mission executives and Princeton alumni. Speer, the indefatigable missionary administrator, claimed that between 1812 and 1875, one in eighteen graduates of Princeton became missionaries and that between 1875 and 1912 the percentage was one in nine.[69]

There is something unique about the combination of American Protestant frontier religion, the belief in voluntarism, and the drive toward entrepreneurship that provided the key ingredients for the success of the SVM, as well as many other missionary associations. Like other moral causes, such as abolition or the temperance and suffrage movements, overseas mission was another opportunity for an American spiritual crusade. Interestingly, as quickly as the movement gained popularity and momentum it fizzled out, just as the institutions of the church were gearing up. By 1918, World War I shattered the ideals of those young Americans hoping to go abroad and change the world. American students began looking to other domestic moral causes at home, or some even chose the lure of the self-indulgent lifestyles of the 1920s.[70]

The genius of the SVM was that it was predominantly student organized and led. It relied on paid student secretaries to travel and recruit and speak on behalf of the cause of missions. The SVM also organized courses and book clubs to read the biographies of renowned missionaries or descriptions of missionary life. Occasionally the SVM would also publish tracts or pay for the reprinting of previous books on missions, such as *A Handbook of Comparative Religions* by Samuel Kellogg and James Dennis's *Social Evils of the Non-Christian World*. These small booklets were intended to be studied by student groups, outside of the required college or seminary curriculum. These pamphlets often led students to take issue with the trends in the study of comparative religions.

Regarding Islam, the most prominent pamphlet published by the SVM was Samuel Zwemer's *Islam: A Challenge to Faith* in 1907. This booklet was written to encourage students to "take the oath" and become missionaries, specifically to work "among Mohammedans." The "problem and the peril of Islam" were challenges, not something to be feared but to be embraced, assured Zwemer. In an address to the SVM convention, later included as part of this booklet, Zwemer proclaimed, "The battle is the Lord's and the victory will be his also. . . . Why should we not attack vigorously when the enemy is beginning to waver?"[71] "The time is ripe for a world-wide spiritual crusade."[72]

Zwemer's booklet provides information on the history of Islam, the beliefs of Muslims, and the latest then known data on Muslims around the world. He firmly believed that by "objectively" analyzing Muslim societies, Christians would be able to arm themselves with information that would yield success in the evangelization of those Muslim communities. Like many of his predecessors, Zwemer argued that Islam was morally and spiritually decrepit and was "disintegrating" from within. For Zwemer, Islam was "a concoction . . . mixing old ingredients into a new panacea for human ills, and forcing it down by means of the sword."[73]

Islam: A Challenge to Faith became the basis for a one-page brochure published for the 1913 SVM convention. The foldout brochure, *Islam*, was a "cheat sheet" for Christian students to understand Islam from an evangelical and polemical perspective. The left-hand column provided information on the history of Islam. "Mohammedanism," it claimed, had its origins from three main traditions: Arabian heathenism, Judaism,

Islam.

God so Loved the World that He gave His only begotten Son.

The Challenge of Islam.

Alone of non-Christian faiths.
Islam claims to have judged and superseded Christianity.

Islam Affirms.	Islam Denies.
The Unity of God. A conception majestic in simplicity but sterile. God is aloof, passionless, needing no-one, loving no-one. Character is overlooked in emphasising unity.	**The Fatherhood of God.** "Like as a Father pitieth His children."
The Might of God. Absolute, autocratic will-power, acting apart from reason and love. A greatness that crushes. Submission to such a God tends to fatalism.	**The Holiness of God.** "Thus saith the High and Lofty One Whose Name is Holy, I dwell with him that is of a contrite and humble spirit to revive the spirit of the humble."
The Mercy of God. The spasmodic clemency of a despot, lenient to sin as well as to the sinner. No deep hatred of sin; no sense of the cost of forgiveness. No need for atonement.	**The Mystery of the Incarnation.** "One God and one Mediator between God and men, the Man, Christ Jesus." "The Son of God Who loved me and gave Himself for me."
The Fact of a Sinless Prophet—Jesus. Son of Mary. "Word of God," "Spirit of God" who worked miracles, ascended to Heaven and will come again.	**The Fact of the Cross.** "Christ Crucified the Power of God and the Wisdom of God."
The Unique Relation to God of a Sinful Prophet—Mohammed. Final revealer of God to men.	**The Presence of the Holy Spirit.** "He shall guide you into all Truth. He shall glorify ME."

" Islam defies your King."
(Cable sent by Cairo Student Volunteers to the 1900 Conference.)

On the gateway of the Church of St. John the Baptist
at Damascus, now a Mosque, still stand the words

Thy Kingdom, O Christ,
Is a Kingdom of all Ages.

A Call to Prayer

"That they may know Thee
the only true God
and Jesus Christ Whom Thou hast sent."

Thy Kingdom Come.

Figure 6.1. Student Volunteer Movement tract on "Islam" (1914), from Internet Archive.

and a "Corrupt Christianity." The central column described the "Challenge of Islam" and Islam's central tenets in comparison to the beliefs of Christianity. Here the pamphlet claims that in the Islamic understanding, God is described as "autocratic" and a "spasmodic . . . despot," while the Christian view is that God is loving. The final right-hand column highlights the missionary nature of Islam. It includes several passages from the Qur'an that describe "Islamic daw'wah": its demands to kill "idolaters" and "[put] to the sword those who do not submit" (notably the "sword verses" from surah 9). Finally, at the bottom of the brochure is a list of recommended books, including Elmwood Wherry and Samuel Zwemer's *Islam and Missions* (1911) and Zwemer's full book *Islam: A Challenge to Faith* (1909, 2nd ed.).[74]

The Development of Mission Schools

By the last decade of the nineteenth century, a curriculum for Christian missions began to take shape in many seminaries. Christian mission as a viable profession was popular due to clear vocational options. Domestically, missionary organizations in urban spaces, like the YMCA and the YWCA, attracted many young students to a different kind of ministry. Student mission organizations continued to draw many in through their organized programs. In addition, American interests in the wider world were beginning to take on an imperial form. The United States annexed Hawaii in 1897 after a de facto period of rule and began to flex its international muscles, fighting over Cuba with Spain. While there were serious debates about the morality of American imperialism, within the seminaries there was no doubt that American Christians had a role to play in the opportunities of Christian evangelization around the world. There was a general interest in the world, and mission societies provided opportunities. Finally, there was a major revolution taking place in higher education at this time. Graduate schools and programs as we know them today began to take shape as research institutions. Specialized courses began to be offered as electives for advanced-level students. These electives allowed students with particular interests to expand their horizons, rather than simply follow a general seminary curriculum. There was a "professionalization" of theological disciplines for both professors and students.[75] It is within this context of a changing role of graduate education that the study of Christian missions began to take shape.

By 1895, a one-hour Christian Missions course was introduced into the third year of the curriculum at Princeton. The course was comprehensive in nature, including history, theology, and the practical theology of missions. Beginning the following year, it was offered biannually for both second-year and third-year students together, and was taught by different faculty, including Professors Greene, Vos, De Witt, Loetscher, and Erdman. However, because missions was not considered its own discipline yet, there was no one person assigned to teach it. It was covered from a variety of perspectives—biblical, theological, historical, and practical, depending on the faculty instructor.

In 1899, Hartford began to offer an "Organized Course on Foreign Missions" open to Hartford students, students from other seminaries interested in missions, and missionaries appointed by their mission boards. Rather than a degree program, this was a specific set of lectures that was offered by various seminary faculty, a professor from Trinity College in Hartford, and missionaries who happened to be on furlough. The seminary catalog described this course in this way:

> The theory of missions, the missionary obligation as taught in Scripture and supplemented by the conditions of heathen lands, as well as the apologetic value of missionary achievements, will be set forth; the history of different periods and of special lands will be reviewed; the methods of various Christian bodies will be compared and tested; the different forms of missionary activity will be fully described; *the religious conditions of the heathen and Mohammedan world will be examined*, and particular attention will be given to non-Christian religions; practical topics, such as the missionary's health, will not be omitted; and peculiar problems, such as self-support, will be discussed; some definite instruction and training in pedagogy will also be given.[76]

Although there are no statistics to indicate the number of students enrolled in this program, more lectures were added in 1901 and again in 1904.[77] The program became the model for the later Kennedy School of Missions, which was established at Hartford in 1911. A primary reason for the success of this program was twofold; first was the leadership of

President Mackenzie, whose role in Edinburgh will be further noted, and second was the expertise of two faculty members, Edwin Knox Mitchell (1853–1934), the professor of Graeco-Roman and Eastern church history, and Duncan Black Macdonald, then associate professor of Semitic languages.

Edwin Knox Mitchell was a graduate of Union seminary in 1884. He was ordained in the Presbyterian Church and served a congregation in Florida from 1886 to 1890 until he came to Hartford in 1901. He taught early church history and patristics. For this program, however, he lectured on the "history and methods of Missions in the first six centuries, Nestorian Missions, and the rise and spread of Mohammedanism."[78] In addition to his regular teaching at the seminary, Mitchell also played a prominent role within the ministerium of Hartford, being president of the Hartford Council of Churches. He and his wife, Hetty Marquand Enos, were active in the Bushnell Park association of Hartford. Their local activities undoubtedly raised the profile of Hartford seminary among the clergy of what was then one of the wealthiest cities in America. Duncan Black Macdonald, who had arrived at Hartford in 1892, gave lectures on the theology of Islam and on Muslim views of Christian and Jewish scriptures, as well as teaching Hebrew, Arabic, Syriac, and Coptic. Next to Samuel Zwemer, there was no seminary professor who was more influential in the American study of Islam than Macdonald. Yet the two provided very different perspectives on the teaching of Islam in American seminaries.

Ecumenical Missionary Conference of New York

At the conclusion of the nineteenth century, not only was there a burning missionary zeal among students in the United States and missionary agencies that were eager to employ them, but there was a growing appetite for American intervention abroad. The annexation of Hawaii, Guam, the Philippines, and Puerto Rico in 1898 signaled that the United States had assumed a formal role as an imperial power. As with all other European nations, international politics was supported by a religious zeal to save and to civilize. The two ideas were inexorably bound together. Just two years after these annexations, in 1900, the largest missionary conference ever assembled was convened at Carnegie Hall in New York City.[79]

One of the primary organizers and participants of the New York Ecumenical Missionary Conference was the president of Hartford seminary, Chester D. Hartranft. Hartranft spoke at the conference on "social progress and the peace of the world," arguing for the moral superiority of Protestant Christianity in the development and progression toward a Christian civilization.[80] This was a common theme shared by another prominent speaker at the event, John Henry Barrows, the former chair of the Parliament of the World Religions, now the president of Oberlin College. However, Barrows, reflecting on religious pluralism several years after his sojourn around the world, was now convinced "that Christianity is not merely one of many competing religions, but is God's way of salvation, is the final, authoritative message from heaven to earth, written in the blood of the Cross and stamped with the seal of the resurrection."[81] He was not the proponent of theological pluralism that the Parliament of the World Religions has become today.

The New York conference was held for ten days throughout downtown Manhattan and included twenty-five hundred delegates. It was so large that various sessions were held at different churches around the city. And it was such a popular event that even President William McKinley and New York governor Theodore Roosevelt attended. Both were strong proponents of American expansion overseas, including American missionary work as an important source of American influence and soft power.

Sessions were divided by regions of the world and specific topics of missions. On one afternoon, the subcommittee on "Mohammedan Lands: Turkey, Persia, Syria, Arabia, Egypt, North Africa" convened at the Madison Avenue Reformed Church. There reports were given about the various types of mission work in Muslim-majority countries. The bulk of the time, however, was given over to reports from Turkey, where Americans had established several different missions and schools. In addition, reports of the killing of Assyrians and Armenians by the Turks between 1894 and 1896 had begun to surface, and protection of the religious and ethnic minorities in Turkey became a controversial subject in the United States. There were significant calls for the US government to protect these Christian-minoritized communities and converts to Christianity.[82] This was something that the American administration was in favor of. Yet, the established American missionary institutions had to walk a fine line of not publicly criticizing the Turkish government, for fear that they might be shut down. Many American missionaries in Turkey urged caution in political matters. The president of Robert College, George Washburn, spoke at length of the sole mission of American missionaries, which was to conduct educational and spiritual work and to leave all politics aside.[83] This waffling would all change after the 1915 genocide. Cables from mission stations and reports from missionaries provided the first accounts of the massacres. This turned the tide of public support in favor of an American Mandate, which was ultimately rejected by President Wilson.[84]

If Americans were still uncertain about claiming their role as an imperial force in the new century, many had no qualms about utilizing the international order set by European colonial powers. Some American missionaries, especially those working in the Near East, were publicly grateful for this world order and the opportunities for Christian mission among Muslims. They saw the advantages of imperial rule as an opportunity to evangelize.

1906 Cairo Conference

While the New York ecumenical conference focused on world Christian mission, it was the 1906 Cairo conference, organized by Samuel Zwemer and Elwood Wherry, that led to initiatives for the evangelization of the Muslim world, including the promotion of the study of Islam in American seminaries. Zwemer was a graduate of New Brunswick in 1890, and an active secretary of the Student Volunteer Movement during his seminary years. He went out to be a peripatetic missionary in the Arabian Gulf, later being called by the Reformed Church's Arabian Mission from 1899 until 1912, when he was appointed by several mission agencies to set up a missionary study center in Cairo. In 1928, he would be hired as the professor of the history of religion and Christian mission at Princeton seminary. However, it was his organization of a missionary conference in Cairo that gained him notoriety among Protestants as the premier missionary-scholar on Islam. He became known affectionately among evangelicals as "The Apostle to Islam."[85]

While serving in the Arabian Gulf, Zwemer desired to bring together administrators of mission boards and missionaries working in Muslim contexts to examine data and information on Muslim communities

around the world. He believed that this "scientific" approach would provide practical information for the furthering of Christian evangelization
among Muslims. In the end, sixty-two missionaries and administrators
came together for one week in Cairo, Egypt, in the spring of 1906. This
was the first time in the modern age that Christians assembled specifically to discuss the "Mohammedan missionary problem," so dubbed by
Henry Jessup (1832–1910), the first missionary speaker at the conference.
In his opening address, Jessup candidly stated that "it is a fact not to
be ignored or lightly regarded that almost the only really open doors
to reach Islam, are in countries where Moslems are under Christian or
non-Moslem rule."[86]

Henry Jessup was highly respected as a missionary and authority on
all things "Oriental." He traveled to Syria as a missionary of the ABCFM
immediately upon graduation from Union and then his ordination into
the Presbyterian Church in 1855. He served fifty-three years as a missionary in Syria, becoming the doyen of the American missionaries in
the Levant until his death in 1910. He was well known and well respected
among his Presbyterian peers in the United States and missionary colleagues around the world. In 1857, he was offered the position of professor of biblical literature at Union, which he thoughtfully and prayerfully
declined.[87] In 1878, he was elected the moderator of the Presbyterian
Church at its national assembly. This time, he reluctantly agreed and
stayed in the United States throughout the year to serve in that position. However, he returned to Syria the following year when his one-year
term ended, preferring his life as a missionary abroad.

Over the course of his long career, Jessup had four furloughs in the
United States, in 1857, 1868, 1878–1879, and 1882–1884, when he engaged
in public speaking to raise money on behalf of the Mission Board. During these furloughs he not only spoke at churches and local missionary
associations but lectured at nine different seminaries, including Andover and Union.[88] His most influential speech about Islam, however, was
his address to the Presbyterian General Assembly at Saratoga Springs,
New York, in 1879. The speech was so well received that he was asked to
expand it, and it was then published by the denomination as *The Mohammedan Missionary Problem*.

In his presentation, Jessup outlined for his fellow Presbyterians the
challenges of proselytizing Muslims, as well as the hopeful signs of their

"eventual" conversion. The laundry list of challenges and opportunities is built around "rancorous" and "vile" descriptions of the Oriental Muslim, to use the words of Samir Khalaf.[89] Jessup underlines for his audience what he describes as various social problems, including Muslim intolerance, immorality, untruthfulness, and degradation of women. While Jessup recognizes that Muslims do believe in the one God and that Islam does have a kernel of truth that has been gleaned from bits and pieces of Judaism and Christianity, Islam is in the end morally and spiritually sick. But, he assured his audience that there was a remedy for the illness.

Jessup was a proponent of British colonization. He believed that God was using the British Empire to extend the opportunities of the "Anglo-Saxon race" to preach the Gospel around the world. And, due to the high character and quality of the British, Jessup naively asserted that "in the wise providence of God, who causes even the wrath of man to praise him, an Anglo-Saxon Christian queen, already the ruler of forty-one millions of Mohammedans in India, stands up before the world as the protectress of the whole Turkish empire in Asia. As we are not writing from the political standpoint, but only from the position of students of the divine providence, we cannot but look on with wonder and gratitude to God."[90]

Jessup underlines this point by highlighting that it was not a coincidence that the Anglo-Saxons were introduced to Christianity in the sixth century just as Muhammad began preaching his religion in Arabia. Standing before his American audience, Jessup asserted that the American missionary role was not to rule the empire but to provide schools, distribute the Bible, and evangelize. And, they were to be part of this Christian mission by financially supporting the missionary schools and ministries for the future of God's kingdom. For Jessup, the Protestant faith not only saves an individual from sin but will ultimately create a modern, moral, free, and prosperous society. In a variation on the theme introduced by Archibald Alexander at the Princeton chapel back in 1823, Jessup emphasizes that Islam is uncultured and leads societies to decline. "The religion of Mohammed and its legal code are adapted to a simple pastoral or nomad state of society. It cannot adapt to modern commerce and civilization and is in direct conflict with them."[91] Confident in the ultimate victory of evangelical work in the Muslim world, Jessup assured his American Presbyterian audience that someday soon "the sun will rise in the west, and a cold, odoriferous wind blow from Syria which will sweep away the souls of all believers and the Koran itself."[92] Only an enlightened American Protestantism will inevitably bring about the salvation of the East. As Deanna Ferree Womack notes, Jessup believed "in the congruity between Protestant Christianity and modern civilization."[93] For Jessup, European colonialism made it possible for Christian missionaries to work freely, speak, write, and convert without fear of government interference to bring about this congruence.

This was not always the case, however. At various times during the imperial age, British and Dutch trading companies as well as Portuguese or Spanish colonial governors saw the missionaries as intervening in their colonial enterprises and potential profits by raising questions about the rights of indigenous peoples. Methodist and Mennonite missionaries in particular were outspoken opponents of the slave trade and plantations in the Caribbean, for example. However, by the late nineteenth century it was rare for Protestant denominations not to support the civilizing task of Christian mission work in its various forms, even among those who did not promote or espouse active Christian missionary work abroad.[94] We witnessed this in the writings and speeches of John Barrows at the Parliament of the World Religions, for example. For Barrows at the parliament, dialogue—not preaching—was an opportunity for exploring how God spoke to all communities of the world. In the end, Barrows was convinced that adherents of other religions would naturally see a benevolent Protestant Christianity as the pinnacle of God's intention for humanity. Zwemer and Jessup were critical of this comparative-religions approach, however. They believed that preaching and repentance were necessary actions. Robert Speer, who attended Princeton and became the influential secretary of the Presbyterian Board of Foreign Missions, agreed. In his presentation at Cairo, he remarked that "there is a great ignorance of the real doctrine and moral character of Islam. Some think of it as a purely monotheistic system and see no need of attempting to proselytize its followers. Others think of it as next best to Christianity and perhaps the best practicable religion for the Africans and Arabs . . . that Mohammed was a great and true prophet of God, and that his religion, if not quite as good as Christianity is yet a great and good religion and well suited to the needs of a large section of the human race."[95] Zwemer was even more poignant in his criticism of the comparative religions approach and specifically about the 1893 parliament in Chicago. He wrote, "America entertained perverts to Islam at a Parliament of Religions, while throughout vast regions of the Mohammedan world millions of Moslems have never so much as heard of the incarnation and the atonement of the Son of God, the Saviour of the world."[96] We can assume that Zwemer is critiquing what he believes is theological perversion of Christianity.

In the end, the Cairo conference issued a statement calling for a new generation of missionaries to receive specialized training in Islam, for the development of publications and the distribution of evangelistic literature for Muslims, and for the "fresh occupation of important centers" in the Muslim world (particularly Cairo). These proposals would be successfully implemented. As a result, the Oriental Study Center was organized in Cairo in 1912, a new missionary journal, the *Moslem World*, was established, and missionaries began to study Islam specifically. In fact, the Cairo conference was so successful, and its organizers so committed, that several other missionary conferences on Islam would be organized: in Lucknow, India, in 1911 and Jerusalem in 1924.[97] It seemed, at the time, as if the Christian evangelization of the Muslim-majority world was finally succeeding. The final statement of the Cairo conference concluded with the forceful "God wills it," reminiscent of the Crusaders' call, "*Deus le volt!*"[98]

The World Missionary Conference at Edinburgh and Islam

While the New York conference was the largest ecumenical missionary conference ever to date, it was the Edinburgh conference that would become the high-water mark of the Western Protestant missionary era. In 1910, 1,215 delegates from missionary agencies in Europe and North America gathered in Edinburgh, Scotland. The event was a massive administrative undertaking that capitalized on the goodwill among missionary agencies at the height of ecumenical confidence. Representatives from European and American missionary agencies and churches spent eight days reviewing extensive reports and data to provide the best strategies for evangelizing the world.[99] Ironically, this public display of goodwill and confidence was exhibited only four years before all hopes would be shattered in the face of the carnage of a European world war, where all of the goodwill was trashed.

Commission V of the World Missionary Conference was given the task of examining the preparation of missionaries at colleges, seminaries, and training centers. Of the twenty-four members of this committee, only six were American, including Douglas Mackenzie, the new president of Hartford seminary, who was also chair of the commission. In preparation for the conference, the committee sent out questionnaires to mission boards, seminaries, and training centers, as well as to missionaries already working abroad, and asked them to reflect on the effectiveness of training methods for mission work. Surprisingly, given the great investment in personnel and finances to support foreign mission, the responses demonstrated that there had not been adequate training of missionaries to study the languages, cultures, or religions of their "target" community. Rather, missionaries indicated that they usually had to "learn on the job." They either sank or swam. In particular, the commission noted deficiencies of most missionaries in knowledge of the field of comparative religions, a general knowledge of the history of Christian missions, or an understanding of sociology (in order to accurately assess and understand the general trends and shifts in the societies in which they served), good pedagogical methods for teaching the faith, and, finally and most importantly, adequate language proficiency in the languages used where the missionaries lived and worked. The report did note that there were some well-qualified linguists who had mastered the languages of their adopted lands, but many missionaries were not sufficiently able to communicate in vernacular languages.[100]

As a result of this study, the commission proposed the establishment of missionary training centers and mission departments within seminaries or divinity schools to raise the standards of missionary service.[101] This recommendation led to the establishment of the Hartford Kennedy School of Missions (1911), the Department of Foreign Service at Union with Columbia University (1914), and the School of Religions at Princeton (1914).[102] In addition, a number of faculty chairs in Christian missions were created throughout the country, including at Union, Gettysburg, and Andover.[103] Finally, many seminaries, including five of those that are the focus of this book, added annual lectureships on some aspect of Christian missions to be offered by specialists or missionaries on furlough. By the 1920s, the study of Christian missions was a growing area of theological education. Ironically, this was at a time when student interest in missions was waning. After World War I, fewer students were interested in going abroad. Rather, there was a new growing interest in ministries within US urban spaces, where the Social Gospel movement was taking shape.

Christian mission was still an option for ministerial service, but it had lost the luster of its heyday during the Great Awakening. Moreover, missionary service in Muslim-majority lands was only one area of specialized ministry in a larger network of mission communities. Of the seven seminaries included in this book, only Hartford and Princeton would establish courses in the specific study of Islam: Duncan Black Macdonald in the "Muhammadan Department" at Hartford and Samuel Zwemer as the professor of the history of religion and Christian mission at Princeton.

Commission IV of the Edinburgh conference was responsible for gathering information from missionaries on the various "non-Christian Religions" around the world. Twenty-nine missionaries in Islamic contexts completed the questionnaire. Of those correspondents, thirteen were Americans from the ecumenical ABCFM, the Dutch Reformed Church in America, and the Presbyterian Church, USA. Twelve of these thirteen Americans attended Andover, Hartford, New Brunswick, Princeton, or Union seminaries. Thus, the seminaries on which we have been focusing produced many of the missionaries who served in Muslim-majority contexts and contributed directly to the shaping of the report on Islam at Edinburgh.[104]

The Commission IV report highlighted an important opportunity as well as several roadblocks in evangelizing Muslims. First, the report indicated that local indigenous piety or traditions played an important role in the possibility of conversion. It was through the specific daily lived religion of Muslims that missionaries would find opportunities for proselytization, rather than by publicly debating Christian doctrines. However, there were numerous roadblocks to successful proselytization. The report claimed that many Muslims were dissatisfied with Islam because it did not speak to their moral needs, but rather it supported immoral behavior (e.g., polygamy and divorce). However, the report also bemoaned that indigenous Christians were often not an appropriate model to take advantage of because they engaged in their own immoral acts of "drinking and prostitution."[105] (Of course, many of the indigenous Christians in Muslim-majority countries of the Near East were of Orthodox or Catholic communions, which were often seen as polytheists by some Protestant missionaries.) Second, rather paternalistically, the report claimed that Muslims were not truly able to comprehend the purpose of the Trinity as an experience of God rather than an ontological reality. The Islamic doctrine of *tawhid*, God's oneness, challenges the concept of the Trinity. So, in response the report simply called for missionaries to double down on the need to point out Muslims' moral laxity, that the death of Jesus as God's true mercy to humanity was the only answer to the problem of their sin. Only by accepting their need to repent and receive forgiveness would Muslims understand God's divine presence in the person of Christ. This was a prescription for a problem, however, that Muslims did not see as a problem. Finally, the report concluded its challenges by noting that converts to Christianity faced ostracism or worse from their own families or communities, which inhibited public conversions.[106]

The underlying theme of the report from Commission IV regarding the challenges of mission work among Muslims was that Muslims were simply unable to understand their true existence—as sinful persons in need of repentance. According to Samuel Zwemer, one of the missionary respondents of the survey, when the Gospel is "properly presented" to Muslims, then any who feel a sense of guilt or remorse for their sin will naturally convert.[107] The best way that this can be achieved, writes Zwemer, is through the example of the personal piety of a missionary who must serve as an exemplary role model of the true inward spiritual life. Thus, the report highlights the need for thoroughly training committed and pious missionaries who could be effective witnesses in a new age of mission.

Remarkably, there is only one small reference in the report to the larger geopolitical events that shaped the great missionary age—the opportunities that global colonialism provided for missionaries. This is certainly surprising given the global geopolitics and imperialism of the day. The report briefly mentions the "global Pan-Islamic hopes among the Moslem peoples under Christian rule; and the association of Christianity with the foreign yoke."[108] The "moral laxity" of individual Muslims is highlighted, yet there is no mention of the negative effects of or association with imperialism. To the contrary, on the opening night of the conference numerous letters of support for the success of the conference were read, including one from the German Colonial Office in Berlin: "The German Colonial Office recognises with satisfaction and gratitude that the endeavours for the spread of the Gospel are followed by the blessings of civilisation and culture in all countries. In this sense, too, the good wishes of the Secretary of State of the German Imperial Colonial Office accompany your proceedings."[109] The silence in naming colonization and imperialism as stumbling blocks to Western Christian evangelization at Edinburgh is deafening. Rather, Zwemer and Jessup saw the political map of the world as "the finger of God" providing new "open doors" for the spiritual "occupation" of the Muslim world. They both talked openly of the spiritual occupation of Muslim lands. They regularly spiritualized violent language—writing and speaking about a spiritual crusade, calling for reinforcements to advance forward in the battle against Islam. In reality, Jessup's and Zwemer's hopes and dreams were built on the actual political and military occupation of foreign lands by a system of international colonialism. As Americans, they could wash their hands of any national implications of political imperialism. They held themselves to what William Hutchison called America's "moral equivalent of imperialism."[110] Yet, their success was impossible without actual commercial and political networks that required physical domination.

Duncan Black Macdonald and the Kennedy School of Missions

President Mackenzie of Hartford returned from the Edinburgh conference determined that Hartford would be the location of one of the newly proposed mission centers. Mackenzie's vision for Hartford was to relocate the seminary from its downtown Hartford campus to a new site in the West End of the city. A new thirty-acre campus was purchased in 1913, but the project stalled as World War I intervened. Donors and students began to show hesitation in committing to foreign mission work during the conflagration of a world war. However, due to his persistence, the project continued after the war and by 1927 a new neo-Gothic campus was completed that was to serve as a primary site for missionary training up through the 1970s. What would ultimately be called the Kennedy School of Missions was established in 1911 with a donation of $250,000 by Mrs. Emma Baker Kennedy of New York, with an additional sum of $50,000 added by the estate of the late Cleveland H. Dodge, and another sum by John D. Rockefeller. The first course was organized by the new dean, Edward Capen, professor of sociology, in September, less than one year after the Edinburgh conference. There were fourteen students enrolled in the first mission school program.[111]

As a small mission school, Hartford quickly became a center for those interested in mission to the Muslim-majority world. With a specific "Muhammadan Department," Hartford sent 135 graduates to Turkey, Egypt, Syria, and Persia between 1911 and 1935.[112] This was due to the presence of several key faculty members, including Edwin Mitchell, John E. Merrill (1872–1960), who was a former missionary in Turkey, and Duncan Black Macdonald (1863–1943). No one person has contributed more to the field of Islamic studies in America than Macdonald. He was responsible for putting the small school of Hartford on the international map. His name was memorialized in 1973 when a center for the study of Islam and Christian-Muslim relations was established in his name. However, Macdonald had already been well known during his lifetime as the premier Islamicist in North America.

Originally from Scotland, Macdonald earned his divinity degree at the University of Glasgow. He had already begun reading Arabic along with his Hebrew instructor at the university. Smitten by the intricacies of Arabic grammar, he continued his studies in Berlin under the German Orientalist Eduard Sachau. It was at this point that Hartford seminary's second president, Chester Hartranft, was looking to greatly expand the faculty. Hartranft hired both Edwin Mitchell for the department of church history and Macdonald for the biblical studies department in 1892. As the professor of Semitic languages, Macdonald had the primary role of teaching Hebrew. However, he offered elementary Arabic alongside Hebrew in his first year and then advanced Arabic the following year.

Macdonald would continue to teach Arabic, along with colloquial Egyptian Arabic, Coptic, and, occasionally, Malay. It was through his study of the Arabic language that he began reading Islamic texts. And it was through these Islamic sources that he introduced his students to

Islam. This was unusual at an American seminary. To this point Islam had been taught primarily through Christian sources—either in church history classes or through European Orientalist sources. In addition to having students read the Qur'an, he introduced them to the medieval commentary of al-Badawi, al-Ghazzali's *Ihya 'Ulum al-Din*, and Ibn Khaldun's *Muqaddima*, among others. Later he would add to his teaching repertoire *The Arabian Nights*, which he believed provided not only a unique pathway into the worldview of the ancient Near East but also new insights into the popular piety of Muslims in the medieval period.[113] It is interesting that later in his career, Macdonald became interested in the occult, including spiritualist practices such as those of the Theosophical Society. His 1909 book, *The Religious Attitude and Life in Islam*, originally given as the Haskell lectures at the University of Chicago, focused on the "unseen dimension of reality" for Muslims, using examples from Sufism and the life of the Prophet to highlight his spiritualism, a popular trend among many in the 1890s.[114]

Macdonald began offering a course on Islam in 1895, the fourth year of his tenure at Hartford and before the founding of the Kennedy School of Missions. However, it is because of his popularity as a teacher that Macdonald's legacy has become embroiled in a debate about his relationship with the mission school. Najib Awad has noted the criticisms of Macdonald for his "missionary-like Orientalist condescension."[115] Critics of Macdonald, including contemporary Muslim scholars, look back on his prominent role in the training of missionaries to the Muslim world, casting him alongside Zwemer as villains of Christian Orientalism at worst or as having a paternalist naiveté at best.[116] They point to his language and characterization of Muslims as "childlike." However, supporters of a more congenial evaluation of Macdonald's legacy often turn to his own reflections on teaching missionaries, where he intimates that it was merely through mission studies that he was able to "smuggle" in Islamic studies, implying that he put up with the missionary agenda in order to pursue his own interests in Islamic studies.[117]

There is no question that Macdonald was instrumental in training missionaries whose ultimate goal was the conversion of Muslims. His most well-known students included the British missionary Temple Gairdner and the American Reformed missionary Edwin Calverley (who would go on to become the editor of the *Muslim World* when it relocated from Princeton to Hartford in 1938). Macdonald was also instrumental in teaching a growing number of women missionaries who came to the Kennedy School while on furlough.[118] Macdonald had an important role at the Kennedy School relating to how to train missionaries "properly"—that is, by seeing Islam "from within," as Muslims would understand it.

Macdonald would have an impact on missionary training even beyond Hartford. After Edinburgh, he was appointed a member of the Committee for the Preparation of Missionaries Appointed to the Near East in the then newly formed ecumenical Board of Missionary Preparation.[119] In his own contributions to this committee, Macdonald would encourage missionaries not to focus on preaching repentance of sin but rather to try "to understand their [the Muslims'] religious life" and accept their interest in Christ from whatever perspective they might have.[120] In a most congenial assessment of Macdonald's legacy, Jan Bodine argues that "his writings and teaching were devoted to helping the missionary gain both understanding and liking for the people as well as for points of contact between Christianity and Islam. Throughout his writing, Macdonald advocates approaching the Muslim as a person, as a human being who has his or her own value and religion, which must be understood and appreciated before any effort can be made to present Christianity to him or her."[121]

While it is not accurate to state that Macdonald was interested in dialogue with Islam, he was more interested in learning about Islam from the spiritual aspects of a Muslim believer, rather than debating aspects of Christian doctrine as Zwemer regularly did in his writings. Macdonald began his career as a Semitic linguist and became a Christian Islamicist. The year after his arrival at Hartford, the seminary received the Mueller Semitic Library. This library purchase provided Macdonald with the opportunity to begin his Islamic studies completely separately from his role in training missionaries. He also avidly purchased his own Islamic books as he had occasion, especially during his sabbatical in the Near East in 1908. His impressive library was donated to the Hartford seminary library after his death. Ultimately, his remarkable command of Islamic sources and the Arabic language laid the groundwork for him to become recognized as the premier North American scholar of Islam. In the end, he contributed eighty-two entries to the second edition of *The Encyclope-*

dia of Islam, published in Leiden. This alone demonstrates his respected status as an Islamicist among Europeans, including Ignaz Goldziher.[122]

Much like the previous generation of biblical scholars, Macdonald was entrenched in philology. But rather than reading Arabic as a cognate biblical language, he became fascinated with the language and its usage by Arab Muslims. His earliest writings, especially the widely acclaimed *Development of Muslim Theology, Jurisprudence, and Constitutional Theory* (1903), focused on texts. However, after a sabbatical in 1908–1909 when he spent several months in Cairo, Jerusalem, and Damascus, he came away with a deeper appreciation for Muslim spirituality. During his time in Cairo, he deliberately kept away from missionary establishments and meetings, especially Zwemer's Oriental Institute, where he might have been enlisted to lecture. Rather, Macdonald spent his days visiting Islamic sites and conversing with Egyptians and Syrians in the old quarters of the cities, drinking tea and even praying with Muslims. He wanted to experience religion as they did.[123]

Macdonald emerged from his only experience in a Muslim-majority context with a nuanced view of Islam: as doctrinal on the one hand and as a lived religion on the other. The publication of *The Religious Attitude and Life in Islam* in 1909 was the ultimate result of his sabbatical. In it, he focuses on the lived religion of Muslims whom he encountered, including the Sufis, who were of particular interest to him. Certainly, Yahya Michot is correct in his view that Macdonald's exploration of Islamic spirituality says more about Macdonald's interests, and perhaps his idiosyncrasies regarding his own dabbling in "parapsychological theories of his day," than about Islam of that time in general.[124] Nevertheless, his methods were unique among those of other American scholars who continued to focus only on texts and doctrines to learn about the "unchanging East."

If Macdonald can be assessed accurately as a Christian Islamicist who trained missionaries, he was also a biting critic of Western imperialism. He returned from sabbatical with the additional insights of how Muslims of the Near East experienced Western Christendom as imperialism. Looking back over his career on the occasion of his seventieth birthday, in 1933, he provided a final word of warning to his students, many of whom were now in academic positions at seminaries and universities, as well as missionaries and directors of mission boards:

The West is imposing its whole materialistic, mechanized civilization on the East. The East knows it, resents it, but is defenceless. Its own culture, its own religious and philosophical systems of thought and conduct, are falling like card houses. . . . So it is very plain that the religion of the West must go to the East as an essential part of its civilization, and that can only be done through Christian Missions of the old-fashioned kind. Missions which carry and preach as a divine fact the Incarnate Life of the Lord Christ. That this is a frankly supernatural doctrine makes no difficulty for the East; for it a religion must be supernatural; otherwise it is nothing.[125]

In perhaps a naïve assertion, Macdonald contended that Western missionaries were needed to save Eastern Muslims from the inescapable lures of the secularist West. And, if Macdonald can be accused of seeing Muslim belief as "childlike"—the same can be said for his own view of Christianity, which was also built on supernatural beliefs, as noted through his unique interests in the paranormal world. Unlike Zwemer, who saw empire as a friend of Christian mission, as the world was embroiled in a second world war, Macdonald felt that missionaries needed to steer clear of any kind of Western imperial connection themselves, which became an impossible task. Nevertheless, the legacy of Macdonald is that Islamic studies undertaken from a Christian perspective became well entrenched at Hartford. Subsequent professors of Islamic studies, including Kenneth Cragg, Willem Bijlefeld, David Kerr, and Jane Smith all continued the tradition of attempting a positive "Christian engagement with Islam."[126]

Samuel Zwemer at Princeton

As we have seen, Princeton was the first seminary to include a mission requirement in 1837, however short-lived it was. It was not until after Edinburgh that a department of missions was created at Princeton, in 1915. The department was staffed by Dr. J. Ross Stevenson, the newly installed president and professor of history of religion and Christian missions. Ross was a supporter of Christian mission abroad and had two children serving as Presbyterian missionaries in China. He was ultimately responsible for bringing Samuel Zwemer to Princeton as the new professor of the history of religion and Christian mission in 1928, a post

Zwemer held until his own retirement in 1938. Zwemer became the most influential "scholar-missionary" of Islam. His international reputation preceded Edinburgh, as he had organized the 1906 Cairo conference on Islam. And, in many ways, Edinburgh was merely a support for his already successful career as the preeminent "Apostle to Islam." Edinburgh provided the public support and international interest for him to establish the *Moslem World* journal in Cairo in 1911. The journal received international support from Christian mission agencies and was widely read and contributed to by missionaries serving in Muslim contexts around the world. It was published by the Presbyterian Synod of the Nile's Nile Mission Press from 1906 until 1938, when it was transferred to Hartford seminary and the Kennedy School of Missions upon Zwemer's retirement.[127]

Certainly, Zwemer's arrival in Princeton in 1929 was an important feather in the cap for Stevenson and for Princeton seminary. However, the landing was not as smooth as Zwemer anticipated. Coming back to New Jersey, only miles from where he began his theological studies at New Brunswick, was something of a homecoming for Zwemer. However, he would find that the New Jersey of the late twenties was not the same place he had left in 1899. The "roaring 20s" was a period when American society emerged out of the Great War with a new sense of joie de vivre. The debates over the public sale of alcohol that resulted in the Eighteenth and Twenty-First amendments to the Constitution, and the contentious suffragette movement that eventually led to the legal right to vote for women, were examples of an American society experiencing dramatic social changes.

For theological conservatives in the American Protestant Church this was a time to insist on the bedrock beliefs of "the Fundamentals," including biblical inerrancy. The very year that Zwemer arrived at Princeton, the seminary had just fractured due to the fundamentalist-modernist debates. These debates were, in part, a result of the Scopes Trial of 1925 that pitted evolutionary theory against biblical creationism.[128] Some of the faculty and the board of Princeton left as they felt the seminary was too "modern," that is, too liberal. They left to create Westminster Seminary. For all intents and purposes, Zwemer probably would have been more comfortable leaving with J. Gresham Machem and the others who founded Westminster.

However, nearer to Zwemer's heart, the American Protestant Church was even debating the ethics of missionary work. In 1932, the publication of *Laymen's Report* on mission, an ad hoc, ecumenical study, promoted the shift away from traditional proselytizing in missionary work toward relief, development, and social services. This report reflected a split in Protestant churches between those who held to traditional methods of evangelization and those who thought Christian mission should be more a "foreign service of ambassadorship."[129] The primary author of the *Report* was William E. Hocking, who had taught comparative religions at Andover before he became a well-known philosopher of religion at Harvard. Given Zwemer's already-noted disdain for the comparative religions approach, the fact that Hocking's position was widely accepted by mainline churches must have stung him bitterly.

During his time at Princeton, Zwemer's publications focused less on specific research on Muslim communities and more widely on supporting Christian mission in general. He was doing what he could, he believed, to stem the tides that had taken center stage in many mainline church denominations. In many ways, Zwemer's appointment at Princeton was too late. The Great Missionary Age had ended, and so had the energy of the ecumenical church to evangelize the Muslim world. But, Zwemer had left his mark. His publications would continue to be used, and his methods are still followed. He is still known as the "Apostle to Islam." Such commitments to evangelize the Muslim world would continue in the evangelical seminaries, such as Dallas and Fuller. And active proselytization in the Muslim world is left to small evangelical parachurch organizations.

1910 as the High-Water Mark

Protestant missionaries who were educated and trained in the seminaries in the nineteenth and early twentieth centuries were key figures in the dissemination of information on Islam back to their alma maters, their networks of fellow classmates, and the public at large. As Samir Khalaf notes, while many different kinds of Americans traversed Muslim-majority lands in the late nineteenth century—"merchants, diplomats, travelers, military and naval personnel"—the missionaries had the longest sustained interaction and more intimate knowledge of the cultures and religions with which they interacted.[130] They wrote and spoke about Islam to their constituents back home and were thus considered the experts. Several missionaries who succeeded at communicating on the home front to support the proselytization of Muslims were Henry Jessup, James Dennis, and Samuel Zwemer. Indefatigable in their public speaking engagements in the United States and through their manifold publications, they successfully managed to provide images of Islam, Muhammad, and the Qur'an as the products of what they believed to be a misguided and pitiful religion.

It was relatively easy to convince one's constituency of the misguidedness of the poor "childlike" Orientals in need of salvation and civilization. For those sitting in their parlors of Seneca, New York, or even the rural crossroads of Gettysburg, Pennsylvania, Islam was truly foreign. Muslims were part of the exotic and yet depraved Orient. Jessup and Zwemer condemned not only the religious and theological claims of Islam but the moral and ethical lives of all Orientals. The East was in need of saving because it was immoral. One wonders, however, what Jessup and others might have been like if they had become "home" missionaries in the cities of the East Coast or the frontier of the expanding "Wild West." Would Jessup have found a more moral Christian America on the street corners of New York City or the gambling parlors of Tombstone, Arizona, compared to Beirut or Urumia?

There were others, like Cyrus Hamlin, William Shedd, and Duncan Black Macdonald, who did come to appreciate Islam or Muslims, or at least sought to explain the complexities of Eastern cultures and Islam to American Christians in more generous terms. Representatives of this thinking were, in the end, still interested in evangelizing individuals rather than civilizations. Among all of those reviewed in our seminaries, Macdonald stands out as the only nonmissionary who engaged in a sustained study of Islam by reading deeply Muslim sources "from within." Because of this, he was widely recognized as a scholar of Islam in North America and Europe.

The Edinburgh missionary conference was the high-water mark of the Protestant Age of Mission. There would never again be an international conference of its size and stature. While Zwemer and Wherry would continue the message of evangelization of the Muslim world, American society began to lose interest. After the Great War, young Americans began to turn to other types of crusades. Protestant denominations would begin debating the foundations and purpose of missionary work. Some mission boards continued in their proselytizing missions, while others began promoting humanitarian relief or development as a Christian witness. Following the tragedies of World War I and the massacres of Armenians and Assyrians, as well as a famine in Syria, many church organizations focused on contributing to the Near East Relief efforts—the missionary turned relief and development agency. Many mainline and progressive churches would put their eggs in this basket, focusing on relief work and social service rather than individual faith and piety. Some churches ultimately moved toward a model of interfaith dialogue in their engagement with other religions. It was the *Laymen's Report* of 1933 that finally gave voice to what some churches had wanted to hear—that it was okay to focus on international philanthropy as a valid form of Christian mission. Nevertheless, after 1910 graduates from seminaries who served as missionaries in Muslim-majority contexts were considered the primary authorities on Islam for Americans for the next forty years until they were replaced by diplomats, oil company executives, and academics in university Middle East study centers.[131]

Conclusion

There has been a growing body of literature recently on early American engagement with the Near East and the Orient. The role of American missions to the Muslim world has also become an active area of study not only for theologians or missiologists but for American historians and those students interested in what is now known as the Middle East. This book fills a gap in this growing body of literature. It has traced how Islam was taught in seminaries and experienced by students studying for the Protestant Christian ministry throughout the nineteenth century, and shortly thereafter. We have found that the history of Islam, the life of the Prophet Muhammad, and Arabic as a scriptural language were readily visible topics in the curricula of seven different seminaries along the eastern coast of the newly emerging American republic.

As we have argued, beginning in 1808 American Protestant seminaries came into existence to provide a new type of theological education to supply the growing number of American Protestant denominations with educated ministers. Seminaries were established as the United States territories and populations were expanding. There was a need for Protestants to train pastors in a more efficient manner than had been done during the colonial period, when seasoned pastors took on apprentices. Seminaries were also the places where denominations distinguished themselves from the other church bodies by teaching and upholding their own traditions and theological understandings of the faith.

The first years of existence for these seven seminaries were difficult. There were not enough funds, physical resources, books, faculty, or students. However, as the years went by, the seminaries succeeded in constructing campuses, hiring well-respected instructors, building some of the most prominent theological libraries in North America, and admitting aspiring but not always well-qualified students. Among the earliest professional graduate schools, seminaries by and large had good reputations, usually spawning church colleges to provide religious education to undergraduates as well.

Early on, seminary faculty were often seasoned pastors who had only a general knowledge of their fields. However, they quickly developed into a guild of highly specialized professionals. Enamored with the German educational system, many American seminary graduates traveled to Germany to learn the latest theological methods or tools of biblical exegesis. While there was a great deal of freedom in Germany to push the boundaries of research, in America faculty were often challenged by their constituents. Each school was created by its own denomination to support the traditions and guard the orthodoxy of its brand of the Protestant faith. Professors often had to deal with the intrachurch politics of denominationalism. It was not unusual that faculty came under fire and were held liable for teaching suspicious doctrine or biblical heresy, especially as their fields of study became more specialized. Despite these challenges, seminary faculty became expert researchers who advanced their respective subjects. They were hired to engage in technical studies of theology, biblical exegesis, and, later, the new fields of practical ministry that included training in educational pedagogy, psychology, and sociology.

Given these developments and focus on the knowledge and skills of Christian ministry, it is perhaps surprising that during these initial years of graduate Protestant theological education, we find Islam and Arabic addressed widely throughout the seminary experience, and not just within the courses related to Christian missionary activity. In fact, Christian missions as a field of study developed relatively late compared to the fields of biblical studies, theology, church history, and others related to pastoral ministry.

As we have seen, the libraries contained a wide variety of resources on Islam from the very beginning. Often these books were European Orientalist works and translations of the Qur'an. Two of the most common European resources available in all the seminary libraries were Humphrey Prideaux's ubiquitous critique of Muhammad, and George Sale's translation of the Qur'an with his "Preliminary Discourse" that included more positive information on the history of Islam. These two sources framed the life of the Prophet very differently from one another. Later, German scholarship on Islam, especially studies of the life of Muhammad, were translated into English, providing even further interpretations of the Prophet in relation to Judaism and Christianity. Given the specific purpose and scope of these seminary libraries to advance biblical knowledge and Christian theological reflection, it is surprising how much information about Islam was available. However, very few seminaries invested in finding primary Islamic literature. Most seminarians read and learned about Islam and Muhammad from Christian sources. The only professor who had students engage directly with Islamic literature to learn rather than develop polemics was Duncan Black Macdonald. Macdonald stands out as the only North American seminary scholar who engaged Islamic sources to learn about Islam "from within." While Samuel Zwemer had command of Arabic and knew Islamic sources, he was keen on developing Christian apologetics in response to Islamic claims. Macdonald was the premier scholar of Islam of his day who contributed significantly to the origins of Islamic studies in North America. Zwemer was always the Christian evangelist and "Prophet to Islam."

Despite the general lack of other primary Islamic sources, the students of these seminaries did read the Qur'an—even in Arabic. As we have seen, reading the Bible in its original languages was one of the primary skills that students were required to learn at seminary. Exegeting the Word of God for one's congregation was of central importance. The use of cognate languages—Aramaic, Syriac, Akkadian, and Arabic—to assist in exegeting the Hebrew Bible became a standard practice. For example, Moses Stuart, the first Bible professor at Andover seminary, created his own Arabic grammar to teach students Arabic as a biblical cognate language. By 1888, John G. Lansing at New Brunswick had also published a thorough Arabic grammar. He included surahs of the Qur'an in his Arabic chrestomathies in Hebrew class and generated interest in the Arab Islamic world. A remnant of this period of seminary education is still evident in the latest edition of Brown, Driver, and Briggs's *Hebrew and English Lexicon*.

As this book has shown, information about Islam and its history was also gleaned from translated Eastern Christian records or histories of the church. Usually, these histories focused on the geopolitics of Latin Christendom and Islamic empires, but they rarely examined Islam as a religion. Except for Frederick Kinsman at General seminary, American church historians did not repeat the same Latin themes of Islam as fulfilling apocalyptic portents from the Bible or retell the medieval fables about Muhammad's life. However, there was a significant shift in American views of Islam with the translated work of Augustus Neander and his student Philip Schaff. For Neander, Muhammad was not a charlatan or a heretic, the commonly held views among Christians; rather, he was an Arab leader whose "awakened consciousness of God" motivated him to lead his people away from idolatry.[1] Schaff translated Neander's history and contributed his own views on Islam to his students through his lectures and the book *Through Bible Lands*. Like Duncan Black Macdonald, Schaff had the opportunity to travel to the Near East and experience firsthand a Muslim-majority culture. Yet, the two had profoundly different experiences. Schaff was hosted by many of the American missionaries serving in Egypt and Palestine. Macdonald, on the other hand, kept away from missionary establishments and spent time walking and talking with local Arab Muslims. However, despite still exuding an American Orientalist perspective, at least Schaff did not promote antagonism between Christianity and Islam.[2] For Schaff, Islam was not a rival religion or civilization though it promoted a culture that was antiquated and superseded by American Protestant Christianity.

The presence of Islam and Muhammad in seminary curricula was significant, especially with the creation of the new field of comparative religions. Using the work of Max Müller and James Freeman Clarke, nineteenth-century Americans organized and categorized the languages, religions, and races of people into a hierarchy. Within this "Darwinian canopy" of social and religious Darwinism, Islam came to be seen as a product of an inferior culture. Muhammad came to be viewed as an Arab leader who attempted to lead his people out of their primitive state, only to succumb to the inevitable lure of power. For some seminary professors and clergy, however, Muhammad was admired for his role in moving the religious ball forward among his native Arabs. He was to be lauded for his role in helping to build up human civilization, only to hand over the baton to others. Yet still, for many professors and missionaries, Muhammad was viewed as giving in to the wiles of immorality and passing such tendencies along to his followers.

According to some American scholars, despite the personal shortcomings of Muhammad, Islam was an integral part of Jewish-Christian monotheism. Reading the German works on Muhammad by Abraham

Geiger and Gustav Weil, Henry Preserved Smith argued that Muhammad lived in a Jewish and Christian milieu. There was much to learn about Christianity and Judaism by examining the life of Muhammad, he wrote. For Smith, Islam was part of the Judeo-Christian religious tradition in its particular Arab cultural guise. In response to this comparative perspective, Samuel Zwemer and James Dennis reminded their constituencies that Muslims were spiritually and morally sick and needed to be cured. Only a spiritual crusade could save them. Those who had lived and worked in the Muslim-majority world as missionaries with the intent to proselytize Muslims were confirmed in their views that Islam led societies down a path of immorality. When reports of Turkish massacres of Armenians and Assyrians became widely spread, the Turks were held accountable for their fanaticism, barbarism, and despotism. Even those missionaries who articulated that there was a difference between Islam in its purer forms and its Turkish expressions, like Cyrus Hamlin and William Ambrose Shedd, believed that Protestant Christianity was the answer to civilizing the Turks.

In the end, this book has demonstrated that seminaries provided the earliest sustained instruction about Islam among educational institutions in North America. Given that these seven seminaries trained thousands of pastors for ministry in the mainline churches of the United States, the impact of such an education cannot be underestimated. Philip Schaff alone was responsible for teaching thousands of students. Given the accolades of Schaff at his death by many of these students, his views and perspectives had an effect in how they viewed Islam. The same, of course, can be said for Macdonald and Zwemer, but in very different ways. Macdonald left a legacy of Islamic studies in America that evolved into a commitment to Christian-Muslim dialogue. Zwemer's indefatigable insistence on the conversion of Muslims is alive and well among many evangelical and even mainline churches. However, while the teaching and learning was extensive and diverse, one theme was common. Islam was a foreign entity. It was not American. It may have been part of the march of progress of Near Eastern culture and religion, which could be looked back upon with appreciation. But it was seen to be superseded by an American Protestant Christianity. American Orientalism and American Biblical Orientalism became entrenched into views of Islam among American seminaries.

By the mid-twentieth century, American universities took over the role of research on Islam from seminaries. Near Eastern and Middle Eastern studies programs at large universities acquired private and public funding to engage in all manner of study on Islam. This was especially true after World War II when the Middle East became a major front of the Cold War. American mainline Protestant Christianity also retreated from the center of American life and lost much of its cachet as a voice of Americana. More liberal denominations joined the World Council of Churches and National Council of Churches and dabbled in dialogue with Islam.[3] The more "fundamental" traditions kept their focus on the evangelization of Muslims, especially after the Lausanne Conference, called the International Congress on World Evangelization, organized by Billy Graham in 1974.

Moving forward, is there anything, then, that might be gleaned from this study for contemporary Protestant theological education as it relates to Islam? There are at least three lessons that we can take from this research as to how Islam was taught and experienced in seminaries during the first hundred years of seminary education that might be applied to twenty-first-century American Protestant seminary curricula, as different as they are today from the way they were over two hundred years ago. For those engaged in the structure and pedagogy of formal American Christian theological education, these three lessons are important for the training of ministerial students within a globalized and interreligious twenty-first-century North America.

First, exposure to Islamic sources is an important step in discovering more accurate information about Islam. While this might seem self-evident, much of the early education about Islam was filtered through second- or third-hand Christian sources. Certainly, many classes, lectures, and books provided seminary students with a wide variety of views about Islam. However, there were few opportunities to read Islamic sources—except the Qur'an, which was widely available. Yet, reading the Qur'an in translation without some kind of Islamic framework or guide generally succeeded in delivering only what the Christian reader assumed or desired. Simply cracking open Sale's or Palmer's translation of the Qur'an would not assist in gaining an understanding of Islam "from within." Learning about Islam requires not simply reading a translation of the Qur'an by itself. Failing to provide a larger Islamic theological framework in which to read the Qur'an is akin to asking a non-Christian to read the book of Leviticus to understand how Christians understand the Bible. Just as Protestants have different biblical and theological perspectives, so too do Muslim communities and individual Muslim scholars. To expect to learn about Islam without engaging diverse contemporary Islamic sources flies in the face of contemporary standards of American theological education, which seeks to uncover diverse Muslim "own" voices.

Second, and relatedly, Americans taught and learned about Islam through an American Orientalist lens that perceived Islam as foreign and culturally Other. Whether students were in a church history, comparative studies, or biblical studies class, attending a public lecture, or meeting in a student missionary society, in nineteenth-century seminary education Islam was not experienced as part of American life and culture. While Muslims had been on the continent long before the creation of the United States as part of the Iberian explorations of North America and were brought as enslaved persons on ships from Africa, Islam was viewed and experienced by White Protestants as an "Oriental" religion.[4] It was seen as part of an antiquated and backward world that a modern and forward-looking Protestant American could judge.

Such a narrative framework simply does not hold up to honest intellectual or moral scrutiny today. Thankfully, we are now beginning to recognize the important contributions of enslaved Muslims to American history and culture. In addition, since the nineteenth century, immigrant Muslim communities have come to the United States and established themselves, adding to the fabric of American life. Muslims are now neighbors, coworkers, friends, and fellow citizens. Islam has become part of the American civil, social, and religious experience. Regardless of a seminary's particular theological perspective, whether other religious traditions are seen as dialogue partners or as objects for proselytization, it is no longer possible to study Islam without engaging an American Islam. There are a wide variety of opportunities by which seminaries can engage in interreligious engagement, study, and learning with American Muslims.

Finally, the loss of the Arabic language in the role of seminary education, even as an ancillary part of biblical studies, has been detrimental to our understanding of the worlds of Christianity and Islam. While it is generally assumed that Arabic is a "Muslim language," Arabic served as an important language for Jewish and Christian Arabs in the Near East. The Arabic Christian theological tradition is a critical part of the world Christian movement that began, according to the New Testament, at Pentecost, and is alive and well even today. Arabic is a "Christian language" for tens of millions around the world. Recapturing Arabic as a language that is part of the Christian experience will open American seminary students to an important part of the cultural legacies of world Christianity.[5] In addition, as Briggs, Lansing, and Macdonald demonstrated, the use of Arabic translations of the Hebrew Bible or even the New Testament may provide important insights into a Christian reading of the Qur'an. Reading passages from the Qur'an in parallel with Arabic translations of the Psalms may generate fresh insights into both scriptures for Muslims and Christians alike.

Throughout the nineteenth century, the United States became a "land of sects." Seminaries came into existence as Protestant denominations sought to preserve and protect their own historical, theological, and ethnic traditions. They provided a safe haven for the transmission of biblical and theological interpretation of the world and encouraged their graduates to both defend and share their faith. By the beginning of the twentieth century, Christian ecumenism was the new modus operandi for most mainline Protestants. The ecumenical impulse expanded even further after Vatican II as Catholics and Protestants slowly found opportunities for conversations and shared social ministries in local communities, despite attempts to hide from the important differences and fraught historical relationships. With the increasing public role of non-Christian religious communities in American society, Christian seminaries might look backward and double down on their own origin stories, finding solace by providing an education that shapes and forms candidates for ministry within a theological echo chamber, or they may take advantage of the diversity of "own" religious voices and experiences in American society to assist seminarians to appreciate the "land of sects" as a place of both religious opportunity and religious expression. Rather than seeing other religious traditions, especially Islam, as inherently culturally and spiritually "other," American theological education might provide opportunities for seminarians to learn about and experience how their own tradition of Christianity is distinctive, but might surprisingly also reveal the shared human desire for a prosperous spiritual and national life. And, as noted in the preface, and as Virginia Theological Seminary discovered through a study of its own graduates in 2013, those seminary students who are not exposed to other religions in seminary will feel ill equipped to engage in ministry in an interreligious twenty-first-century America.

NOTES

PREFACE

1 Gortner, Wood, and Hawkins, "Faithful Christians, Faithful Neighbors," 59.
2 Gortner, Wood, and Hawkins, "Faithful Christians, Faithful Neighbors" 61.

INTRODUCTION

1 "Lecture on Mohammedanism," Charles Hodge Papers; Manuscripts Division, Department of Special Collections, Princeton University Library. The quotation comes from Anderson's lecture as recorded by Samuel Schmucker. "MS Notes on A. Alexander's lectures on Polemics at Princeton Theological Seminary 1820," Collected Papers of Samuel Simon Schmucker, Lectures on Theology, Wentz Memorial Library Archives, United Lutheran Seminary, Gettysburg, PA.
2 For more on the impact of the Barbary Wars see, Robert J. Allison, *The Crescent Obscured: The United States and the Muslim World, 1776–1815* (New York: Oxford University Press, 2000); Lawrence A. Peskin, *Captives and Countrymen: Barbary Slavery and the American Public, 1785–1816* (Baltimore, MD: Johns Hopkins University Press, 2009).
3 The term "Orientalism" was coined by Edward Said in *Orientalism* (New York: Random House, 1978).
4 For an excellent overview of American views of Islam throughout these diplomatic and military incidents, see Denise Spellberg, *Thomas Jefferson's Qur'an: Islam and the Founders* (New York: Vintage, 2014), 124–57.
5 Fisk, *A Sermon, Preached in the Old South Church Boston*, 31.
6 Hubers, *I Am a Pilgrim, a Traveler, a Stranger*, 103.
7 Grafton, *An American Biblical Orientalism*, 78–86.
8 See Thomas S. Kidd, *American Christians and Islam: Evangelical Culture and Muslims from the Colonial Period to the Age of Terrorism* (Princeton, NJ: Princeton University Press, 2009), 1–57; and Marr, *The Cultural Roots of American Islamicism*, 1–133.
9 Edward Elbridge Salisbury, *An Inaugural Discourse on Arabic and Sanskrit Literature, New Haven, Aug. 16, 1843* (New Haven, CT: B.L. Hamlen, 1843).
10 Roberta L. Dougherty, "Edward E. Salisbury," in *Christian-Muslim Relations 1500–1900*, ed. David Thomas, 16: 272–78.
11 William Warren Sweet, "The Rise of Theological Schools in America," *Church History* 6, no. 3 (September 1937): 267.

243

12 Miller, *Piety and Profession*, 6.

13 Kidd, *American Christians and Islam*, 1–18.

14 A. L. Tibawi, *American Interests in Syria, 1800–1901: A Study of Educational, Literary, and Religious Work* (Oxford: Clarendon, 1966); and Lyle Vander Werff, *Christian Mission to Muslims* (Pasadena, CA: William Carey Library, 1977).

15 Habib Badr, "The Origins of American Protestant Interest in the Middle East (1780–1823)," *Theological Review* 13, no. 2 (1992): 79–106; Adam Becker, *Revival and Awakening: American Evangelical Missionaries in Iran and the Origins of Assyrian Nationalism* (Chicago: University of Chicago Press, 2015); Grafton, *An American Biblical Orientalism*; Samir Khalaf, *Cultural Resistance: Global and Local Encounters in the Middle East* (London: Saqi Books, 2002) and *Protestant Missionaries in the Levant*; Hans Lukas-Keiser, *Nearest East: American Millennialism and Mission to the Middle East* (Philadelphia: Temple University Press, 2010); Ussama Makdisi, *Artillery of Heaven: American Missionaries and Failed Conversion of the Middle East* (Ithaca, NY: Cornell University Press, 2008); Heather J. Sharkey, ed., *Cultural Conversions: Unexpected Consequences of Christian Missionary Encounters in the Middle East, Africa, and South Asia* (Syracuse, NY: Syracuse University Press, 2013); Emrah Şahin, *Faithful Encounters: Authorities and American Missionaries in the Ottoman Empire* (Montreal: McGill-Queen's University Press, 2018); and Uta Zeuge-Buberl, *The Mission of the American Board in Syria: Implications of a Transcultural Dialogue*, trans. Elizabeth Janik (Stuttgart: Frans Steiner Verlag, 2017).

16 Beth Baron, *The Women's Awakening in Egypt: Culture, Society, and the Press* (New Haven, CT: Yale University Press, 1994). See also Ellen L. Fleischmann, "'Our Moslem Sisters': Women of Greater Syria in the Eyes of American Protestant Missionary Women," *Islam and Christian–Muslim Relations* 9, no. 3 (1998): 307–23; Christine B. Lindner, "'Long, Long Will She Be Affectionately Remembered': Gender and the Memorialization of an American Female Missionary," *Social Sciences and Missions* 23, no. 1 (2010): 7–31; Deanna Ferree Womack, *Protestants, Gender, and the Arab Renaissance in Late Ottoman Syria* (Edinburgh: Edinburgh University Press, 2019); and Fruma Zachs and Sharon Halevi, *Gendering Culture in Greater Syria* (London: I. B. Tauris, 2015).

17 See James A. Field Jr., *America and the Mediterranean World, 1776–1882* (Princeton, NJ: Princeton University Press, 1961); David H. Finnie, *Pioneers East: The Early American Experience in the Middle East* (Cambridge, MA: Harvard University Press, 1967); John A. DeNovo, *American Interests and Policies in the Middle East, 1900–1939* (Minneapolis: University of Minnesota Press, 1963); and Joseph L. Graybill, *Protestant Diplomacy and the Near East: Missionary Influence on American Policy, 1810–1927* (Minneapolis: University of Minnesota Press, 1971).

18 Jacob Berman, *American Arabesque: Arabs and Islam in the Nineteenth-Century Imaginary* (New York: New York University Press, 2012); Einboden, *The Islamic Lineage of American Literary Culture*; Kidd, *American Christians and Islam*;

Marr, *The Cultural Roots of American Islamicism*; Hilton Obenzinger, *American Palestine: Melville, Twain, and the Holy Land Mania* (Princeton, NJ: Princeton University Press, 2020); Spellberg, *Thomas Jefferson's Qur'an*; and Karine V. Walther, *Sacred Interests: The United States and the Islamic World, 1821–1921* (Chapel Hill: University of North Carolina Press, 2015).

19 Kambiz GhaneaBassiri, *A History of Islam in America: From the New World to the New World Order* (Cambridge: Cambridge University Press, 2010), 1. See also Allan D. Austin, *African Muslims in Antebellum America: Transatlantic Stories and Spiritual Struggles* (Hoboken, NJ: Taylor and Francis, 2012); Edward E. Curtis IV, *The Columbia Sourcebook of Muslims in the United States* (New York: Columbia University Press, 2008); Sylviane A. Diouf, *Servants of Allah: African Muslims Enslaved in the Americas* (New York: New York University Press, 2013); and Michael A. Gomez, *Black Crescent: The Experience and Legacy of African Muslims in the Americas* (New York: Cambridge University Press, 2005).

20 Miller, *Piety and Intellect*, 200–201. In addition, see his additional studies, *Piety and Profession*; and *Piety and Plurality*.

21 Miller, *Piety and Intellect*, 68. Dwight lists seven marks of a seminary, including "adequate funding" and "scholarly understanding of Christian theology," which we have included under the role of the board and the faculty above.

22 Miller, *Piety and Intellect*, 200. I am grateful to Andrew Gardner for his critique of Miller and his work in developing other methods of successful seminary education. See Andrew Gardner, "Mapping Ministerial Matriculation: Theological Education, GIS, and the Production of the 19th Century Protestant Clergyperson" (unpublished paper, 2022). For several helpful critiques of Miller's method, see the book reviews of John M. Adams, *Journal of Church and State* 33, no. 3 (Summer 1991): 628–29; and Robert Bruce Mullin, *Anglican and Episcopal History* 62, no. 4 (December 1993): 584–86.

23 While it has been argued that New Brunswick commenced as Queen's College in 1784, for the purposes of this research we are using Miller's criteria for an independent seminary.

24 Committee of the Board of Trustees, *Newton Theological Institution: A Sketch of Its History, and an Account of the Services at the Dedication of the New Building, September 10, 1866* (Boston: Gould and Lincoln, 1866), 3–12.

25 For the history of the divinity school at Yale see Roland H. Bainton, *Yale and the Ministry: A History of Education for the Christian Ministry at Yale from the Founding in 1701* (New York: Harper & Brothers, 1957). Bainton focuses on the perspectives of the early faculty within the larger Protestant theological debates of the day. For a helpful study on the debates over religious higher education in the early republic and the creation of divinity schools within universities versus independent denominational seminaries, see Marsden, *The Soul of the American University Revisited*, esp. 63–72.

26 The debate over whether New Brunswick Seminary was founded in 1784 as the earliest seminary will be addressed in chapter 2.

27 World Missionary Conference, *World Missionary Conference, 1910*, vol. 3 (Edinburgh: Oliphant, Anderson & Ferrier, 1910), 214–37; and vol. 4, 122–54, respectively.

28 See Willem Abraham Bijlefeld, "The Muslim World: Hundred Years of Continuity and Change," *Muslim World* 100, no. 4 (October 2010): 539–44.

29 Stanley, *The World Missionary Conference, Edinburgh 1910*, 316–17.

30 Grafton, *An American Biblical Orientalism*, 12–15.

CHAPTER 1. EARLY AMERICAN GRADUATE EDUCATION AND AMERICAN SEMINARIES

1 Woods, *History of the Andover Theological Seminary*, 58.

2 Hartford Theological Seminary, *A Memorial of the Semi-centenary Celebration of the Founding of the Theological Institute of Connecticut*, 19.

3 For a study on the transformation of Orthodox Jewish institutions in America, see Vered Sakal, "The Land of the Free? Orthodox Reactions to Religious Freedom in 19th- and Early 20th-Century America," *Jewish Studies Quarterly* 25, no. 1 (2018): 84–98.

4 de Tocqueville, *Democracy in America*, 243.

5 Medical schools often receive recognition for developing the first professional schools. See Abraham Flexner, *Medical Education in the United States and Canada: A Report to the Carnegie Foundation for the Advancement of Teaching* (New York: Carnegie Foundation, 1910). However, see Sweet's comments about the founding of medical schools in the late eighteenth century as they compare with seminaries. Sweet, "The Rise of Theological Schools," 260.

6 Holifield, *God's Ambassadors*, 95, 148.

7 Baird, *Religion in the United States*, 611.

8 Miller, *Piety and Profession*, 127.

9 Arnold, "Martin Luther and Education," 291.

10 Kansfield, "The Origins of Protestant Theological Seminary Libraries in the United States," 10; Miller, *Piety and Intellect*, 444.

11 Woods, *History of the Andover Theological Seminary*, 18.

12 Fraser, *Schooling the Preachers*, 22.

13 See Ronald H. Bailey, *Hartwick College: A Bicentennial History, 1797–1997* (Oneonta, NY: Hartwick College, 1997).

14 Fraser, *Schooling the Preachers*, 15.

15 Kansfield, "The Origins of Protestant Theological Seminary Libraries," 68.

16 Fraser, *Schooling the Preachers*, 21.

17 Holifield, *God's Ambassadors*, 124.

18 Fraser, *Schooling the Preachers*, 85.

19 Fraser, *Schooling the Preachers*, 103.

20 Fraser, *Schooling the Preachers*, 117.

21 Holifield, *God's Ambassadors*, 113.

22 Reformed Church in America, *Centennial of the Theological Seminary of the Reformed Church in America*, 54.

23 Hageman, *Two Centuries Plus*, 36.

24 Selden, *Princeton Theological Seminary*, 28.

25 Baird, *Religion in the United States*, 105.

26 Schaff, *America*, xii.

27 Dawley, *The Story of the General Theological Seminary*, 70.

28 Miller, *Piety and Profession*, 142.

29 Wentz, *History of the Gettysburg Theological Seminary*, 176–92.

30 Contra Bruce Kuklick, who in *Puritans in Babylon* seems to argue that nineteenth-century higher criticism, specifically the results of study of the ancient Near East, led to a crisis in seminaries and the downfall of biblical criticism wherein there was a perceived incompatibility of science and religion. *Puritans in Babylon*, 197–98.

31 See Aubert, *The German Roots of Nineteenth-Century American Theology*; Henry Geitz, Jürgen Heideking, and Jurgen Herbst, eds., *German Influences on Education in the United States to 1917* (New York: Cambridge University Press, 1995), esp. 27–32.

32 Robinson, "Theological Education in Germany." See also Philip Schaff, *Germany: Its Universities, Theology, and Religion: With Sketches of Neander, Tholuck, Olshausen, Hengstenberg, Twesten, Nitzsch, Muller, Ullmann, Rothe, Dorner, Lange, Ebrard, Wichern, and Other Distinguished German Divines of the Age* (Philadelphia: Lindsay & Blakiston, 1857), which provides a comprehensive examination of the theological education in Germany in the middle of the nineteenth century.

33 See Pranger, *Philip Schaff*.

34 Aubert, *The German Roots of Nineteenth-Century American Theology*, 39.

35 Holifield, *God's Ambassadors*, 147.

36 Hill, *Religious Education in the African American Tradition*, 16–22; Holifield, *God's Ambassadors*, 148.

37 Conrad Cherry, "The Study of Religion and the Rise of the American University," in *Religious Studies, Theological Studies, and the University-Divinity School*, ed. Joseph Mitsua Kitagawa (Atlanta, GA: Scholars Press, 1992), 115.

38 Marsden, *The Soul of the American University Revisited*, 100.

39 See for example Seyyed Hossein Nasr and John O. Voll's contributions in Mumtaz Ahmad, Zahid Bukhari, and Sulayman Nyang, eds., *Observing the Observer: The State of Islamic Studies in American Universities* (Washington, DC: International Institute of Islamic Thought, 2012), 12–27 and 28–52, respectively; and Zareena A. Grewal and R. David Coolidge, "Islamic Education in the United States: Debates, Practices, and Institutions," in *The Cambridge Companion to American Islam*, ed. Juliane Hammer and Omid Safi (New York: Cambridge University Press, 2013), 246–65.

40 Veysey, *The Emergence of the American University*, 264.

41 Two very important studies of the creation of the American university are Julie A. Reuben, *The Making of the Modern University* (Chicago: University of Chicago Press, 1996) and Marsden, *The Soul of the American University Revisited*.

42 While there were female seminaries and teachers' colleges as early as the 1850s, Hartford began to admit women to degree programs in 1892. Emile Grace Briggs, daughter of Union's Francis Briggs, was the first woman to take courses and graduate from Union in 1897. For the earliest female seminaries see Leonard I. Sweet, "The Female Seminary Movement and Woman's Mission in Antebellum America," *Church History* 54, no. 1 (March 1985): 41–55.

43 Kuklick, *Churchmen and Philosophers*, 225–26.

44 Miller, *Piety and Profession*, 49–50.

45 For a review of the major studies of the changing role of theological education in the twentieth century see the Kelly Report in Robert L. Kelly, *Theological Education in America* (New York: George H. Doran, 1924) and Mark A. May, *The Education of American Ministers*, vols. 1–2 (New York: Institute of Social and Religious Research, 1934); H. Richard Niebuhr, *The Advancement of Theological Education* (New York: Harper, 1957). For a review of how theological education has looked to the "theory and practice" of other professional schools, see Elizabeth A. Dryer, "Excellence in the Professions: What Theological Schools Can Learn from Law, Business, and Medical Schools," *Theological Education* 33, no. 1 (Autumn 1996): 1–22.

46 Chester David Hartranft, *Some Thoughts on the Scope of Theology and Theological Education: Address Delivered before the Pastoral Union* (Hartford, CT: Press of the Case, Lockwood & Brainard, 1888), 19–25.

CHAPTER 2. SEMINARY LIBRARIES AND ISLAMIC SOURCES

1 Robinson, "Theological Education in Germany," 27.

2 "The Dedication of the Robert E. Speer Library," *Princeton Seminary Bulletin* 51, no. 3, (1958): 52.

3 Demarest, *Centennial of the Theological Seminary of the Reformed Church in America*, 90.

4 Gasero, "The Origins of the Theological Library at New Brunswick," 74.

5 Kansfield, "The Origins of Protestant Theological Seminary Libraries in the United States," 100.

6 Gasero, "The Origins of the Theological Library at New Brunswick," 82.

7 Kansfield, "The Origins of Protestant Theological Seminary Libraries in the United States," 167; Woods, *The History of the Andover Theological Seminary*, 466.

8 Paulus, "Spiritual Culture and the Theological Library," 221, 223.

9 Mitchell, 'Protestant Theological Libraries," 10.

10 Hartford Theological Seminary, *A Memorial of the Semi-centenary Celebration of the Founding of the Theological Institute of Connecticut*, 23.

11 Kansfield, "The Origins of Protestant Theological Seminary Libraries in the United States," 174. See Gibbs, *Catalog of the Library Belonging to the Theological Institution in Andover*.

12 Robinson to Stuart, February 9, 1830, in Williams, ed., *Robinson's Letter—Journal*. I am extremely grateful to Leah Edelman, Outreach Archivist at the Burke Library at Union Theological Seminary, for helping me locate these letters.

13 For a review of the importance of this work and Robinson's scholarly contributions see Grafton, *An American Biblical Orientalism*, 97–126.

14 McCGatch, "A Major Library Acquisition of 1838," 111. See also Matthew Baker, "A Word about Edward Robinson," *Burke Library Blog*, accessed October 3, 2022, https://blogs.cul.columbia.edu/burke/2017/02/17/a-word-on-edward-robinson/.

15 Clark, *Founding the Fathers*, 92; McCGatch, "A Major Library Acquisition of 1838," 13.

16 For a list of the books in the catalog see Andover Theological Seminary Records, Record Group 275, Special Collections, Yale Divinity School Library, Box 18 17, Inventory Catalog 1826–1838. The *Chrestomathie* appears in the 1838 library bulletin. Andover Theological Seminary Records, Record Group 275, Special Collections, Yale Divinity School Library, Box 18 17, Inventory Catalog 1826–1838.

17 Asaph Ben-Tov, "Fides et leges Mohammædis exhibitae ex Alkorani manuscripto duplici, praemissis institutionibus arabicis," in *Christian-Muslim Relations 1500–1900*, ed. David Thomas, 9: 844–49.

18 Hay, *Catalogue of Duplicate Books from the Library of the Theological Seminary*, 1.

19 Niels H. Sonne, *John Pintard and the Early Years of the General Theological Seminary Library* (New York: N.p., 1961). Reprinted with revisions from the *Bulletin of the General Theological Seminary* 47, no. 1 (February 1961): 6–14.

20 The sixty-eight volumes were published between 1826 and 1857. It is unclear exactly which volumes Pintard acquired at that time.

21 Dawley, *The Story of the General Theological Seminary*, 65; General Theological Seminary Library, *A Catalogue of the Library*, 4 and 27, respectively.

22 Dawley, *The Story of the General Theological Seminary*, 121.

23 Kansfield, "The Origins of Protestant Theological Seminary Libraries in the United States," 101; Gasero, "The Origins of the Theological Library at New Brunswick," 77.

24 The 1854 catalog of the college and seminary demonstrates a collection focused on the Hebrew and Greek versions of the Bible. Only Walton's Polyglot reflected any interest in other ancient biblical texts. There is a heavy emphasis on Calvinist and Dutch Reformed Theology.

25 Van Dyke, *Notes on the Sage Library*, 4.

26 Van Dyke, *Notes on the Sage Library*, 8.

27 Root, "As It Was in the Beginning," vol. 1, 10–11.

28 Root, "As It Was in the Beginning," vol. 1, 16.

29 Root, "As It Was in the Beginning," vol. 1, 32.

30 *The Hartford Seminary Record*, vol. 4, October 1893–August 1894 (Hartford, CT: Hartford Seminary Press, 1894), 174.

31 Diocesan Convention of Maryland, *Journal of Proceedings*, 1896, 17. In 1896, the Maryland Diocese also received another donation from the estate of Rev. Edwin A. Dalrymple made up of eight thousand additional volumes.

32 "A Description of the Gift of the Maryland Diocesan Library to General Theological Library by the Diocese of Maryland," Mary O. Klein to Rev. James C. Ransom, November 22, 2005. Special thanks to Mr. Patrick Cates, Library Manager, Christoph Keller Jr. Library at General Theological Seminary, for his assistance in this record. Email correspondence October 20, 2020.

33 Nabil Matar, "The Qur'an in English Writings, 1543–1697," in *Christian-Muslim Relations 1500–1900*, ed. David Thomas, 6: 11–24.

34 Grafton, "Martin Luther's Sources on the Turk and Islam," 671.

35 Lucien van Liere, "Bewys van den waren godsdienst met overige Neerduitsche gedichten," in *Christian-Muslim Relations 1500–1900*, ed. David Thomas, 7: 250–52, 439.

36 Alexander Ross, *Pansebeia; or, A View of All Religions in the World*, 4th edition (London: J. Williams, 1672), 116. See also Clinton Bennett, "Pansebeia; or, A View of All the Religions of the World," in *Christian-Muslim Relations 1500–1900*, ed. David Thomas, 8: 312–20.

37 See Nabil Matar, *Turks, Moors, and Englishmen in the Age of Discovery* (New York: Columbia University Press, 1999); Jo-Ann Esra, "Diplomacy, Piracy, and Commerce: Christian-Muslim Relations between North Africa, the Ottoman Empire, and Britain, c. 1580–1685," in *Christian-Muslim Relations 1500–1900*, ed. David Thomas, 6: 11–24. See also the important history by Paula S. Fichtner, *Terror and Toleration: The Habsburg Empire Confronts Islam, 1526–1850* (London: Reaktion Books, 2008).

38 General Theological Seminary Library, *A Catalogue of the Library*, 1824.

39 Elmarsafy, *The Enlightenment Qur'an*, 28.

40 Bevilacqua, "How to Organize the Orient," 225.

41 Bevilacqua, "How to Organize the Orient," 258.

42 For a review of Robinson's work in nineteenth-century American Bible dictionaries, see Grafton, *An American Biblical Orientalism*, 127–46.

43 See Asaph Ben-Tov, "Fides et leges Mohammaedis exhibitae ex Alkorani manuscripto duplici, praemissis institutionibus arabicis," in *Christian-Muslim Relations 1500–1900*, ed David Thomas, 9: 844–49.

44 Email correspondence with Mr. Chris Glass, Research Services Librarian, Boston Public Library, July 20, 2021.

45 Gibbon, *The History of the Decline and Fall of the Roman Empire*, vol. 3, 126.

46 Gibbon, *The History of the Decline and Fall of the Roman Empire*, vol. 3, 147.

47 For a helpful analysis of Gibbon's work on Muhammad, see Clinton Bennett, "The History of the Decline and Fall of the Roman Empire," in *Christian-Muslim Relations 1500–1900*, ed. David Thomas, 13: 355–68.

48 Nabil Matar, "The True Nature of Imposture Fully Display'd in the Life of Mahomet," in *Christian-Muslim Relations 1500–1900*, ed. David Thomas, 13: 87–95.

49 Alexander, *Evidences of the Authenticity*, 170.

50 For an overview of Alexander's role in the Deist debate see, Leffert A. Loetscher, *Facing the Enlightenment and Pietism: Archibald Alexander and the Founding of Princeton Theological Seminary* (Westport, CT: Greenwood Press, 1983), esp. 177.

51 David D. Grafton, "A Brief Outline of the Evidences of the Christian Religion," *Christian-Muslim Relations 1500–1900*, ed. David Thomas, 16: 93–97.

52 Alexander, *Evidences of the Authenticity*, 179. See Grafton, "An Early American Lutheran Perspective of Islam," 181–96.

53 Alexander, *Evidences of the Authenticity*, 174.

54 Alexander, *Evidences of the Authenticity*, 175.

55 Alexander, *Evidences of the Authenticity*, 177.

56 Alexander, *Evidences of the Authenticity*, 179.

57 See the very helpful article, Graham A. Cole, "'Who Can Refute a Sneer?': Paley on Gibbon," *Tyndale Bulletin* 49, no. 1 (May 1998): 57–70.

58 Paley, *A View of the Evidences of Christianity*, 250–60.

59 See Paul Baepler, "The Barbary Captivity Narrative in American Culture," *Early American Literature* 39 (2004): 217–46; and Jacob Berman, "The Barbarous Voice of Democracy," *American Literature* 79 (2007): 1–27.

60 See the extremely valuable collection of correspondence of the Syrian Mission by Kamal Salibi and Yusuf K. Khoury, eds., *The Missionary Herald: Reports from Ottoman Syria, 1819–1870*, 5 vols. (Amman, Jordan: Royal Institute for Interfaith Studies 1995).

61 Van Vranken, New Brunswick Theological Seminary Archives, New Brunswick, New Jersey, MSS XT8 DT V37, Lecture 2.

62 In addition to Van Vranken's handwritten notes, there are two sets of notes taken by his students J. B. Drury (grad. '61), Van Vranken, New Brunswick Theological Seminary Archives, MSS XT8 DT V37d v. 1, and Joseph Pascal Strong, Special Collections, Rutgers Libraries, MC 641.

63 See Roberto Tottoli's entries on "Ludovico Marracci," in *Christian-Muslim Relations 1500–1900*, ed. David Thomas, 9: 791–800.

64 This is the common language used throughout the Andover, Princeton, and Union seminary catalogs. See Miller, *Piety and Intellect*, 144.

65 Email correspondence with Jeremy Wallace, Head of Collection, Research, and Engagement Strategies, Wright Library, Princeton Theological Seminary (October 28, 2022). Other libraries continued to receive copies of Sale's translation as gifts from graduates throughout the twentieth century.

66 See, Denise Spellberg, *Thomas Jefferson's Qur'an: Islam and the Founders* (New York: Vintage Books, 2013).

67 Clinton Bennett, *The Koran, Commonly Called the Alcoran of Mohammed*, in *Christian-Muslim Relations 1500–1900*, ed. David Thomas, 13: 327–37.

68 Clinton Bennett, "George Sale," in *Christian-Muslim Relations 1500–1900*, ed. David Thomas, 13: 325–27.

69 Matthew Ebenezer, "A Comprehensive Commentary on the Quran," in *Christian-Muslim Relations 1500–1900*, ed. David Thomas, 16: 375–80.

70 *Biblical Repository and Theological Review* 8 no. 1 (1836): 62.

71 Van Dyke, *Notes on the Sage Library*, 7.

72 Herman G. B. Teule, "Ktōbō d-maktbōnut zabnē, Part 1," in *Christian-Muslim Relations 600—1500*, ed. David Thomas, 4: 599–602.

73 For an assessment of Gagnier's work see Clinton Bennett, "De vita et rebus gestis Mohammedis," in *Christian-Muslim Relations 1500–1900*, ed. David Thomas, 13: 184–87; and Gunny, *The Prophet Muhammad in French and English Literature*, 58–60.

74 Gunny, *The Prophet Muhammad in French and English Literature*, 58–60.

75 David D. Grafton, "The Life of Mahomet: Mahomet and His Successors," in *Christian-Muslim Relations 1500–1900*, ed. David Thomas, 16: 166–73.

76 See David D. Grafton, "The Life of Mohammed," in *Christian-Muslim Relations 1500–1900*, ed. David Thomas, 16: 121–24.

77 Bush, *The Life of Mohammed*, 12.

78 Bush, *The Life of Mohammed*, 161.

79 For the most thorough study of this period of Muslim-Christian exchange see Avril Ann Powell, *Muslims and Missionaries in Pre-Mutiny India* (London: Curzon Press, 1993).

80 Miller, "European Judaism and Islam," 828–36.

81 See, Stacy Davis, "Unapologetic Apologetics: Julius Wellhausen, Anti-Judaism, and Hebrew Bible Scholarship," *Religions* 12, no. 8 (2021), accessed May 17, 2023, https://doi.org/10.3390/rel12080560; and Evan Goldstein, "'A Higher and Purer Shape': Kaufmann Kohler's Jewish Orientalism and the Construction of Religion in Nineteenth-Century America," *Religion and American Culture* 29, no. 3 (Fall 2019): 326–60.

82 See, Zachary Purvis, "Transatlantic Textbooks: Karl Hagenbach, Shared Interests, and German Academic Theology in Nineteenth-Century America," *Church History* 83, no. 3 (January 2014): 650–83.

83 Kansfield, "The Origins of Protestant Theological Seminary," 107.

CHAPTER 3. ISLAM IN AMERICAN CHURCH HISTORY

1 Clark, *Founding the Fathers*, 36.

2 Clark, *Founding the Fathers*, 141.

3 Clark, *Founding the Fathers*, 56–75; with reference to Smith, 61.

4 Clark also references the use of Ferdinand Christian Baur's history, *The Church History of the First Three Centuries* from 1853, translated into English by Allan Menzies in 1878. However, we found no evidence that this was used as a textbook in these seminaries.

5 Clark, *Founding the Fathers*, 144–45.

6 Marchand, *Down from Olympus*, vii.

7 Clark, *Founding the Fathers*, 138.

8 Clark, *Founding the Fathers*, 143.

9 As cited in Clark, *Founding the Fathers*, 154.

10 Clark, *Founding the Fathers*, 160.

11 Demarest, *History of Rutgers College*.

12 New Brunswick Theological Seminary Archives, New Brunswick, New Jersey. MSS XT8 Sac D51v RBR, Lecture 7.

13 See Tolan, *Saracens.*

14 Herman G. B. Teule, "Ktābā d-maktab zabnē," in *Christian-Muslim Relations 600–1500,* ed. David Thomas, 4: 599–602.

15 Maria Vaiou, "Chronographia," in *Christian-Muslim Relations 600–1500,* ed. David Thomas, 1: 427–36.

16 The standard edition of *Chronographia* with commentary is that of C. de Boor (2 vols., Leipzig: N.p., 1883–1885). References to the life of Muhammad can be found in vol. 1, 333–34.

17 Clark, *Founding the Fathers,* 86.

18 "Notes on Mohammed and Islam," *Lectures in Church History,* notes taken by David Van Kearne (Monday, November 27, 1865), NBTS archives, MSS XT8 SH W85v. v.2.

19 See Edward Gibbon, *The Decline and Fall of the Roman Empire,* vol. 2, chapter 513. Christian Classics Ethereal Library, accessed June 9, 2020, www.ccel.org.

20 "Notes on Mohammed and Islam."

21 The relationship between Zwemer and Lansing was crucial for Zwemer's life trajectory. Lansing introduced Zwemer not only to Arabic but to the American missionary community in the Middle East.

22 *An Analysis of Systematic Theology,* 2nd ed. (New Brunswick, 1883), New Brunswick Theological Seminary Archives. Copy donated by Elizabeth Zwemer Pickens. I am grateful to James Brumm for pointing out this important artifact to me.

23 Mahan, *A Church History of the First Seven Centuries,* 554–55.

24 See Robert Hoyland, *Seeing Islam as Others Saw It: A Survey and Evaluation of Christian, Jewish, and Zoroastrian Writings on Early Islam* (Princeton, NJ: Darwin Press, 1997), 533–34.

25 Mahan, *A Church History of the First Seven Centuries,* 556–57.

26 Kinsman, *Outlines of the History of the Church,* 149.

27 Kinsman, *Outlines of the History of the Church,* 149.

28 Kinsman, *Outlines of the History of the Church,* 151.

29 Kinsman, *Outlines of the History of the Church,* 152.

30 A biography of Mosheim can be found in the preface to Mosheim, *Institutes of Ecclesiastical History,* iii–viii. It is Murdock's 1839 second edition that serves as the basis of this study.

31 For Mosheim's method of organizing the history of the church see, introduction, *Institutes of Ecclesiastical History,* xvii–xx.

32 Mosheim, *Institutes of Ecclesiastical History,* vol. 1, 426.

33 Mosheim, *Institutes of Ecclesiastical History,* vol. 2, 13.

34 Mosheim, *Institutes of Ecclesiastical History,* vol. 2, 360.

35 Mosheim, *Institutes of Ecclesiastical History,* vol. 2, 420.

36 Mosheim, *Institutes of Ecclesiastical History,* vol. 2, 360–61.

37 Mosheim, *Institutes of Ecclesiastical History,* vol. 1, 430.

38 Mosheim, *Institutes of Ecclesiastical History,* vol. 1, 427.

39 Mosheim, *Institutes of Ecclesiastical History,* vol. 1, 431.

40 Mosheim, *Institutes of Ecclesiastical History*, vol. 1, 429.

41 Clark, *Founding the Fathers*, 77.

42 Samuel Davidson, "The Life and Writings of Geiseler," in Johan Karl Ludwig Geiseler, *A Textbook of Church History*, vol. 1 (New York: Harper and Bros., 1868), v–xiv.

43 Clark, *Founding the Fathers*, 400, n. 134.

44 Geiseler, *Textbook*, vol. 1, 535

45 Geiseler, *Textbook*, vol. 1, 535.

46 Geiseler, *Textbook*, vol. 1, 536.

47 See footnote 7, Geiseler, *Textbook*, vol. 1, 536.

48 See John Tolan, "Eulogius of Cordova," and Kenneth B. Wolf, "Paul Alvarus," in *Christian-Muslim Relations 600—1500*, ed. David Thomas, 1: 679–80, and 1: 645–48, respectively.

49 Geiseler, *Textbook*, vol. 2, 256.

50 For a review of Schaff's praise and critiques of Neander's method of history see Clark, *Founding the Fathers*, 80–81.

51 Neander, *General History*, vol. 5, 117.

52 Neander, *General History*, vol. 5, 114.

53 Neander, *General History*, vol. 5, 113.

54 Neander, *General History*, vol. 5, 113.

55 Neander, *General History*, vol. 5, 118.

56 Neander, *General History*, vol. 3, 340.

57 Neander, *General History*, vol. 3, 345.

58 Neander, *General History*, vol. 3, 340.

59 Neander's comments on this topic reflect the concept of a "people's history" of Muslim-Christian relations as explored in David D. Grafton, "Interesting, Varied, and Messy Lives: A People's History of Christian-Muslim Relations," in *Georgetown Companion to Interreligious Studies*, ed. Lucinda Mosher (Washington, DC: Georgetown University Press, 2022), 232–42.

60 Neander, *General History*, vol. 4, 60–61.

61 See also, John V. Tolan, *Saint Francis and the Sultan: The Curious History of a Christian-Muslim Encounter* (New York: Oxford University Press, 2009).

62 Neander, *General History*, vol. 4, 60.

63 See Samuel Marinus Zwemer, *Raymond Lull: First Missionary to the Moslems* (New York: Funk & Wagnalls, 1902).

64 See Tolan, *Saracens*, xix.

65 Shriver, *Philip Schaff*, 101.

66 Shriver, *Philip Schaff*, 108. See also the biography by Schaff's son, David S. Schaff, *The Life of Philip Schaff: In Part Autobiographical* (New York: C. Scribner's Sons, 1897). For a full list of Schaff's writings see Pranger, *Philip Schaff*, 293–95.

67 See Barrows, ed., *The World's Parliament of Religions*, vol. 2, 1192–1201.

68 See David D. Grafton, "German Lutherans and Assimilation: Lessons in the Current Atmosphere of Islamophobia," *Journal of Lutheran Ethics* (May/June 2011), accessed July 3, 2023, www.elca.org.

69 Pranger, "Philip Schaff: His Role," 213–26.

70 Papers of UTS Faculty and Students, Union Theological Seminary Archives, 3 1 10–11 Schaff's UTS lectures, Charles R. Gillett, 1877.

71 Schaff, *Through Bible Lands*, 110.

72 The term "Bible Lands" had been coined by the missionary Isaac Bird. See *Bible Work in Bible Lands; or, Events in the History of the Syria Mission* (Philadelphia: Presbyterian Board of Publication, 1872).

73 For the role of pilgrimages in American Protestant piety see Stephanie S. Rogers, *Inventing the Holy Land: American Protestant Pilgrimage to Palestine, 1865–1941* (Lanham, MD: Lexington Books, 2011).

74 Schaff, *Through Bible Lands*, 14. For the importance of these two works in generating American views of the Near East see Grafton, *An American Biblical Orientalism*, 118–21 and 173–77.

75 Schaff, *Through Bible Lands*, 35.

76 Schaff, *Through Bible Lands*, 36.

77 Schaff, *Through Bible Lands*, 370.

78 Schaff, *Through Bible Lands*, 234.

79 Schaff, *Through Bible Lands*, 391.

80 Schaff, *Through Bible Lands*, 112. The comparison had been popularized by Henry Mayhew and Charles Mackay in *The Mormons; or, Latter-Day Saints* (London: Office of the National Illustrated Library, 1851). See Christine Talbot, "The Mormons," in *Christian-Muslim Relations 1500–1900*, ed. David Thomas, 16: 180–84.

81 Schaff, *Through Bible Lands*, 111.

82 Schaff, *Through Bible Lands*, 112.

83 Schaff, *History of the Christian Church*, vol. 4, 400.

84 Philip Schaff, *Slavery and the Bible: A Tract for the Times* (Chambersburg, PA: M. Kieffer, 1861).

85 Schaff, *Through Bible Lands*, 111–12.

86 For a very helpful overview of Schaff's conception of history see Pranger, *Philip Schaff (1819–1893)*, 230–34.

87 Schaff, *History of the Christian Church*, vol. 4, 182.

88 Schaff, *History of the Christian Church*, vol. 4, 143–201.

89 See Rodwell, *el-Kor'ân*, xix–xx.

90 Rodwell, *el-Kor'ân*, xxiii.

91 Schaff, *History of the Christian Church*, vol. 4, 145.

CHAPTER 4. ARABIC AS A BIBLICAL LANGUAGE AND THE STUDY OF THE QUR'AN

1 Robinson, "Oriental Literature," 195. My emphasis.

2 For more on Robinson see Haim Goren, *"The Loss of a Minute Is Just So Much Loss of Life": Edward Robinson and Eli Smith in the Holy Land* (Belgium: Brepols, 2020); Grafton, *American Biblical Orientalism*, 97–147; and Jay G. Williams, *The*

Times and Life of Edward Robinson: Connecticut Yankee in King Solomon's Court (Atlanta, GA: Society of Biblical Literature, 1999).

3 Packard, "The Claims of the Arabic Language," 436.

4 Packard, "The Claims of the Arabic Language," 430.

5 Nabil Matar, "Edward Pococke," in *Christian-Muslim Relations 1500–1900*, ed. David Thomas, 8: 445–48. See also Umar Ryad, "'Rather Turkish Than Papist': Islam as a Political Force in the Dutch Low Countries in the Early Modern Period," *Muslim World: The Reformation and Islam; Special Edition* 107, no. 4 (October 2017): 724–25; and Gerard Wiegers, "Thomas Erpenius," in *Christian-Muslim Relations 1500–1900*, ed. David Thomas, 8: 567–70.

6 Toomer, *Eastern Wisedome*, 14–16.

7 As cited in Erika Rummel, "Humanists, Jews, and Judaism," in *Jews, Judaism, and the Reformation in Sixteenth-Century Germany*, ed. Dean Phillip Bell and Stephen G. Burnett (Leiden: Brill, 2006), 14.

8 Toomer, *Eastern Wisedome*, 42. See Luther's "Lectures on Genesis," *Luther's Works*, vol. 2, ed. Jaroslav Pelikan (St. Louis, MO: Concordia, 1960).

9 Reliance on the Vatican's library for some of the more recent publications on Arabic biblical texts can be seen in Hikmat Kashouch, *The Arabic Versions of the Gospels and Their Families* (Berlin: De Gruyter, 2012), and Ronny Vollandt, *Arabic Versions of the Pentateuch: A Comparative Study of Jewish, Christian, and Muslim Sources* (Leiden: Brill, 2015).

10 For the curious origins and identity of the Maronites as a Christian community see Kamal Salibi, *Munṭalaq tarikh Lubnan, 634–1516* (Beirut: Nawfal, 1992); or his *Maronite Historians of Mediaeval Lebanon* (Beirut: Catholic Press, 1959), which was based on his PhD dissertation from School of Oriental and Asian Studies in London.

11 Joseph Moukarzel, "Maronite Christians," in *Handbook of Christianity in the Middle East*, ed. Mitri Raheb and Mark A. Lamport (Lanham, MD: Rowman & Littlefield, 2021), 292–93. We can also highlight the important role of the Assyrian-born Jesuit Louis Cheikho (1859–1927), who created and edited the important Arabic journal *al-Mashriq* to edit and revive Arabic Christian texts.

12 Burman, *Reading the Qur'an in Latin Christendom*, 103–10.

13 The authorship of this translation is usually credited to the Scotsman Alexander Ross (d. 1654). However, for a helpful review of this debate see Clinton Bennett, "Alexander Ross, Hugh Ross, Thomas Ross," *Christian-Muslim Relations 1500–1900*, ed. David Thomas, 8: 290–98.

14 Nabil Matar, "The Qur'an in English Writings, 1543–1697," in *Christian-Muslim Relations 1500–1900*, ed. David Thomas, 8: 11–24.

15 See the excellent study by Hala Auji, *Printing Arab Modernity: Visual Culture and the American Press in Nineteenth-Century Beirut* (Leiden: Brill, 2016).

16 See Richard Rex, "The Earliest Use of Hebrew in Books Printed in England, Dating Some Works of Richard Pace and Robert Wakefield," *Transactions of the Cambridge Bibliographical Society* 9 (1990): 517–25; and David Tene, "Earli-

est Comparisons of Hebrew with Aramaic and Arabic," in *Progress in Linguistic Historiography: Papers from the International Conference on the History of the Language Sciences, Ottawa, 28–31 August 1978*, ed. E. F. K. Koerner (Amsterdam: John Benjamins Publishing, 1980), 355–72.

17 Wakefield was not the first to make such claims; in fact, the famous medieval French rabbi David Kimchi (d. 1235), in his *Radicum*, or the Book of Roots, had argued this. Robert Wakefield, *On the Three Languages* (1524), trans. Gareth Lloyd Jones (Binghamton, NY: Medieval and Renaissance Texts and Studies, 1989), 116.

18 Wakefield, *On the Three Languages*, 216.

19 Ages, "Luther and the Rabbis," 64. See also, Gerhard Falk, *The Jew in Christian Theology: Martin Luther's Anti-Jewish Vom Schem Hamphoras, Previously Unpublished in English, and Other Milestones in Church Doctrine concerning Judaism* (Jefferson, NC: McFarland, 1992), part I: 166–90, part II: 190–224.

20 Ryad, "'Rather Turkish Than Papist,'" 722.

21 Jones, "Thomas Erpenius," 15–25.

22 Jones, "Thomas Erpenius," 21.

23 Jones, "Thomas Erpenius," 24.

24 Jones, "Thomas Erpenius," 20–21.

25 Jones, "Thomas Erpenius," 25.

26 Brekka, "The Antwerp Polyglot Bible," 29.

27 See G. A. Russell, *The "Arabick" Interest of the Natural Philosophers in the Seventeenth Century* (Leiden: Brill, 1994).

28 Brekka intimates that the Antwerp Polyglot did not include Arabic simply because there were not sufficient Arabic fonts available for the printing. Brekka, "The Antwerp Polyglot Bible," 121.

29 See Peter N. Miller, "The 'Antiquarianization' of Biblical Scholarship and the London Polyglot Bible (1653–57)," *Journal of the History of Ideas* 62 (2001): 463–82.

30 Henry J. Todd, *Memoirs of the Life and Writings of the Right Rev. Brian Walton*, vol. 2 (London: N.p., 1821), 40.

31 There is currently a resurgence in Arabic New Testament textual studies. See n. 9 of this chapter.

32 Todd, *Memoirs of the Life*, vol. 2, 227.

33 Grafton, *An American Biblical Orientalism*, 17–18. See also, Fuad Shaban, *For Zion's Sake: The Judeo-Christian Tradition in American Culture* (London: Pluto Books, 2005), 61–100.

34 Torrey, "The Beginnings of Oriental Study at Andover," 250.

35 Goldman, ed., *Hebrew and the Bible in America*, 229.

36 Marr, *The Cultural Roots*, 262–98.

37 Einboden, *The Islamic Lineage*, 12.

38 Einboden, *The Islamic Lineage*, 34.

39 Marr, *The Cultural Roots*, 165.

40 Torrey, "The Beginnings of Oriental Study at Andover," 251.

41 Torrey, "The Beginnings of Oriental Study at Andover," 257.

42 Stuart, *Hebrew Grammar*, iv.

43 Gesenius, *Geschichte der hebraischen Sprache und Schrift*, 182–218. See R. Miller, "The Debate over the Vowel Points and the Crisis in Orthodox Hermeneutics," *Journal of Medieval and Renaissance Studies* 10 (1980): 53–72.

44 Goldman, "Biblical Hebrew in Colonial America," 176–77.

45 Smith, *A Hebrew Grammar*, 154.

46 Stuart notes, "The question whether the written vowels of the Hebrew language were coeval with the consonants, or at least very ancient, has been agitated with great interest and much learning, by a great number of critics, for three centuries past. On the one side it has been maintained that the vowel points were coeval with the writings of the Old Testament, or at least with the time of Ezra; on the other, that they are an invention of the Masorites, at some period between the fifth and tenth centuries." Stuart, *Hebrew Grammar*, 16.

47 Brown, Briggs, and Driver, eds., *A Hebrew and English Lexicon*, i.

48 Stuart, *Hebrew Grammar*, 3.

49 Gesenius and Rödiger, *Gesenius' Hebrew Grammar*, 6.

50 Stuart, *Hebrew Grammar*, 1.

51 Miller, *Piety and Intellect*, 113; J. F. McCurdy, "Dr. Green's Contribution to Semitic Scholarship," *Celebration of the Fiftieth Anniversary of the Appointment of Professor William Henry Green as an Instructor in Princeton Theological Seminary* (New York: Scribner's, 1896), 16.

52 McCurdy, "Dr. Green's Contribution," 33.

53 For example, in *Aryo-Semitic Speech: A Study in Linguistic Archaeology* (Andover, MA: Warren F. Draper, 1881), McCurdy develops a detailed argument of the development of proto-Aryan and proto-Semitic languages.

54 Dawley, *The Story of the General Theological Seminary*, 281.

55 Dawley, *The Story of the General Theological Seminary*, 240.

56 Dawley, *The Story of the General Theological Seminary*, 281.

57 *Catalogue of the Officers and Students of the General Theological Seminary of the Protestant Episcopal Church in the United States* (New York: [The Seminary], 1893), 26.

58 Gottheil was appointed the professor of Semitic Languages and Rabbinical Literature at Columbia in 1887. His initial area of study was Hebrew and Aramaic, but he also taught Arabic, Syriac, Assyrian, and Ethiopic. By 1903–1904, Gottheil was teaching Arabic by using the annals of Tabari. For a short biography see the Encyclopedia Iranica online, accessed February 13, 2021, https://iranicaonline.org.

59 As a result of Briggs's inaugural address, he was charged by the Presbyterian Church with heresy. This famous "Briggs trial" in 1892 led to his renouncing his ordination with the Presbyterian Church and his subsequent ordination as an Episcopal priest. More importantly, the heresy trial led to an official break between Union Seminary and the Presbyterian Church. This was the first of several debates between church denominations and seminary faculty over the issue of freedom of inquiry. See Henry Preserved

Smith, "Charles Augustus Briggs," *American Journal of Theology* 17, no. 4 (1913): 497–508. Interestingly, Briggs's daughter, Emile Grace Briggs, was the first woman to take courses and graduate from Union in 1897 and became a member of the Society for Biblical Literature and Exegesis, and an exegete in her own right.

60 Briggs, *Biblical Study*, 50.

61 J. Preston Searle, Obituary, (1906), RCA Archives, Gardner Sage Library, "John G. Lansing" Box 24, File 25. The discovery of Lansing's Arabic library is a fascinating story. "Forgotten Arabic Books and Tablet Discovered in the Denver Public Library," *Denver Mountain News*, August 29, 1939. New Brunswick Theological Seminary Archives, "John G. Lansing," Box 24, File 25, Item 6.

62 Lansing, *Inaugural Address*, 39–67. Those who were on record for making such an argument were Albert Schultens (1686–1750) in *Dissertatio theologico-philologica de utilitate linguae Arabicae in interpretenda sacra lingua* (1706), and Eberhard Schrader (1836–1908) in *Studien zur Kritik und Erklärung der biblischen Urgeschichte* (1863), as well as Samuel Driver (1846–1914).

63 Lansing, *Inaugural Address*, 47.

64 These same arguments are repeated in his Arabic grammar; Lansing, *A Manual of Arabic*, vii–viii.

65 Lansing, *Inaugural Address*, 47.

66 Lansing, *Inaugural Address*, 54.

67 For the most up-to-date biography see, Michot, "Duncan Black Macdonald."

68 Michot, "Duncan Black Macdonald."

69 Macdonald, *The Development of Muslim Theology*.

70 Macdonald, *The Hebrew Literary Genius*, 93.

71 Duncan Black Macdonald, The Haskell Lectures, no. 6 (1914), 6–11, Hartford International University Archives, Duncan Black Macdonald Papers, 106, fol. 2090, item 54935.

72 Duncan Black Macdonald, The Haskell Lectures, no. 2 (1914), 5, Hartford International University Archives, Duncan Black Macdonald Papers, 106, fol. 2090, item 54931.

73 Macdonald, The Haskell Lectures, no. 2 (1914), 5.

74 Macdonald was way ahead of his time in using literary analysis during a period in which form and source criticism were the primary methods of higher critical inquiry. His earlier work in interpreting Islam focused primarily on human experience of religion, especially ecstatic experiences, rather than theology or other historical arguments. See *The Religious Attitude and Life in Islam* (Chicago: University of Chicago Press, 1909). Macdonald viewed the *Arabian Nights* as cultural tales that lie behind much of the religious and cultural framework of pre-Islamic and medieval Islamic Arabic culture.

75 Macdonald, The Haskell Lectures, no. 3 (1914), 4. Hartford International University Archives, Duncan Black Macdonald Papers, 106, fol. 2090, item 54932.

76 Macdonald, The Haskell Lectures, no. 6, 2.

77 In the twentieth century, New Testament textual studies focused on the search for the original Greek texts. Arabic versions were considered to be late and weak translations. See Bruce M. Metzger, *The Text of the New Testament: Its Transmission, Corruption, and Restoration* (New York: Oxford University Press, 1964), 85.

78 Grafton, *The Contested Origins of the 1865 Arabic Bible*, 202–3. See also the important article by Kenneth E. Bailey and Harvey Staal, "The Arabic Versions of the Bible: Reflections on Their History and Significance," *Reformed Review* 36, no. 1 (Autumn 1982): 3–11.

79 See Griffith, *The Church in the Shadow of the Mosque*. The book is a monograph that is the culmination of years of research on Arabic Christian literature. See the bibliography within *The Church in the Shadow of the Mosque*, 191–94, for the full list of Griffith's contributions in this area.

80 The field of medieval Arabic Christian literature is vast and growing. Its roots stem from Carl Brockelmann, *Geschichte der Arabischen Literatur*, 2 vols. (Weimar: Felber, 1898–1902), Georg Graf's dissertation, *Die christlich-arabische Literatur: bis zur fränkischen Zeit (Ende des 11. Jahrhunderts)* (Freiburg im Breisgau: Herder, 1905), later expanded and published as *Geschichte der christlichen arabischen Literatur*, 5 vols. (Rome: Vatican City, 1944–1953) and Louis Cheikho, *Le Christianisme et la littérature chrétienne en Arabie avant l'Islam*, 3 vols. (Beirut: N.p., 1913–1923). For Theodore Abu Qurra, see Najib George Awad, *Orthodoxy in Arabic Terms: A Study of Theodore abu Qurrah's Theology in Its Islamic Context* (Boston: De Gruyter, 2016); Sidney Harrison Griffith, *The Beginnings of Christian Theology in Arabic: Muslim-Christian Encounters in the Early Islamic Period* (New York: Routledge, 2002); John C Lamoreaux, *Theodore Abū Qurrah* (Provo, UT: Brigham Young University Press, 2005).

81 Peter Balakian, "From Ezra Pound to Theodore Roosevelt: American Intellectual and Cultural Responses to the Armenian Genocide," in *America and the Armenian Genocide of 1915*, ed. Jay Winter (New York: Cambridge University Press, 2003), 240–41.

82 Grafton, *An American Biblical Orientalism*, 5–7.

83 John Starkey, "Arabists in the USA," *Saudi Aramco Magazine*, July–August 1965, 16–25.

84 Columbia University, *A History of Columbia University*, 278–80.

CHAPTER 5. THE STUDY OF ISLAM AS A "COMPARATIVE RELIGION"
1 elMarsafy, *Enlightenment Qur'an*, 9.

2 Rothschild et al., eds., *The History of Religions School Today*, 2. See also Wayne Meeks's chapter, "History of Religions School," in *The New Cambridge History of the Bible*. Vol. 4, *From 1750 to the Present*, ed. J. Riches (Cambridge: Cambridge University Press, 2015), 127–38.

3 Masuzawa, *Invention of World Religions*, 41.

4 Sharpe, *Comparative Religion*, 33

5 Jordan, *Comparative Religion*. In 1951, the School of Oriental and African Studies (SOAS) established the Jordan Lectures in Comparative Religion in his honor. See SOAS, University of London, "Jordan Lectures in Comparative Religion," accessed August 9, 2022, www.soas.ac.uk.

6 Jordan, *Comparative Religion*, 63.

7 Jordan, *Comparative Religion*, xi.

8 See Friedrich Max Müller, *My Autobiography: A Fragment* (London: Longmans, Green, 1901). See also Lourens P. van den Bosch, *Friedrich Max Müller: A Life Devoted to the Humanities* (Leiden: Brill, 2002).

9 Masuzawa, *Invention of World Religions*, 24.

10 See the excellent discussion of Masuzawa's critique of Müller by Walter Bruggemann: Brueggemann, "The Invention and Persistence of Wellhausen's World," *Catholic Biblical Quarterly* 75, no. 1 (January 2013): 18–19.

11 As cited in Sharpe, *Comparative Religions*, 41.

12 Müller, *Introduction to the Science of Religion*, esp. 283–334.

13 Müller, "Mohammedanism and Christianity," 302–12.

14 Masuzawa, *Invention of World Religions*, 197.

15 Einboden, *The Islamic Lineage*, 46–47.

16 Einboden, *Jefferson's Muslim Fugitives*, 33–41.

17 See Jeffrey Einboden, "New England Unitarians," in *Christian-Muslim Relations 1500–1900*, ed. David Thomas, 16: 297–310.

18 Adams, *A Dictionary of All Religions*, 161.

19 I am grateful to Victoria Jesswein, archivist at Wentz Memorial Library, United Lutheran Seminary at Gettysburg, for this information.

20 Schmucker's reference to the "Hasbemians" is to Abu Hashim Abd al-Salam (d. 933), "Nohamians" more than likely refers to the school of Abu Ishak Ibrahim al-Nazzam (d. 845), and the "Jabheians" to al-Jahiz (d. 869), a student of al-Nazzam. All these individuals subscribed to various forms of Mu'tazila thought.

21 Smucker, *History of All Religions*, 172.

22 As cited in Masuzawa, *Invention of World Religions*, 78.

23 Clarke, *Ten Great Religions*, 3.

24 Clarke, *Ten Great Religions*, 2.

25 Clarke, *Ten Great Religions*, 15–16.

26 Clarke, *Ten Great Religions*, 448.

27 Clarke, *Ten Great Religions*, 451.

28 Clarke, *Ten Great Religions*, 456.

29 Clarke, *Ten Great Religions*, 465.

30 Clarke, *Ten Great Religions*, 471.

31 Clarke, *Ten Great Religions*, 471 and 468, respectively.

32 Clarke, *Ten Great Religions*, 484.

33 See chapter 2. See also, David D. Grafton, "A Brief Outline of the Evidences of the Christian Religion," in *Christian-Muslim Relations 1500–1900*, ed. David Thomas, 16: 94–97.

34 For a brief biography of Moffat see John DeWitt, "The Memorial Tablet to Dr. James C. Moffat," *Princeton Theological Review* 1, no. 4 (1905): 624–30.

35 Moffat, *A Comparative History*, 23.

36 Moffatt, *A Comparative History*, 29.

37 Moffatt, *A Comparative History*, 181.

38 Moffatt, *A Comparative History*, 244.

39 Patton, *Syllabus of Prof. Patton's Lectures.*

40 Princeton Theological Seminary, Library. Princeton, NJ. Special Collections, The Francis Landey Patton Manuscript Collection, SCM 066, Box 1, printed "Lectures on Theism," 1888, with marginal notes by student (Robert E. Speer), 1890.

41 New York State Historical Documents, Albany, NY, "Lecture notes by unidentified student of Dr. Cady's lectures on Christian evidences," 1889 (NIC)NYNE589-710-0012.

42 Union Theological Seminary, *Annual Catalogue: Union Theological Seminary*, 1902–1903, 38.

43 Musazawa, *Invention of World Religions*, 101, n. 33.

44 *Annual Catalogue: Union Theological Seminary*, February 1893, 5.

45 Ellinwood, *Oriental Religions and Christianity*, vi.

46 James Patterson, "Ellinwood, Frank Field (1826–1908)," in *Biographical Dictionary of Christian Missions*, ed. Gerald H. Anderson (New York: Macmillan Reference USA, 1998), 197–98.

47 Ellinwood, *Oriental Religions and Christianity*, 338.

48 Ellinwood, *Oriental Religions and Christianity*, 190, 192, 194, respectively.

49 Ellinwood, *Oriental Religions and Christianity*, 196.

50 Ellinwood, *Oriental Religions and Christianity*, 203.

51 Ellinwood, *Oriental Religions and Christianity*, 218.

52 For the importance of Germany in the development of American higher education see, Marsden, *The Soul of the American University*, 89–90.

53 Smith published his biography at the end of his life to defend his views. See Henry Preserved Smith, *The Heretic's Defense: A Footnote to History* (New York: C. Scribner's Sons, 1926).

54 Evans and Smith, *Biblical Scholarship*, 82.

55 Evans and Smith, *Biblical Scholarship*, 68. Smith uses for his sources Muir, Nöldeke, Thomas Hughes's *Dictionary of Islam*, and Palmer's translation of the Qur'an as published in Müller's *Sacred Books of the East.*

56 Smith, "The Apologetic Interpretation of Scripture," 364.

57 Evans and Smith, *Biblical Scholarship*, 71.

58 Smith, *The Bible and Islam.*

59 Henry Preserved Smith Papers, series 2, box 3, and folder 5, "History of Religion. Lecture I. Plan of the course," page 1. Papers of UTS Faculty and Students, Union Theological Seminary, Columbia University in the City of New York.

60 Henry Preserved Smith Papers, series 2, box 3, and folder 5, "History of Religion. Lecture I. Plan of the course," page 20. Papers of UTS Faculty and Students, Union Theological Seminary, Columbia University in the City of New York.

61 Henry Preserved Smith Papers, series 2, box 3, and folder 5, "Islam," page 3. Papers of UTS Faculty and Students, Union Theological Seminary, Columbia University in the City of New York.

62 David D. Grafton, "The Bible and Islam," in *Christian-Muslim Relations 1500–1900*, ed. David Thomas, 16: 339–40.

63 Smith, *The Bible and Islam*, 63.

64 Smith, *The Bible and Islam*, 317.

65 Smith, "The Apologetic Interpretation of Scripture," 370.

66 See N.A., *Levi Payson Stone: A Memorial* (privately printed, 1885), 17, 27; and L. P. Stone letter to the board of directors of Princeton Seminary, July 27, 1883. Stone, Levi P. PTS Directors, Trustees, and Benefactors Reference Collection. Special Collections, Wright Library, Princeton Theological Seminary.

67 David D. Grafton, "Samuel Henry Kellogg," in *Christian-Muslim Relations 1500–1900*, ed. David Thomas, 16: 351–52.

68 Kellogg, *The Genesis and Growth of Religion*, 26. The lectures were later published as *A Handbook of Comparative Religion* (Philadelphia: Westminster, 1899).

69 Kellogg, *The Genesis and Growth of Religion*, 248.

70 Griffith, *The Church in the Shadow of the Mosque*, 96–97.

71 Kellogg, *The Genesis and Growth of Religion*, 261.

72 Kellogg, *The Genesis and Growth of Religion*, 248.

73 Kellogg, *A Handbook of Comparative Religion*, 96.

74 Kellogg, *A Handbook of Comparative Religion*, 125. See David D Grafton, *A Handbook of Comparative Religions*, in *Christian-Muslim Relations 1500–1900*, ed. David Thomas, 16: 353–56.

75 *American Lectures on the History of Religions* (New York: Putnam, 1896), v.

76 Hart, "Religious and Theological Studies," 727.

77 See "American Lectures in the History of Religions," American Academy of Religions, accessed July 25, 2022, www.aarweb.org/.

78 Hart, "Religious and Theological Studies." The Hart study noted that in 1990 there was significant disagreement as to "*what* is studied and *how* it is studied and *who* studies it [religion]," 724. The study also showed that scholars at seminaries in theological studies and those at secular university religion departments felt their methodologies and perspectives were misunderstood by both the other cohort of scholars and the public at large (752).

79 "Mission and Vision," Parliament of the World Religions, accessed August 3, 2022, https://parliamentofreligions.org.

80 Barrows, *John Henry Barrows*, 30.

81 Barrows, *John Henry Barrows*, 258.

82 Barrows, *John Henry Barrows*, 271.

83 Barrows, *John Henry Barrows*, 255.

84 Barrows, *John Henry Barrows*, 262–63.
85 Barrows, *The World's Parliament of Religions*, 1568.
86 Barrows, *John Henry Barrows*, 361.
87 The lectures he gave during his year-long tour were published as *Christianity, the World-Religion: Lectures Delivered in India and Japan* in 1897. He also published *A World Pilgrimage* in the same year as part of his travels in developing the lectures.
88 Barrows, *John Henry Barrows*, 359.
89 See Grabill, *Protestant Diplomacy*.
90 Barrows, *The Christian Conquest of Asia*, 27.
91 Barrows, *The Christian Conquest of Asia*, 31.
92 Barrows, *The Christian Conquest of Asia*, 36.
93 Barrows, *The Christian Conquest of Asia*, 42, 44, respectively.
94 Barrows, *The Christian Conquest of Asia*, 31.
95 Barrows, *John Henry Barrows*, 26.
96 Barrows, *The Christian Conquest of Asia*, 55.
97 Barrows, *The Christian Conquest of Asia*, 35.

CHAPTER 6. MISSIONS TO THE "MOHAMMEDAN WORLD"

1 For the various extant African Muslim slave writings see Allen D. Austin, *African Muslims in Antebellum America: A Sourcebook* (New York: Garland, 1984).
2 Timothy Marr, in *The Cultural Roots of American Islamicism*, notes the colonial exploits of Captain John Smith in the Ottoman Empire, as they were published in *The True Travels, Adventures, and Observations of Captaine John Smith, in Europe, Asia, Affrica, and America, from Anno Domini 1593 to 1629* (London: N.p., 1630), 2–4.
3 One of the most readable and informative studies in this field is still David H. Finnie, *Pioneers East: The Early American Experience in the Middle East*. See also James A. Field Jr., *America and the Mediterranean World, 1776–1882*.
4 For an excellent study on the history of American Middle East studies and Islam see Lockman, *Contending Visions of the Middle East*.
5 Thompson, "The Theological Seminary and Foreign Missions," 86.
6 Myklebust, *The Study of Missions*, 149. Mykelbust provides an overview of the various configurations of mission chairs, full and part-time professors of missions in the seminaries, 269–81.
7 Woodbridge, *Analysis of Systematic Theology*.
8 I am extremely thankful to James Hart Brumm, director of the Reformed Church Center, the Seminary Archives, at the New Brunswick Theological Seminary, for his pointing out Zwemer's copy of Woodbridge's textbook.
9 Schmucker, "MS Notes on A. Alexander's lectures on Polemics at Princeton Theological Seminary 1820," collected papers of Samuel Simon Schmucker, United Lutheran Seminary, Wentz Library, Gettysburg, PA.
10 Myklebust, *The Study of Missions*, 361–62.

11 Originally published as "Present Attitude of Mohammedanism, in Reference to the Spread of the Gospel," in B. Edwards, *American Quarterly Observer* 1 (1833–1834): 103–14; and then reprinted as Smith, *Missionary Sermons and Addresses.*

12 Smith, *Missionary Sermons,* 223. See also David D. Grafton, "Missionary Sermons and Addresses," in *Christian-Muslim Relations 1500–1900,* ed. David Thomas, 16: 128–33.

13 Grafton, *The Contested Origins of the 1865 Arabic Bible,* 17–23.

14 Hamlin, *My Life and Times,* 543. For an extensive and hagiographical account of his life, see Alfred Hamlin, *In Memoriam, Rev. Cyrus Hamlin, D.D., L.L.D.* (Boston: N.p., 1903).

15 Hamlin's archives are housed at Middlebury College Library. There are no lecture notes or outlines, and nothing related to his views on Islam.

16 Hamlin, *Among the Turks,* 286.

17 Hamlin, *Among the Turks,* 282.

18 Hamlin, *Among the Turks,* 346.

19 Hamlin, *Among the Turks,* 348.

20 Hamlin, *My Life and Times,* 243.

21 Hamlin, *Among the Turks,* 351.

22 Hartford Theological Seminary, *A Memorial of the Semi-centenary Celebration,* 76; *Catalogue of the Officers and Students of the Seminary, Andover, MA:* 1867–1868, 5.

23 Dennis, *Christian Missions,* vol. 1, 464.

24 *Biographical Catalogue of Princeton Theological Seminary,* 262.

25 Dennis, *Christian Missions,* vol. 1, ix.

26 Dennis, *Christian Missions,* vol. 1, xv.

27 Dennis, *Christian Missions,* vol. 1, 305.

28 Dennis, *Christian Missions,* vol. 1, 388.

29 Dennis, *Christian Missions,* vol. 1, 305.

30 Dennis, *Christian Missions,* vol. 1, 416.

31 Shedd, *Islam and the Oriental Churches.* The book was later reprinted by the SVM in 1908.

32 Shedd, *Islam,* 11, in reference to a report from *Ecumenical Missionary Conference,* vol. 1, 436.

33 Shedd, *Islam and the Oriental Churches,* 43.

34 Shedd, *Islam and the Oriental Churches,* 3.

35 Shedd, *Islam and the Oriental Churches,* 117.

36 Shedd, *Islam and the Oriental Churches,* 226.

37 See Mary Lewis Shedd, *The Measure of a Man: The Life of William Ambrose Shedd, Missionary to Persia* (New York: George H. Doran, 1922).

38 Wherry, *A Comprehensive Commentary on the Qur'án,* vol. 1, 301.

39 Matthew Ebenezer, "A Comprehensive Commentary on the Qur'án," in *Christian-Muslim Relations 1500–1900,* ed. David Thomas, 16: 375–80.

40 See Avril Ann Powell, *Muslims and Missionaries in Pre-Mutiny India* (Surrey, UK: Curzon, 1993).

41 Wherry, *Islam and Christianity*, 8. For more on Wherry see Matthew Ebenezer and Charles M. Ramsey, "Elwood Morris Wherry," in *Christian-Muslim Relations 1500–1900*, ed. David Thomas, 16: 371–78.
42 Wherry, *Islam and Christianity*, 170.
43 Calhoun, "The Last Command," 478, n. 43.
44 Miller, *Piety and Intellect*, 20–21.
45 Calhoun describes the "Haystack Meeting" at Williams College by four students in 1810. He asserts that from 1812 to 1912, one in every thirteen graduates from Princeton served in the domestic or foreign mission field. Calhoun, "The Last Command," 457, n. 304. See also, Douglas K. Showalter, "The Story of the Haystack Prayer Meeting," *Bulletin of the Congregational Library*, Second Series 3, no. 1 (2006), https://chaplain.williams.edu.
46 Woods, *Memoirs of American Missionaries*, 2.
47 For formation of the society at Gettysburg see Grafton, "An Early American Lutheran Perspective of Islam," 181–96.
48 Handy, *A History of Union Theological Seminary in New York*, 16.
49 Geer, *The Hartford Theological Seminary*, 204.
50 After the War of Independence, the Episcopal Church did not have bishops in the new republic to oversee church activity. Previously, priests had been under the auspices of the Society for the Propagation of the Gospel. The Domestic and Foreign Missionary Society of the Episcopal Church was not formed until 1821, and the first missionaries were sent out to Greece in 1831. It was not until 1835 that a general Board of Missions was organized by the General Convention, and in 1836 it began the next year consecrating bishops for the western parts of America. Perry, *The History of the American Episcopal Church*, 244.
51 Twenty of twenty-one members of the first class were in the society. Up until 1859, about 80 percent of the student body belonged to the society. Bruner, "Inquiring into Empire," 195.
52 Samuel Marinus Zwemer and James Cantine, *The Golden Milestone: Reminiscences of Pioneer Days Fifty Years Ago in Arabia* (New York: Fleming H. Revell, 1938), 18–19.
53 See the extremely valuable collection of correspondence of the Syrian Mission by Kamal Salibi and Yusuf K. Khoury, eds., *The Missionary Herald: Reports from Ottoman Syria, 1819–1870*, 5 vols. (Amman, Jordan: Royal Institute for Interfaith Studies, 1995).
54 See, for example, Rufus Anderson, *History of the Missions of the American Board of Commissioners for Foreign Missions to the Oriental Churches* (Boston: Congregational Publications Society, 1872); see esp. 1–6 for the debate over whether conversion of Muslims was possible.
55 *Condition and Character of Females in Pagan and Mohammedan Countries*, 12.
56 Gayatri Spivak, "Can the Subaltern Speak?" in *Colonial Discourse and Post-Colonial Theory: A Reader*, ed. Patrick Williams and Laura Chrisman (Hemel Hempstead, UK: Harvester, 1993), 93.

57 For an overview of the early American missions in Syria and Turkey see Grafton, *The Contested Origins*, 42–67. For the origins of the American Mission in Egypt see Ramy Marcos, *The Emergence of Evangelical Egyptians* (Lanham, MD: Lexington Books, forthcoming 2024).

58 Mosher, "Horatio Southgate," in *Christian-Muslim Relations 1500–1900*, ed. David Thomas, 16: 134–37.

59 See Laury, *A History of Lutheran Missions*, 115–17. The American Lutherans did have missions in Urumia, Persia, and then Kurdistan, begun by graduates from Luther and Augustana Seminaries, and missions to Muslims in southern India were begun by graduates of Concordia Seminary. Grafton, *Piety, Politics, and Power*, 159–81.

60 Grafton, *Piety, Politics, and Power*, 163–69.

61 Grafton, "An Early American Lutheran Perspective of Islam," 187.

62 Leonard Woods, 256–60.

63 Lansing's record of the founding can be found at Cantine and Zwemer, *The Golden Milestone*, 148–57.

64 Charles D. Matthews, "Reliques of the Rev. Dr. John G. Lansing," *Moslem World* 30, no. 3 (July 1940): 273.

65 Parker, *The Kingdom of Character*, 3.

66 Parker, *The Kingdom of Character*, 50.

67 For the contributions of women missionaries see Dana Robert, "The Influence of American Missionary Women on the World Back Home," *Religion and American Culture* 12, no. 1 (2001): 59–89. For women serving in Muslim-majority contexts see Deanna Ferree Womack, *Protestants, Gender, and the Arab Renaissance in Late Ottoman Syria* (Edinburgh: Edinburgh University Press, 2019), and the work of Christine Lindner, especially "'Long, long will she be affectionately remembered': Gender and the Memorialization of an American Female Missionary," *Mission & Social Sciences* 23, no. 1 (2010): 7–31.

68 Turner, *The Missionary Uprising among Students*, 10. For a shorter history and analysis see Ben Harder, "The Student Volunteer Movement for Foreign Missions and Its Contribution to 20th Century Missions," *Missiology* 8, no. 2 (April 1980): 141–54.

69 Moorhead, *Princeton Seminary*, 282.

70 Parker, *The Kingdom of Character*, 168–69. See also Nathan D. Showalter, "The End of a Crusade: The Student Volunteer Movement for Foreign Missions and the Great War" (ThD Thesis, Harvard University, 1990).

71 Zwemer, *Islam*, 243.

72 Zwemer, *Islam*, 254,

73 Zwemer, *Islam*, 24–25.

74 The SVM also published Zwemer's *Are More Foreign Missionaries Needed?* in 1911, which was a popular pamphlet. It was a call to mission, to step up and replace those lost on the "firing line" of missionary life.

75 Miller, *Piety and Profession*, 49–50.

76 Hartford *Annual Register*, 1899, 5 (my emphasis).
77 Capen and Hodous, *The Kennedy School of Missions*, 2–3.
78 Edwin Knox Mitchell, box 42, folder 696, Hartford International University Archives.
79 Askew, "The New York 1900 Ecumenical Missionary Conference," 146.
80 See the transcript of his speech in Ecumenical Conference on Foreign Missions, *Ecumenical Missionary Conference, New York, 1900*, 347–54.
81 Ecumenical Conference on Foreign Missions, *Ecumenical Missionary Conference, New York, 1900*, 358.
82 See Edwin Munsell Bliss, Edwin A. Grosvenor, and Cyrus Hamlin, *Turkish Cruelties upon the Armenian Christians: A Reign of Terror; From Tartar Huts to Constantinople Palaces* (Chicago: Monarch Book, 1896).
83 Ecumenical Conference on Foreign Missions, *Ecumenical Missionary Conference, New York, 1900*, 452–53.
84 Grabill, *Protestant Diplomacy and the Near East*, 186–212.
85 See Wilson J. Christy, *Apostle to Islam: A Biography of Samuel M. Zwemer* (Grand Rapids, MI: Baker, 1952).
86 Zwemer, Wherry, and Barton, *The Mohammedan World of To-Day*, 19.
87 Henry H. Jessup, *Fifty-Three Years in Syria*, vol. 2 (New York: Fleming H. Revell, 1910), 369.
88 Jessup, *Fifty-Three Years*, vol. 2, 363.
89 Khalaf, *Protestant Missionaries in the Levant*, 88. Khalaf focuses on Jessup's views on Islam in pages 87–93.
90 Jessup, *The Mohammedan Missionary Problem*, 108.
91 Jessup, *The Mohammedan Missionary Problem*, 94.
92 Jessup, *The Mohammedan Missionary Problem*, 105.
93 Womack, "Henry Jessup." See also Ussama Makdisi's assessment of Jessup's role in *Artillery from Heaven: American Missionaries and the Failed Conversion of the Middle East* (Ithaca, NY: Cornell University Press, 2008), 166–79.
94 Bosch, *Transforming Mission*, 303–12.
95 Zwemer, Wherry, and Barton, *The Mohammedan World of To-Day*, 273.
96 Zwemer, *Islam*, 255.
97 See John Raleigh Mott, *Conferences of Christian Workers among the Moslems, 1924: A Brief Account of the Conferences Together with Their Finding and Lists of Members* (New York: Chairman of the Missionary Council, 1924).
98 Zwemer, *Islam*, 250–51.
99 For an insightful analysis and critique of Edinburgh, see Stanley, *World Missionary Conference*, 91–131.
100 Gairdner and Mott, *Echoes from Edinburgh 1910*, 238.
101 Stanley, *World Missionary Conference*, 181.
102 Stanley, *World Missionary Conference*, 317; Myklebust. *The Study of Missions*, 84–94. Yale University had established a mission department with a chair of Mission Studies in 1906.

103 Stanley, *World Missionary Conference*, 317.

104 The only missionary not to attend one of these seminaries was G. F. Holmes, who was a medical doctor and did not attend seminary. The others were Herman Barnum, Kharput, Turkey (ABCFM) [Andover '57]; James Cantine, Muscat (RCA) [NBTS '89]; George F. Herrick, Constantinople (ABCFM) [Andover '59]; Franklin E. Hoskins, Beirut (PC) [Union '88]; Henry H. Jessup, D.D., Beirut (PC) [Union '55]; Phineas B. Kennedy, Albania. (ABCFM) [Princeton '94]; William A. Shedd, Urmia (PC) [Princeton '92]; John Van Ess, Busrah (RCA) [Princeton '02]; Andrew Watson, Cairo (PC) [Princeton '89]; George E. White, D.D., Marsovan (ABCFM) [Hartford '78]; Samuel G. Wilson, D.D., Tabriz (PC) [Princeton '80]; Samuel M. Zwemer, Bahrain (RCA) [NBTS '89]. World Missionary Conference, *World Missionary Conference 1910: Report of Commission IV; The Missionary Message in Relation to Non-Christian Religions* (Edinburgh: Oliphant Anderson & Ferrier, 1910), xvi–xvii.

105 World Missionary Conference, *Commission IV*, 134.

106 World Missionary Conference, *Commission IV*, 137.

107 World Missionary Conference, *Commission IV*, 148.

108 World Missionary Conference, *Commission IV*, 150.

109 Gairdner, *Echoes from Edinburgh 1910*, 45.

110 Hutchison, "A Moral Equivalent for Imperialism," 167.

111 Capen and Hodous, *The Kennedy School of Missions*, 5.

112 Capen and Hodous, *The Kennedy School of Missions*, 17.

113 Blackburn, "Arabic Instruction at Hartford Seminary," 292.

114 For a critique of *Religious Attitude* see Yahya Michot, "The Religious Attitude and Life in Islam," in *Christian-Muslim Relations 1500–1900*, ed. David Thomas, 16: 409–11. For further reading on the Theosophist movement and its interest in Islam see Tim Rudbøg, "Helena Petrovna Blavatsky," in *Christian-Muslim Relations 1500–1900*, ed. David Thomas, 16: 279–83.

115 Najib George Awad, "'Understanding the Other From-Within': The Muslim Near East in the Eyes of Duncan Black Macdonald," *Muslim World* 106, no. 3 (July 2016): 524.

116 For the critique of Macdonald see Pruett, "Duncan Black Macdonald: Christian Islamicist," 125–67; and the more nuanced appreciation and criticism of Michot, "Duncan Black MacDonald."

117 Awad, "'Understanding the Other from Within,'" 527; Bodine, "The Legacy of Duncan Black Macdonald," 162; and Bijlefeld, "Editorial Introduction," 72. These claims stem from his "autobiographical notes," put together by the librarian at Hartford. Elizabeth Root, unpublished "Biography of Duncan Black Macdonald," 12–13, The Hartford International University for Religion and Peace Archives.

118 Blackburn, "Arabic Instruction," 293.

119 Frank Knight Sanders, ed., *The Fourth Report of the Board of Missionary Preparation* (New York: Board of Missionary Preparation, 1914), 184–220.

120 Macdonald, *The Vital Forces of Christianity and Islam*, 239.

121 Bodine, "The Legacy of Duncan Black Macdonald," 163.

122 For the impressive bibliography of Macdonald's writings see William G. Shellabear et al., *The Macdonald Presentation Volume: A Tribute to Duncan Black Macdonald Consisting of Articles by Former Students, Presented to Him on His Seventieth Birthday, April 9, 1933* (Princeton, NJ: Princeton University Press, 1933), 473–87.

123 Macdonald's letters and journal written during his time in Cairo can be found in the archives of Hartford. See the Duncan Black Macdonald Papers, Hartford International University for Religion and Peace Archives.

124 Michot, "The Religious Attitude and Life in Islam."

125 Macdonald, "The Essence of Christian Missions," 330.

126 Salem, "One Hundred Twenty-Five Years of Islamic Studies at Hartford Seminary," 254.

127 For a history of the journal see W. A. Bijlefeld, "The Muslim World: Hundred Years of Continuity and Change," *Muslim World* 100 (2010): 539–44; and David D. Grafton, "The Moslem World," in *Christian-Muslim Relations 1500–1900*, ed. David Thomas, 16: 451–54.

128 For a very interesting example of how these debates were carried out among missionary institutions and among Arab Christians see, Marwa Elshakry, *Reading Darwin in Arabic, 1860–1950* (Chicago: University of Chicago Press, 2013).

129 Moorhead, *Princeton Seminary*, 342. See William Ernest Hocking, ed., *Re-Thinking Missions: A Laymen's Inquiry after One Hundred Years* (New York: Harper and Brothers, 1932).

130 Khalaf, *Protestant Missionaries*, 87.

131 Kaplan, *The Arabists*, 87–99.

CONCLUSION

1 Neander, *General History*, 113.

2 Grafton, *An American Biblical Orientalism*, 12–15.

3 See the work of Marston Speight, *Christian-Muslim Relations: An Introduction for Christians in the United States of America* (Hartford, CT: Task Force on Christian-Muslim Relations, National Council of the Churches of Christ in the U.S.A., 1983).

4 For an excellent overview of early Muslims in America see Kambiz Ghanea-Bassiri, *A History of Islam in America: From the New World to the New World Order* (New York: Cambridge University Press, 2012), 9–58.

5 For example, see Mark Lamport and Mitri Raheb, eds., *The Rowman & Littlefield Handbook of Christianity in the Middle East* (Lanham, MD: Rowman & Littlefield, 2021).

BIBLIOGRAPHY

ARCHIVES

Andover Theological Seminary Records. Special Collections. Yale Divinity School. New Haven, CT.

Collected Papers of Samuel Simon Schmucker. United Lutheran Seminary. Wentz Library. Gettysburg, PA.

Directors, Trustees, and Benefactors Reference Collection. Special Collections. Wright Library. Princeton Theological Seminary. Princeton, NJ.

Duncan Black Macdonald Papers. Hartford International University for Religion and Peace Archives. Hartford, CT.

The Francis Landey Patton Manuscript Collection. Special Collections. Wright Library. Princeton Theological Seminary Library. Princeton, NJ.

The Hartford International University for Religion and Peace Archives. Hartford, CT.

New York State Historical Documents. Albany, NY.

Papers of UTS Faculty and Students. Union Theological Seminary Archives. Columbia University in the City of New York.

Park Family Archives at Yale. Yale Divinity School Library. New Haven, CT.

The Seminary Archives. New Brunswick Theological Seminary. New Brunswick, NJ.

Special Collections & University Archives. Rutgers University Libraries. Rutgers University. New Brunswick, NJ.

CATALOGS AND PERIODICALS

American Quarterly Observer
Annual Catalogue: Union Theological Seminary
Annual Register of the Hartford Theological Seminary
Biblical Repository and American Observer
Biblioteca Sacra and Theological Review
Biographical Catalogue of Princeton Theological Seminary

Bulletin of the General Theological Seminary

Catalog of the Library Belonging to the Theological Institution in Andover

Catalogue of the Library Belonging to the General Theological Seminary of the Protestant Episcopal Church in the United States

Catalogue of the Officers and Students of the Theological Seminary, Andover, MA.

Diocesan Convention of Maryland, Journal of Proceedings, 1896

The Hartford Seminary Record

The Princeton Seminary Bulletin

PRIMARY SOURCES

Adams, Hannah. *A Dictionary of All Religions and Religious Denominations, Jewish, Heathen, Mahometan, and Christian, Ancient and Modern: With an Appendix, Containing a Sketch of the Present State of the World, As to Population, Religion, Toleration, Missions, Etc., and the Articles in Which All Christian Denomination Agree.* 4th ed. New York: James Eastburn, 1817.

Alexander, Archibald. *Evidences of the Authenticity, Inspiration, and Canonical Authority of the Holy Scriptures.* Philadelphia: J. Whetham & Son, 1836.

American Lectures on the History of Religions. New York: Putnam, 1896.

Barrows, John Henry. *The Christian Conquest of Asia: Studies and Personal Observations of Oriental Religions: Being the Morse Lectures of 1898.* New York: Scribner's, 1899.

———, ed. *The World's Parliament of Religions.* 2 vols. Chicago: Parliament, 1893.

Barrows, Mary Eleanor. *John Henry Barrows: A Memoir.* Chicago: Fleming H. Revell, 1904.

A Brief Account of the Rise, Progress, and Present State of the Theological Seminary of the Presbyterian Church in the United States at Princeton. Philadelphia: A. Finley, 1822.

Briggs, Charles A. *Biblical Study: Its Principles, Methods, and History: Together with a Catalogue of Books of Reference.* 3rd ed. New York: Scribner's, 1887.

Brown, Francis, W. Briggs, and C. A. Driver, eds. *A Hebrew and English Lexicon of the Old Testament: With an Appendix Containing the Biblical Aramaic, Based on the Lexicon of William Gesenius as Translated by Edward Robinson.* 1st ed. Boston: Houghton Mifflin, 1906.

Bush, George. *The Life of Mohammed: Founder of the Religion of Islam, and of the Empire of the Saracens.* New York: J. & J. Harper, 1830.

Capen, Edward Warren, and Lewis Hodous. *The Kennedy School of Missions: A Sketch of Twenty-Five Years of Service.* Hartford, CT: Press of the Hartford Seminary Foundation, 1936.

Clarke, James Freeman. *Ten Great Religions: An Essay in Comparative Theology.* Boston: James R. Osgood, 1871.

Columbia University. *A History of Columbia University, 1754–1904*. New York: Columbia University Press, 1904.

Condition and Character of Females in Pagan and Mohammedan Countries. 2nd ed. Boston: Perkins & Marvin, 1831.

Demarest, David D. *Centennial of the Theological Seminary of the Reformed Church in America. (Formerly Ref. Prot. Dutch Church), 1784–1884*. New York: Board of Publication of the Reformed Church in America, 1885.

Demarest, William H. S. *History of Rutgers College; or, An Account of the Union of Rutgers College, and the Theological Seminary of the General Synod of the Reformed Dutch Church*. New York: Anderson & Smith, Printers, 1833.

Dennis, James S. *Christian Missions and Social Progress: A Sociological Study of Foreign Missions*. Vols 1–3. New York: Fleming H. Revell, 1897.

———. *Social Evils of the Non-Christian World*. New York: Student Volunteer Movement for Foreign Missions, 1899.

Ecumenical Conference on Foreign Missions. *Ecumenical Missionary Conference, New York, 1900: Report of the Ecumenical Conference on Foreign Missions, Held in Carnegie Hall and Neighboring Churches, April 21 to May 1*. Vols. 1 and 2. New York: American Tract Society, 1900.

Ellinwood, Frank F. *Oriental Religions and Christianity: A Course of Lectures Delivered on the Ely Foundation before the Students of Union Theological Seminary*. New York: Scribner and Sons, 1892.

Evans, Llewelyn John, and Henry Preserved Smith. *Biblical Scholarship and Inspiration: Two Papers*. Cincinnati, OH: Robert Clarke, 1891.

Fisk, Pliny. *A Sermon, Preached in the Old South Church Boston, Sabbath Evening, October 31, 1819, Just before the Departure of the Palestine Mission*. Boston: Samuel T. Armstrong, 1819.

Gairdner, W. H. T., and John R Mott. *Echoes from Edinburgh, 1910*. New York: Fleming H. Revell, 1910.

General Catalog of Andover Theological Seminary. Andover, Massachusetts, 1808–1908. Boston: Thomas Todd, 1908.

General Theological Seminary Library. *A Catalogue of the Library Belonging to the General Theological Seminary of the Protestant Episcopal Church in the United States*. New York: Vanderpool & Cole, Printers, 1824.

Gesenius, Wilhelm. *Geschichte der Hebraischen Sprache und Schrift*. Leipzig: N.p., 1815.

Gesenius, William, and Emile Rödiger. *Gesenius' Hebrew Grammar*. 17th ed. Trans. Jefferson T. Conant. New York: N.p., 1856.

Gibbon, Edward. *The History of the Decline and Fall of the Roman Empire*. Vol. 3. New York: E. Duyckinck, 1822.

Gibbs, Josiah W. *Catalog of the Library Belonging to the Theological Institution in Andover*. Andover, MA: Flagg and Could, 1819.

Hamlin, Cyrus. *Among the Turks*. New York: R. Carter, 1877.

———. *My Life and Times*. Boston: Congregational Sunday-School and Publ. Society, 1893.

Hartford Theological Seminary. *A Memorial of the Semi-centenary Celebration of the Founding of the Theological Institute of Connecticut.* Hartford, CT: Press of the Case, Lockwood & Brainard, 1884.

Hartranft, Chester David. *Some Thoughts on the Scope of Theology and Theological Education: Address Delivered before the Pastoral Union.* Hartford, CT: Press of the Case, Lockwood & Brainard, 1888.

Hay, Charles A. *Catalogue of Duplicate Books from the Library of the Theological Seminary, at Gettysburg, Pa: Offered for Sale by Order of the Board. By (Charles Augustus), 1821–1893.* Theological Seminary of the General Synod of the Evangelical Lutheran Church in the United States. Library. Gettysburg, PA: Star and Sentinel Office, 1869.

Jessup, Henry H. *Fifty-Three Years in Syria.* Vols. 1 and 2. New York: Fleming H. Revell, 1910.

———. *The Mohammedan Missionary Problem.* Philadelphia: Presbyterian Board of Publication, 1879.

Kansfield, Norman J. "The Origins of Protestant Theological Seminary Libraries in the United States." Dissertation, University of Chicago, Chicago, IL, 1970.

Kellogg, Samuel H. *The Genesis and Growth of Religion: The L. P. Stone Lectures for 1892, at Princeton Theological Seminary.* New York: Macmillan, 1892.

———. *A Handbook of Comparative Religion.* Philadelphia: Westminster, 1899.

Kinsman, Frederick. *Outlines of the History of the Church.* Milwaukee, WI: Morehouse, 1916.

Lansing, John G. *Inaugural Address of the Rev. John G. Lansing as the Gardner A. Sage Professorship of Old Testament and Exegesis, September 23, 1884.* New York: Board of the Reformed Church in America, 1884.

———. *A Manual of Arabic.* 2nd ed. New York: Scribner's, 1891.

Macdonald, Duncan Black. *The Development of Muslim Theology, Jurisprudence, and Constitutional Theory.* New York, Charles Scribner's Sons, 1903.

———. "The Essence of Christian Missions." *Moslem World* 22, no. 4 (1932): 327–30.

———. *The Hebrew Literary Genius: An Interpretation Being an Introduction to the Reading of the Old Testament.* Princeton, NJ: Princeton University Press, 1935.

———. *The Vital Forces of Christianity and Islam: Six Studies by Missionaries to Moslems.* New York: Oxford University Press, 1914.

Mahan, Milo. *A Church History of the First Seven Centuries.* 2nd ed. New York: Pott, Young, 1878.

Moffat, James C. *A Comparative History of Religions.* New York: Dodd & Mead, 1871.

Mosheim, Johann Lorenz. *Institutes of Ecclesiastical History.* Trans. James Murdock. 2nd ed. New York: Harper Bros., 1839.

Müller, F. Max. *Introduction to the Science of Religion: Four Lectures Delivered at the Royal Institution; With Two Essays, on False Analogies and the Philosophy of Mythology.* London: Longmans, Green, 1873.

———. "Mohammedanism and Christianity." *Nineteenth Century*, February 1894, 302–12.

Neander, Augustus. *General History of the Christian Religion and Church*. Vol. 5. Trans. Joseph Torrey. Edinburgh: T&T Clark, 1855.

Packard, Joseph. "The Claims of the Arabic Language and Literature." *Biblical Repository and the Quarterly Observer* 8 (1836): 429–47.

Paley, William. *A View of the Evidences of Christianity*. Philadelphia: J. J. Woodward, 1836.

Patton, Francis L. *Syllabus of Prof. Patton's Lectures on Theism*. Princeton, NJ: Princeton University Press, 1893.

Reformed Church in America. *Centennial of the Theological Seminary of the Reformed Church in America*. New York: Board of Publication of the Reformed Church in America, 1885.

Robinson, Edward. "Oriental Literature." *Biblical Repository* 1, no. 1 (1831): 194–98.

———. "Theological Education in Germany." *Biblical Repository* 1, no.1 (Jan. 1831): 1–51; 1, no. 2 (April 1831): 199–226; 1, no. 3 (July 1831): 409–51; 1, no. 4 (Oct. 1831): 613–37.

Ross, Alexander. *Pansébeia; or, A View of All Religions in the World: With the Several Church-Governments, from the Creation, to These Times: Also, a Discovery of All Known Heresies in All Ages and Places, and Choice Observations and Reflections throughout the Whole: to Which Are Annexed, the Lives, Actions, and Ends of Certain Notorious Hereticks, with Their Effigies in Copper-Plates*. 4th ed., enlarged and perfected. [London]: Printed for J. Williams, 1672.

Schaff, Philip. *America: A Sketch of the Political, Social, and Religious Character of the United States of North America, in Two Lectures, Delivered at Berlin, with a Report Read before the German Church Diet at Frankfort-on-the-Maine, Sept., 1854*. New York: C. Scribner, 1855.

———. *Through Bible Lands: Notes of Travel in Egypt, the Desert, and Palestine*. New York: American Tract Society, 1878.

Shedd, William Ambrose. *Islam and the Oriental Churches: Their Historical Relations*. Philadelphia: Presbyterian Board of Publication and Sabbath-School Work, 1904.

Smith, Eli. *Missionary Sermons and Addresses*. Boston: Perkins, 1833.

Smith, Henry Preserved. "The Apologetic Interpretation of Scripture in Islam and in Christianity." *Journal of Religion* 4, no. 4 (1924): 361–71.

———. *The Bible and Islam; or, The Influence of the Old and New Testaments on the Religion of Mohammed*. London: J. Nisbet, 1897.

Smith, John. *A Hebrew Grammar without Points*. Boston: N.p., 1803.

Smucker, Samuel M. *History of All Religions: Containing a Statement of the Origin, Development, Doctrines, Forms of Worship, and Government of All the Religious Denominations in the World*. Philadelphia: Crawford, 1881.

Stuart, Moses. *Hebrew Grammar with a Copious Syntax and a Praxis*. Andover, MA: Flagg and Gould, 1821.

Thompson, A. C. "The Theological Seminary and Foreign Missions." In *A Memorial of the Semi-centenary Celebration of the Founding of the Theological Institute of Connecticut*. Graham Taylor and Pastoral Union of Connecticut. Hartford, CT: Press of the Case, Lockwood & Brainard, 1884. 74–87.

Van Dyke, John Charles. *Notes on the Sage Library of the Theological Seminary at New Brunswick*. New Brunswick, NJ: N.p., 1888.

Wakefield, Robert. *On the Three Languages (1524)*. Trans. Gareth Lloyd Jones. Binghamton, NY: Medieval and Renaissance Texts and Studies, 1989.

Wherry, Elwood M. *A Comprehensive Commentary on the Qur'án. Comprising Sale's Translation and Preliminary Discourse, with Additional Notes and Emendations*. Vols. 1 and 2. Boston: N.p., 1884.

——. *Islam and Christianity in India and the Far East*. New York: Fleming H. Revell, 1907.

Wherry, W. M., S. M. Zwemer, and C. G. Mylrea. *Islam and Missions: Being Papers Read at the Second Missionary Conference on Behalf of the Mohammedan World at Lucknow, January 23–28, 1911*. New York: Fleming H. Revell, 1911.

Williams, Hermine Weigel. *Robinson's Letter—Journal (1826–1829): Written from Europe by Edward Robinson to His Sister, Elisabeth*. Bloomington, IN: iUniverse, 2010.

Woodbridge, Samuel Merrill. *Analysis of Systematic Theology*. New Brunswick, NJ: N.p., 1883.

Woods, Leonard. *History of the Andover Theological Seminary*. Boston: George S. Baker, 1885 [Ann Arbor, MI: Univ. Microfilms Int., 1981].

——. *Memoirs of American Missionaries, Formerly Connected with the Society of Inquiry Respecting Missions, in the Andover Theological Seminary: Embracing a History of the Society with an Introductory Essay*. Boston: Peirce and Parker, 1833.

World Missionary Conference. *World Missionary Conference, 1910: Report of Commission V; The Preparation of Missionaries*. Edinburgh: Oliphant, Anderson & Ferrier, 1910.

Zwemer, Samuel. *Islam: A Challenge to Faith*. New York: Student Volunteer Movement for Foreign Missions, 1907.

Zwemer, Samuel Marinus, and James Cantine. *The Golden Milestone: Reminiscences of Pioneer Days Fifty Years Ago in Arabia*. New York: Fleming H. Revell, 1938.

Zwemer, S. M., E. M. Wherry, and James L. Barton, eds. *The Mohammedan World of To-Day: Being Papers Read at the First Missionary Conference on Behalf of the Mohammedan World Held at Cairo, April 4th–9th, 1906*. New York: Fleming H. Revell, 1906.

SECONDARY SOURCES

Ages, Arnold. "Luther and the Rabbis." *Jewish Quarterly Review*, New Series, 58, no. 1 (July 1967): 63–68.

Arnold, Matthieu. "Martin Luther and Education." *Lutheran Quarterly* 33, no. 3 (Fall 2019): 287–303.

Askew, Thomas A. "The New York 1900 Ecumenical Missionary Conference: A Centennial Reflection." *International Bulletin of Missionary Research* 24, no. 4 (October 2000): 146–50, 152, 154.

Aubert, Annette G. *The German Roots of Nineteenth-Century American Theology*. New York: Oxford University Press, 2013.

Awad, Najib George. "'Understanding the Other from Within': The Muslim Near East in the Eyes of Duncan Black Macdonald." *Muslim World* 106, no. 3 (July 2016): 523–38.

Baird, Robert. *Religion in the United States*. Glasgow: Blackie and Son, 1844.

Bell, Dean Phillip, and Stephen G. Burnett, ed. *Jews, Judaism, and the Reformation in Sixteenth-Century Germany*. Leiden: Brill, 2006.

Bevilacqua, Alexander. "How to Organize the Orient: D'Herblot and the 'Biblioteche Orientale.'" *Journal of the Warburg and Courtauld Institutes* 79 (2016): 213–61.

Bijlefeld, Willem Abraham. "Editorial Introduction." *Muslim World* 57, no. 2 (April 1967): 72–73.

Blackburn, Steven. "Arabic Instruction at Hartford Seminary: A History since the Nineteenth Century." *Muslim World* 108, no. 2 (April 2018): 289–98.

Bodine, J. Jermain. "The Legacy of Duncan Black Macdonald." *Occasional Bulletin of Missionary Research* 4, no. 4 (1980): 162–65.

Bosch, David. *Transforming Mission: Paradigm Shifts in Theology of Mission*. Maryknoll, NY: Orbiss, 1999.

Brekka, Pamela Merrill. "The Antwerp Polyglot Bible (1572): Visual Corpus, New World Hebrew-Indian Map, and the Religious Crosscurrent of Imperial Spain." PhD dissertation, University of Florida–Gainesville, 2012.

Bruner, Jason. "Inquiring into Empire: Princeton Seminary's Society of Inquiry on Missions, the British Empire, and the Opium Trade, ca. 1830–1850." *Mission Studies* 27, no. 2 (2010): 194–219.

Burman, Thomas E. *Reading the Qur'ān in Latin Christendom, 1140–1560*. Philadelphia: University of Pennsylvania Press, 2007.

Calhoun, David B. "The Last Command: Princeton Theological Seminary and Missions, 1812–1862." PhD dissertation, Princeton Theological Seminary, Princeton, NJ, 1983.

Christiansen, Torben, and William R Hutchison, eds. *Missionary Ideologies in the Imperialist Era, 1880–1920*. Aarhaus, Denmark: Forlaget Aros, 1982.

Clark, Elizabeth A. *Founding the Fathers: Early Church History and Protestant Professors in Nineteenth-Century America*. Philadelphia: University of Pennsylvania Press, 2011.

Davidson, Samuel. "The Life and Writings of Geiseler." *A Textbook of Church History*. Vol. 1. New York: Harper and Bros., 1868.

Dawley, Powel Mills. *The Story of the General Theological Seminary: A Sesquicentennial History, 1817–1967*. Eugene, OR: Wipf and Stock, 1999.

Ebenezer, Matthew. "A Comprehensive Commentary on the Qur'án." In *Christian-Muslim Relations 1500–1900*, ed. David Thomas. Vol. 16. Leiden: Brill, 2020. 375–80.

Edwards, B. B., and Edwards Amasa Park. *Writings of Professor B. B. Edwards with a Memoir*. Vol. 1. Boston: J.P. Jewett, 1853.

Einboden, Jeffrey. *The Islamic Lineage of American Literary Culture: Muslim Sources from the Revolution to Reconstruction*. New York: Oxford University Press, 2016.

———. *Jefferson's Muslim Fugitives: The Lost Story of Enslaved Africans, Their Arabic Letters, and an American President*. New York: Oxford University Press, 2020.

Elmarsafy, Ziad. *The Enlightenment Qur'an: The Politics of Translation and the Construction of Islam*. London: Oneworld Publications, 2014.

Fraser, James W. *Schooling the Preachers: The Development of Protestant Theological Education in the United States, 1740–1875*. Lanham, MD: University Press of America, 1988.

Gairdner, W. H. T., and John R Mott. *Echoes from Edinburgh, 1910: An Account and Interpretation of the World Missionary Conference*. New York: Fleming H. Revell, 1910.

Gasero, Russell L. "The Origins of the Theological Library at New Brunswick." In *Servant Gladly: Essays in Honor of John W Beardslee III*, ed. Jack D. Klunder. Grand Rapids, MI: Eerdmans, 1989. 73–88.

Geer, Curtis M. *The Hartford Theological Seminary, 1834–1934*. Hartford, CT: Case, Lockwood, and Brainard, 1934.

Giltner, John H. *Moses Stuart: The Father of Biblical Science in America*. Atlanta, GA: Scholars Press, 1988.

Goldman, Shalom. "Biblical Hebrew in Colonial America: The Case of Dartmouth." *American Jewish History* 79, no. 2 (1989): 173–80.

———, ed. *Hebrew and the Bible in America: The First Two Centuries*. Hanover, VT: University Press of New England, 1993.

Gortner, David T., Katherine Wood, and J. Barney Hawkins IV. "Faithful Christians, Faithful Neighbors: How Do Episcopal Parishes Relate to Other Faiths—Especially Islam?" *Virginia Theological Seminary Journal* (December 2013): 57–66.

Grabill, Joseph L. *Protestant Diplomacy and the Near East: Missionary Influence on American Policy, 1810–1927*. Minneapolis: University of Minnesota Press, 1971.

Grafton, David D. *An American Biblical Orientalism: The Construction of Jews, Christians, and Muslims in Nineteenth-Century American Evangelical Piety*. Lanham, MD: Lexington Books/Fortress, 2019.

———. "The Bible and Islam." In *Christian-Muslim Relations 1500–1900*, ed. David Thomas. Vol. 16. Leiden: Brill, 2020. 339–40.

———. *The Contested Origins of the 1865 Arabic Bible*. Leiden: Brill, 2015.

———. "An Early American Lutheran Perspective of Islam: Lewis Eichelberger and His Sources." *Journal of the Lutheran Historical Conference*. Proceedings of the 2008 Lutheran Historical Conference, Wagner College, Staten Island, New York (October 11–14, 2008): 181–96.

———. "Martin Luther's Sources on the Turk and Islam in the Midst of Fear of Ottoman Imperialism." *Muslim World: The Reformation and Islam* 107, no. 4 (October 2017): 665–83.

———. *Piety, Politics, and Power: Lutherans Encountering Islam in the Middle East*. Eugene, OR: Pickwick Publications, 2009.

———. "Samuel Henry Kellogg." In *Christian-Muslim Relations 1500–1900*, ed. David Thomas. Vol. 16. Leiden: Brill, 2020. 351–52.

Griffith, Sidney H. *The Church in the Shadow of the Mosque: Christians and Muslims in the World of Islam*. Princeton, NJ: Princeton University Press, 2012.

Gunny, Ahmad A. *The Prophet Muhammad in French and English Literature, 1650 to the Present*. New York: Kube Publishing, 2015.

Hageman, Howard G. *Two Centuries Plus: The Story of New Brunswick Seminary*. Grand Rapids, MI: Eerdmans, 1984.

Handy, Robert T. *A History of Union Theological Seminary in New York*. New York: Columbia University Press, 1987.

Hart, Ray L. "Religious and Theological Studies in American Higher Education: A Pilot Study." *Journal of the American Academy of Religion* 59, no. 4 (Winter 1991): 715–827.

Hill, Kenneth H. *Religious Education in the African American Tradition: A Comprehensive Introduction*. Des Peres, MO: Chalice Press, 2012.

Holifield, E. Brooks. *God's Ambassadors: A History of the Christian Clergy in America*. Grand Rapids, MI: Eerdmans, 2007.

Hubers, John. *I Am a Pilgrim, a Traveler, a Stranger: Exploring the Life and Mind of the First American Missionary to the Middle East, the Rev. Pliny Fisk (1792–1825)*. Eugene, OR: Pickwick Publications, 2016.

Hutchison, William R. "A Moral Equivalent for Imperialism: Americans and Promotion of Christian Civilization, 1880–1910." In *Missionary Ideologies in the Imperialist Era, 1880–1920*, ed. Torben Christiansen and William R Hutchison. Aarhaus, Denmark: Forlaget Aros, 1982. 167–78.

Jones, Robert Jon. "Thomas Erpenius (1584–1624) on the Value of the Arabic Language." *Manuscripts of the Middle East* 1 (1986): 15–25.

Jordan, Louis Henry. *Comparative Religion: Its Genesis and Growth*. New York: Scribner, 1905.

Kansfield, Norman J. "The Origins of Protestant Theological Seminary Libraries in the United States." Dissertation, University of Chicago, Chicago, IL, 1970.

Kaplan, Robert D. *The Arabists: The Romance of an American Elite*. New York: Free Press, 1993.

Khalaf, Samir. *Protestant Missionaries in the Levant: Ungodly Puritans, 1820–1860*. New York: Routledge, 2012.

Kitagawa, Joseph Mitsua, ed. *Religious Studies, Theological Studies, and the University-Divinity School*. Atlanta, GA: Scholars Press, 1992.

Kuklick, Bruce. *Churchmen and Philosophers: From Jonathan Edwards to John Dewey*. New Haven, CT: Yale University Press, 1985.

———. *Puritans in Babylon: The Ancient Near East and American Intellectual Life, 1880–1930*. Princeton, NJ: Princeton University Press, 1996.

Laury, Preston A. *A History of Lutheran Missions*. Reading, PA: Pilger Publishing House, 1899.

Lockman, Zachary. *Contending Visions of the Middle East: The History and Politics of Orientalism*. Cambridge: Cambridge University Press, 2010.

Marchand, Suzanne L. *Down from Olympus: Archaeology and Philhellenism in Germany, 1750–1970*. Princeton, NJ: Princeton University Press, 1996.

Marr, Timothy. *The Cultural Roots of American Islamicism*. New York: Cambridge University Press, 2006.

Marsden, George M. *The Soul of the American University Revisited: From Protestant to Postsecular.* 2nd ed. New York: Oxford University Press, 2021.

Marty, Martin. *Righteous Empire.* New York: Dial Press, 1970.

Masuzawa, Tomoko. *Invention of World Religions; or, How European Universalism Was Preserved in the Language of Pluralism.* Chicago: University of Chicago Press, 2005.

Matar, Nabil. *Islam in Britain, 1558–1685.* New York: Cambridge University Press, 1998.

Matthews, Charles D. "Reliques of the Rev. Dr. John G. Lansing." *Moslem World* 30, no. 3 (July 1940): 269–79.

McCGatch, Milton. "A Major Library Acquisition of 1838: Three Vignettes and a Reflection." In *The American Theological Library Association: Essays in Celebration of the First Fifty Years*, ed. M. Patrick Graham, Valerie R. Hotchkiss, and Kenneth E. Rowe. Evanston, IL: N.p., 1996. 103–21.

Michot, Yahya. "Aspects of Islam." In *Christian-Muslim Relations 1500–1900*, ed. David Thomas. Vol. 16. Leiden: Brill, 2020. 409–12.

———. "Duncan Black MacDonald." In *Christian-Muslim Relations 1500–1900*, ed. David Thomas. Vol. 16. Leiden: Brill, 2020. 401–5.

Miller, Glenn T. *Piety and Intellect: The Aims and Purposes of Ante-Bellum Theological Education.* Studies in Theological Education. Atlanta, GA: Scholars Press, 1990.

———. *Piety and Plurality.* Eugene, OR: Cascade Books, 2014.

———. *Piety and Profession.* Grand Rapids, MI: Eerdmans, 2007.

Miller, Michael L. "European Judaism and Islam: The Contribution of Jewish Orientalists." In *A History of Jewish-Muslim Relations: From the Origins to the Present Day*, ed. Abdelwahab Meddeb and Benjamin Stora. Princeton, NJ: Princeton University Press, 2013. 828–36.

Mitchell, Christine R. "Protestant Theological Libraries: Past, Present, and Future." MA thesis, University of North Carolina–Chapel Hill, 2005.

Moorhead, James H. *Princeton Seminary in American Religion and Culture.* Grand Rapids, MI: Eerdmans, 2012.

Mosher, Lucinda. "Horatio Southgate." In *Christian-Muslim Relations 1500–1900*, ed. David Thomas. Vol. 16. Leiden: Brill, 2020. 134–37.

Myklebust, Olav Guttorm. *The Study of Missions in Theological Education.* Vol. 2. Oslo: Egede Instituttet, 1957.

Packard, Joseph. "The Claims of the Arabic Language and Literature." *Biblical Repository and the Quarterly Observer* 8 (1836): 429–48.

Park, Edwards A. *Writings of Prof. B. B. Edwards, with a Memoir.* 2 vols. Boston: John P. Jewett, 1853.

Parker, Michael. *The Kingdom of Character: The Student Volunteer Movement for Foreign Missions, 1886–1926.* Lanham, MD: University Press of America; American Society of Missiology, 1998.

Parliament of the World Religions. "Mission and Vision." https://parliamentofreligions.org/our-work/mission/. Accessed October 20, 2023.

Paulus, Michael J., Jr. "Spiritual Culture and the Theological Library: The Role of the Princeton Theological Seminary Library in the Religious Life of Theological

Students in the Nineteenth Century." *ATLA Summary of Proceedings* 60 (2006): 220–28.

Perry, William Stevens. *The History of the American Episcopal Church, 1587–1883.* Boston: J. R. Osgood, 1885.

Pranger, Gary K. *Philip Schaff (1819–1893): Portrait of an Immigrant Theologian.* New York: Peter Lang, 1997.

———. "Philip Schaff: His Role in American Evangelical Education." In *German Influences on Education in the United States to 1917,* ed. Henry Geitz, Jürgen Heideking, and Jurgen Herbst. Washington, DC: German Historical Institute, 2006. 213–26.

Pruett, Gordan E. "Duncan Black Macdonald: Christian Islamicist." In *Orientalism, Islam, and Islamists,* ed. Asaf Hussain, Robert Olson, and Jamil Qureshi. Brattleboro, VT: Amana Books, 1984. 125–67.

Robinson, Edward, and Eli Smith. *Biblical Researches in Palestine, Mount Sinai, and Arabia Petraea: A Journal of Travels in the Year 1838.* Boston: Crocker & Brewster, 1841.

Rodwell, J. M. *el-Kor'ân; or, The Koran, Translated from the Arabic, the Suras Arranged in Chronological Order, with Notes and Index.* London: Bernard Quaritch, 1876.

Root, Elizabeth de Welden. "As It Was in the Beginning: Reminiscences of Life in the Hartford Seminary Foundation and a History of the Case Memorial Library." Vols. 1 and 2. Unpublished manuscript, 1968, Hartford International University for Religion and Peace Archives, Hartford, CT.

Rothschild, Clare K., et al., eds. *The History of Religions School Today: Essays on the New Testament and Related Ancient Mediterranean Texts.* Tubingen, Germany: Mohr Siebeck, 2014.

Rowe, Henry K. *History of Andover Theological Seminary.* Newton, MA: N.p., 1933.

Salem, Feryal. "One Hundred Twenty-Five Years of Islamic Studies at Hartford Seminary." *Muslim World* 108, no. 2 (April 2018): 254–88.

Selden, William K. *Princeton Theological Seminary: A Narrative History, 1812–1992.* Princeton, NJ: Princeton University Press, 1992.

Sharpe, Eric J. *Comparative Religion: A History.* 2nd ed. La Salle, IL: Open Court, 1986.

Shriver, George H. *Philip Schaff: Christian Scholar and Ecumenical Prophet; Centennial Biography for the American Society of Church History.* Macon, GA: Mercer University Press, 1987.

Stanley, Brian. *World Missionary Conference, Edinburgh, 1910.* Grand Rapids, MI: Eerdmans, 2009.

Thomas, David, ed. *Christian-Muslim Relations: A Bibliographic History 600-1500.* Vols. 1–5. Leiden: Brill, 2009-2013.

———, ed. *Christian-Muslim Relations: A Bibliographic History 1500-1900.* Vols. 6–16. Leiden: Brill, 2014-2020.

de Tocqueville, Alexis. *Democracy in America.* London: Wadworth, 1998.

Todd, Henry J. *Memoirs of the Life and Writings of the Right Rev. Brian Walton.* Vol. 2. London: N.p., 1821.

Tolan, John. *Saracens: Islam in the Medieval European Imagination.* New York: Columbia University Press, 2002.

Toomer, G. J. *Eastern Wisedome and Learning: The Study of Arabic in Seventeenth-Century England*. Oxford: Clarendon, 1996.

Torrey, Charles C. "The Beginnings of Oriental Study at Andover." *American Journal of Semitic Languages and Literatures* 13, no. 4 (July 1897): 249–66.

Turner, Fennell P. *The Missionary Uprising among Students: Being an Account of the Origin, Work, and Results of the Student Volunteer Movement*. New York: Student Volunteer Movement for Foreign Missions, 1915.

Veysey, Laurence R. *The Emergence of the American University*. Chicago: University of Chicago Press, 1965.

Wentz, Abdel Ross. *History of the Gettysburg Theological Seminary of the General Synod of the Evangelical Lutheran Church in the United States and of the United Lutheran Church in America, Gettysburg, Pennsylvania, 1826–1926*. Philadelphia: Printed for the Seminary by the United Lutheran Publication House, 1927.

Williams, Hermine Weigel, ed. *Robinson's Letter—Journal (1826–1829): Written from Europe by Edward Robinson to His Sister, Elisabeth*. Bloomington, IN: iUniverse, 2010.

Williams, Patrick, and Laura Chrisman, eds. *Colonial Discourse and Post-Colonial Theory: A Reader*. Hemel Hempstead, UK: Harvester, 1993.

Winter, Jay, ed. *America and the Armenian Genocide of 1915*. New York: Cambridge University Press, 2003.

Womack, Deanna Ferree. "Henry Jessup." In *Christian-Muslim Relations 1500–1900*, ed. David Thomas. Vol. 16, Leiden: Brill, 2020. 385–88.

INDEX

Adams, Hannah, 155–57. *See also* comparative religions

African American Muslims, 8, 22, 40, 111, 239, 245n19, 264n1

Alexander, Archibald, 1–3, 48, 63–67, 134, 161, 206, 217

American Biblical Orientalism, 237

American Board of Commissioners of Foreign Missions (ABCFM), 65, 188–90, 192, 193, 204, 205, 216, 221

American Civil War, 11, 14, 23, 37, 40, 75, 106, 115, 161

American evangelicalism, 20, 203, 230, 237. *See also* Great Awakenings; Lausanne Conference

American Lectures on the History of Religions, origins of, 175–76

American merchants, 1–2, 8, 126, 230

American Orientalism, 2, 18, 237, 225. *See also* Orientalism

American Oriental Society, 4, 91

Andover Seminary, 3, 4, 9–11, 14, 19, 23, 27, 32–35, 46, 49–51, 59, 60, 67, 68, 71, 73, 75, 91, 99, 116, 128, 130, 132, 134, 168, 177, 183, 188, 192, 203–6, 216, 220, 221, 230, 235. *See also* Philips Academy

Anglicans, 10, 11, 20, 21, 30, 32, 43, 58, 65, 124, 135, 167. *See also* Episcopal Church

anti-Judaism, 74, 121, 252n81

anti-Semitism, 152, 154

apocalypticism, 72, 88, 115, 236

Armenians, 120, 200, 205; genocide of, xi, 3, 144, 180, 181, 192, 214, 232, 237

Association of Theological Schools (ATS), ix, xi

Assyrians, 133, 162, 197–200; genocide of, xi, 3, 144, 180, 181, 192, 214, 232, 237; language of, 133

Baptists, 10, 11, 22, 23, 29, 35, 37, 204

Barbary Wars, 1, 2, 6, 65, 127

Barrows, John Henry, 176–83, 190, 214, 218. *See also* World Parliament of Religions

Bentley, William, 121, 155

Bible: polyglot Bibles, 53, 54, 56, 120, 143, 146, 152; Saadia Gaon's Arabic translation, 136, 140, 143

Bible Lands, 107, 108; *Through Bible Lands*, 108–14. *See also* Schaff, Philip

biblical archaeology, 141, 149

Boulainvillers, Henri, 94

Briggs, Charles Augustus, 17, 33, 34, 136, 137, 144, 145, 168, 175, 240, 256n59

Brown-Driver-Briggs (BDB), 130–32, 143

Bush, George, 71, 72, 74, 76, 96, 115

Cairo conference, 206, 215–19, 229

Calvinism, 11, 19, 29, 32, 86

Catholicism, 22, 57, 58, 89, 94, 119

Catholicism, eastern rites, 120, 144, 222

Chaldean (Aramaic), 17, 121, 133, 134

Chicago World's Fair, 17, 145, 176, 177. *See also* World Parliament of Religions

ABOUT THE AUTHOR

DAVID D. GRAFTON is Professor of Islamic Studies and Christian-Muslim Relations at Hartford International University for Religion and Peace. Dr. Grafton holds a PhD in Islamic Studies from the University of Birmingham, England. He is the author of several books, including *The Contested Origins of the 1865 Arabic Bible* (2015) and *An American Biblical Orientalism* (2019). He was also the North American Sections editor for *Christian-Muslim Relations: A Biographical History, 1500–1900*.